THE TASTE OF
MEXICO

THE TASTE OF
MEXICO

Patricia Quintana

Photography by Ignacio Urquiza

Marilyn Wilkinson, Consulting Editor

Text by William A. Orme, Jr.

STEWART, TABORI & CHANG

NEW YORK

Published by Stewart, Tabori & Chang, Inc.
740 Broadway, New York, New York 10003

Library of Congress Cataloging-in-Publication Data
Quintana, Patricia.
    The taste of Mexico.
    Includes index.
    1. Cookery, Mexican.   1. Wilkinson, Marilyn.
II. Title.
TX716.M4Q56   1986   641.5972   86-5817
ISBN 0-941434-89-3

Distributed by Workman Publishing
1 West 39th Street, New York, New York 10018

Printed in Japan

86 87 88 89 10 9 8 7 6 5 4 3 2 1
First Edition

page 2: *Caramelized Milk (see recipe on p. 60) is served on a typical ceramic dish from Guanajuato. Formerly, irons were used to melt and caramelize the sugar on top.*
opposite: *The Yucatán is known for its tasty breads and pastries.*

Mexicali

BAJA
CALIFORNIA
NORTE

GULF OF CALIFORNIA

BAJA
CALIFORNIA
SUR

SONORA

Hermosillo

CHIHUAHUA

Chihuahua

T H E   N O R T H

Monterrey

NUEVO
LEÓN

SINALOA

Culiacán

La Paz

TROPIC OF CANCER

N O R T H   P A C I F I C   C O A S T

PACIFIC
OCEAN

SAN LUIS
POTOSÍ

San Luis Potosí

Guanajuato

THE BAJIO

Guadalajara

Querétaro

HIDALGO

JALISCO

Pachuca

CENTRAL
MEXICO

Morelia

STATE OF
MEXICO

MICHOACÁN

Colima

COLIMA

Tlaxcala

TLAXCALA

Mexico City

Puebla

PUEBLA

VERACRUZ

Veracru

TH

GUERRERO

Chilpancingo

Oaxaca

OAXAC

S O U T H   P A C I F I C

0   KILOMETERS   500

0   MILES   300

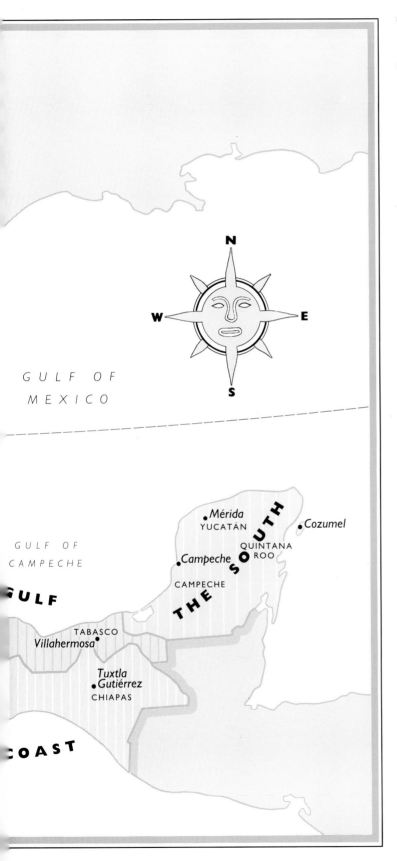

CONTENTS

THE BASICS

Ancient Mexican cultures bequeathed two invaluable foodstuffs to future generations: corn and chiles. Although many foods are indigenous to the New World, these two remain unchallenged as staples of the Mexican diet and social fiber.

CORN: A GIFT FROM THE GODS

Prehistoric Indians domesticated corn in the Valley of Mexico between 5000 and 4000 B.C., according to anthropologists. The Indians called it *toconayo*, "our meat." The ancients, in fact, believed that the gods had molded humans from corn, and the Mexicans, for a time, were known as "the men made from corn."

Although modern religion does not deify corn, Mexicans continue to revere this age-old source of sustenance. The uses and benefits of corn as a foodstuff have multiplied because of technology, advances in agricultural production, and changes in the industry. In Mexico,

Chiles poblanos, bright-yellow squash blossoms, ears of fresh corn, avocados and cilantro—in a molcajete—Mexican chocolate, and a molinillo are among the essentials of Mexican cuisine.

corn is used in everything from popcorn to cornflakes. It is an ingredient in syrups, desserts, corn starch, oil, grits, colorings for caramel, dextrin, glucose flour, and beer, and as a feed for poultry and livestock.

Masa

The most important use of corn is the one that is centuries old. Corn forms *masa*, the dough for tortillas and their variations and for tamales. Since antiquity, a Mexican table without tortillas is an empty table. According to ancient techniques, dried corn kernels are cooked with water and limestone until the kernel skins are soft. After standing for one day, the kernels are skinned, and the hearts are ground to form *masa*. Stone mortars and pestles used to do the job. Today, the process is mechanized in all but remote areas.

Tortillas

Despite mechanization, tortillas in Mexico are far from standardized. They are made from white, yellow, blue, or red corn. They may be small—2 inches in diameter—or large—as wide as 10 inches, as are those sold in the markets of Oaxaca.

Although many Americans are more familiar with wheat than with corn tortillas, the flour ones are more common in the northern states and are used all over Mexico. Unlike corn tortillas, wheat tortillas contain fat. They are rolled rather than flattened in a tortilla press.

TRADITIONAL MASA

2 pounds dried corn kernels
3 to 3½ quarts water
2 tablespoons ground limestone

Bring ingredients to a boil in a large pot. Cook corn kernels over low heat, stirring occasionally, until the skins can be easily removed. Remove from heat. Let stand for 1 day. Skin kernels. Discard skins. Wash kernels thoroughly. Strain through a sieve, and grind in a hand grinder. Add approximately 1½ cups water and a pinch of salt. Knead until a firm, smooth dough is obtained. Add more water if necessary.

MASA AND TORTILLAS FROM MASA HARINA

3 cups masa harina*
½ teaspoon salt
1½ to 2 cups lukewarm water

Mix ingredients in a bowl with a fork. Gather into a ball, and knead dough until smooth and no longer sticky. Cover with a towel, and allow to stand for 1 hour.

To make tortillas, line the base of a tortilla press with a sheet of plastic wrap or with a plastic sandwich bag. Pinch off balls of dough from the masa. (The size will vary, depending on desired tortilla diameter; the balls usually are slightly bigger than a walnut.) Center the masa on the lined tortilla-press base. Cover the masa with a sheet of plastic wrap. Lower the top of the press, and push down the handle. Open. The tortilla will have plastic wrap on top and bottom.

Carefully peel away the plastic on top. Place your left hand (if right-handed) under the tortilla. Flip the tortilla onto the right hand, so the plastic is on top.

Carefully peel away plastic. Flip tortilla onto a preheated, very hot griddle or comal. When the tortilla begins to dry on the edges, flip it over. Cook until the top begins to puff. Tap lightly with your fingertips to allow even puffing, and let cook briefly, about 1½ to 2 minutes. Remove tortillas from the griddle, wrap in a napkin or clean towel, and serve.

Although tortillas do not have to puff in order to be used in most recipes, some dishes call for splitting the puff and stuffing just this part of the tortilla with meats, cheese, or vegetables.

For crisp dishes, such as tostadas and chilaquiles, the tortillas are fried in oil after cooking on the comal. *Masa harina is available in Hispanic grocery stores and some supermarkets.
Makes 1½ pounds masa or about 24 tortillas.

WHEAT (FLOUR) TORTILLAS

4½ cups flour
1 teaspoon salt, or to taste
3 heaping tablespoons solid vegetable shortening
½ cup lukewarm water, approximately

Put flour in a glass bowl. Add salt and vegetable shortening. Mix ingredients until mixture has the texture of coarse meal. Gradually add water, and knead until dough forms a ball and is shiny and elastic. Cover with a dish towel, and let stand for 30 minutes.

To make tortillas, pinch off balls of dough (the size will vary, depending on desired tortilla diameter). With a rolling pin, roll the dough into thin circles on a floured board or pastry cloth. Cook the tortillas on a preheated griddle or comal for 1½ to 2 minutes. Turn and tap lightly with your fingertips. Cook until light-brown splotches appear.
Makes about 14 to 18 tortillas.

clockwise from top left: *A banana leaf is carefully peeled from the tortilla dough. Tortillas were originally prepared by flattening corn dough by hand on a banana leaf, as shown here. Today, the dough is flattened between sheets of plastic wrap in a tortilla press. The dough for flour, or wheat, tortillas is rolled out with a rolling pin on a wooden surface.*

Wheat tortillas cook on an old-fashioned Mennonite stove.

Fresh lard—made with fatback, water, and salt—is sold in most markets and is common to every Mexican household.

Tamales: As Regional as Road Maps

Each region of Mexico has its own style of tamale, a specialty well known outside the country. The classic version, found throughout Mexico, is made with lard mixed with *masa* made from *cacahuazintle* corn kernels, a variety similar to hominy, and baking powder. The best-flavored tamales are prepared with homemade lard, an ingredient common in Mexican recipes and households.

preceding overleaf left: Retablo *paintings are composed of separate images that together present a theme. This one illustrates the importance of both physical and spiritual nourishment by depicting food alongside religious symbols.*
preceding overleaf right: *Jaime Saldivar captures the essence of a Mexican kitchen in this* retablo.

LARD

3⅓   pounds pork fatback, well washed and cut in large chunks
2   quarts water
1½   teaspoons salt

Put pork in a stock pot, and cover with water. Add salt. Bring to a boil. Cook over medium heat at a boil until the pork renders its fat. The fatback will shrink and darken. Remove from heat, and cool slightly. Discard fatback. Strain lard into glass jars, and store in the refrigerator. This lard will have a brownish tint, unlike the store-purchased snow-white variety.

Tamales may be sweet or salty, hot or bland. Sweet tamales are colored with red food coloring and are filled with marmalades and canned or dried fruits. Salty tamales are stuffed with pork, chicken, turkey, fish, shrimp, *mole* sauce, cheese and chiles, *pipián* (pumpkin-seed sauces), beans, and zucchini—to name a few alternatives. Tamales often are eaten for breakfast or as a light dinner.

This book contains several recipes for tamales. Generally, all tamales are made in much the same way.

Soak dried corn husks in water to cover for several hours or until pliable. Spread a few tablespoons of prepared *masa* almost to the edges of a corn husk, making a thin layer. Fold the long edges of the husk lengthwise, overlapping in the center. Fold the top and bottom ends toward the center, overlapping. The tamales often are wrapped in a second husk and secured by being tied with lengthwise strips of corn husks. Arrange tamales upright in a prepared steamer, and cover them with a layer of corn husks and a damp dish towel. Place lid on steamer. Most tamales require steaming for about 1 hour. They are done when the dough no longer sticks to the husk, and the husk can easily be pulled away from the *masa*.

Atole:
The Corn You Drink

Mexicans not only eat corn, but also drink it. *Masa* is the foundation for *atole*, a widely enjoyed beverage prepared by diluting masa in water and boiling it until it thickens to the consistency of a milkshake. The most popular *atoles* are based on white corn. Flavorings such as *piloncillo* (unrefined brown sugar), cinnamon, sugar, fruit, and spices enhance the taste.

Champurrado is a version of sweet *atole* that uses Mexican chocolate. The mixture is whipped to a thick froth with a *molinillo*, a carved wooden beater designed especially for chocolate. The beater has three loose rings that gyrate rapidly when the long handle is spun back and forth between the palms of the hands.

Another well-known *atole* is sweetened with *piloncillo* and is made with milk, cinnamon, or fresh fruits—such as strawberries, oranges, tangerines, and pineapple. Almonds or peanuts sometimes substitute for the fruits. In

Dried corn kernels, a staple of Mexican cuisine.

some regions, such as Chiapas, *atole* is flavored with chile and is served at breakfast or dinner.

CHILES:
HOT, BUT TASTY

It goes without saying that chiles are indispensable to Mexican cooking. The ancient Aztecs and Mayans, who cultivated and consumed them, created recipes that are still in use. The natives believed that chiles had nutritive and medicinal value, a belief confirmed by modern nutritionists.

The fierce, spicy flavor of chiles is captured by their original Indian name, which was derived from *tzir*, "to pierce." In almost all varieties, the hotness can vary from pepper to pepper. Contrary to widespread belief, the fieriness of chiles does not detract from the flavor of food, but enhances its nuances and tastes. Chiles can, of course, be used too abundantly. The result is predictable!

Hundreds of varieties of chiles are grown in Mexico. Some are used in both their fresh and dried forms. Interestingly, the fresh and dried forms of a variety have different names. The most common chiles, with the names of the dried form in parentheses, are:

Chile de árbol   An intense green when fresh, the *chile de árbol* is most often used dried, when it is reddish orange. It is small, uneven in shape, and quite fiery.

Chile chilaca (pasilla)   The *chile chilaca* is deep forest green, about 6 inches long, and slender. Its trademark is a rounded, blunt end. In the United States, it is more widely available in its dried form, the black *chile pasilla*. The *chile pasilla* is dark brown and somewhat less hot than its fresh counterpart. It is pleasantly flavorful. *Pasillas* are used in *mole* and other sauces and are the typical garnish for a bowl of tortilla soup.

Chile chilaca (pasado) or California (Anaheim) chile This long, narrow light green chile is similar to the *chile poblano*. It ranges from mild to hot and is used in northern dishes. The chiles are dried in the sun and are called *chiles pasados*.

Chile habanero The small, lantern-shaped *chile habanero* is peculiar to the Yucatán, where it is used profusely. It is basic to table sauces and is among the hottest of chiles. It is green or reddish orange, depending on its stage of ripeness.

Chile jalapeño or cuaresmeño (chipotle) The *chile jalapeño* is a very popular hot chile. It is bright green and, compared with the *chile serrano*, somewhat large and plump, which makes it a good chile to stuff. The *jalapeño* is often prepared *en escabeche* (pickled). It is also prepared *en rajas*, or "in thin strips," and is used to flavor hot sauces, both cooked and uncooked, and *moles*. When dried and smoked, the *chile jalapeño* becomes the *chile chipotle*. Until recently, this delicacy was little known outside Mexico. The *chile chipotle* is deep rust or brown, with a rich, smoky flavor. After drying, *chipotles* often are canned in an *adobo* (vinegar sauce). They are very, very hot.

Chile manzano (cascabel) The apple-shaped *chile manzano* is pale yellow. It commonly is used dried, as the *chile cascabel*. *Cascabel* means "rattlesnake," and the chile is so called because its seeds rattle and sound like the rattle at the end of that snake's tail. The *chile cascabel* is dark red and very hot.

Chile piquín Used both fresh and dried (mainly dried in the United States), the *chile piquín* is hot. It is often used in its ground form to sprinkle on fruits and corn on the cob and in stews.

Chile poblano (mulato or ancho) The *chile poblano* is best known to Americans as the chile used for *chiles rellenos*, a dish most Mexican restaurants include on their menus. It is also prepared *en rajas*, which may be pickled and canned. It is about the same size as a green bell pepper, but darker green and more slender and pointed.

The *chile poblano* is among the milder peppers, but it has a range that can include hot. It boasts a rich, robust flavor that adds much to *moles*, soups, stews, and cooked and uncooked sauces. When dried, one is darker—the *chile mulato*—and the other is lighter and reddish brown— the *chile ancho*. Both are used extensively in cooked sauces. They are usually mild.

Chile puya (guajillo) The *chile puya* ranges from light to dark green. It is long and thin. It is most commonly used in its dried form, the *chile guajillo*, which is brownish red, slick skinned, and only moderately hot.

Chile serrano (japonés or serrano seco) The *chile serrano* is one of the most commonly used hot chiles, giving piquancy to hot sauces, *moles*, soups, and stews. It is dark green, small, and thin. It often is prepared *en escabeche*. Its dried form, the *chile japonés* is light red.

Preparing Fresh Chiles

Fresh chiles are frequently roasted, peeled, seeded, and deveined before using.

Heat a griddle or comal until very hot. Put chiles on the griddle, and roast until the skin puckers and chars, turning the chiles to roast all sides. Place roasted chiles in a plastic bag, close bag, and "sweat" chiles for 4 to 5 minutes. (Longer sweating will steam the chiles and overcook them.)

Remove the chiles from the bag, and peel them under a stream of cold water. The skin will peel off easily. Discard the skin. If the chiles are to be cut or chopped, remove the stems, and slit the chiles lengthwise in order to remove the seeds and veins. If the chiles are to be stuffed, leave the stems intact. Make a small slit on the side to remove the seeds and veins. Then rinse and dry the chiles with towels or paper towels. Piquancy can be reduced by soaking the chiles in salted water or in a water–vinegar solution for 2 to 3 hours.

Many people find it necessary to wear rubber gloves when working with chiles because their skin becomes

opposite: *Several chiles from Chiapas, along with white, yellow, and red corn kernels.*
overleaf: *The chile xcatik, a long, light-red or light-green chile native to the Yucatán, and the chile habanero, a small but very hot variety used sparingly in recipes.*

burned and irritated. Never touch the face or eyes when working with chiles.

The *chile serrano* receives special preparation called "teasing." The whole, raw *chile serrano* is rubbed between the palms of the hands to loosen the seeds, thus releasing more flavor and accenting the chile's spiciness. Then the whole chile is lightly fried in oil with sliced onion. Prepared in this way, the *chile serrano* and onion are served with broiled meats.

Preparing Dried Chiles

The first step in preparing dried chiles is careful washing. Since they often are sun-dried on the ground, the chiles usually are dusty and dirty. Next, remove the stems (if the chiles are not to be stuffed), and slit the chiles lengthwise in order to remove the seeds and veins. Preheat a griddle, and roast the chiles very lightly, turning to roast all sides. The dried chiles will puff and reconstitute slightly. Be careful not to burn them. Burned dried chiles produce an acrid taste. Some recipes call for frying the cleaned dried chiles rather than roasting them. In this case, heat a little vegetable oil or lard, and lightly fry the chiles. They will puff and reconstitute slightly. Drain the chiles on paper towels.

Dried chiles often are soaked in hot water after they are roasted. Cover the chiles with hot water, and let them stand for 20 minutes. Recipes for many sauces require that some of the soaking water be added for flavor and as a thinning agent.

OTHER BASIC INGREDIENTS

Several ingredients in addition to chiles are roasted (or "toasted") before being used: herbs and spices, whole tomatoes, bell peppers, whole and sectioned onions (white onions are used in Mexico), and peeled and unpeeled garlic cloves. Such spices as cloves and cinnamon stick often are roasted before grinding, as are such herbs as bay leaves and oregano. Roasting adds a robust, distinct flavor to the ingredients and subsequently to the recipes in which they are used. Generally speaking, roasting these and other ingredients begins with heating

Chiles are usually pickled in a mild fruit vinegar.

a dry griddle to very hot. Put the ingredient on the griddle, and allow it to brown or char slightly. It is important to watch spices and herbs closely while roasting them, since burning produces unpleasant flavors. Discard burned spices and herbs, and replace them with a fresh quantity.

Cheeses

Cheeses are so integral to Mexican cooking that it is difficult to believe that they are not native to the New World. Mexicans learned the art of cheese making from the Spaniards when the Europeans introduced cattle in the early sixteenth century. The natives were quick learners and outstanding students. Mexico boasts a bounty of cheeses, from the rich butter cheese of Chiapas to the stringy, mildly acidic variety of Oaxaca. Mennonites who settled in the North are famous for their cheeses, and each wheel is stamped for authenticity. Mexico produces both goat's-milk and cow's-milk cheeses.

There are two basic uses for cheese in Mexican cooking: for toppings and for stuffings. In addition, cheeses may be eaten alone as part of an appetizer, often accompanied by pickled chiles, or with *ates*—the tropical-fruit dessert pastes of Mexico.

Fresh cheeses in Mexico are soft and crumbly, used to sprinkle over tacos, enchiladas, other tortilla concoctions, and *nopal* (cactus-pad) salad. *Queso fresco* (or *queso blanco*) is the generic term, and several brands of *queso fresco* are produced in the United States, especially in areas with large Hispanic populations, such as Chicago and Los Angeles. A mild feta is a good substitute for *queso fresco*.

Queso anejo, an aged cheese, also is used to top some dishes, especially enchiladas. It is hard and dry, not unlike Parmesan and sardo.

Cheeses that string or melt readily are highly prized in Mexico for stuffings. These include *queso asadero* (roasting cheese), *queso* or *quesillo de Oaxaca*, and *queso Chihuahua*—a firm cheese from the North.

Because the quality of cheeses produced in the United States varies so widely, it is impossible to recommend sure substitutes. Choose a good locally available cheese for flavor, creaminess, and stringiness when using cheese for stuffings. Cheeses with these qualities include mozzarella, muenster, brick, and Monterey Jack. A combination of two of these cheeses often produces a good result.

Cilantro and Epazote

Cilantro and *epazote* are two herbs synonymous with Mexican flavors. They are used fresh and have no substitutes, although one is often used in place of the other. They taste nothing alike, but each has a distinctive, sharp, and pungent flavor that imparts authenticity to Mexican dishes.

Cilantro (Chinese parsley or fresh coriander) is increasingly easy to find in the United States. Since it is used in Oriental as well as Mexican cooking, many supermarkets now routinely stock it in the produce department. It resembles flat-leaf parsley, but is a brighter, more yellow green. Use the leaves and tender top stems in recipes, and discard the tough lower stems. Cilantro does not store well. Be sure to keep it dry, because moisture hastens its decay.

Epazote still is almost impossible—if not impossible—to find commercially in the United States. It can, however, be ordered in potted form from several nurseries across the country. Generally thought of as a weed, *epazote* grows wild and is known in the United States as wormseed or *pozote*, among other appellations. Even in Mexico, *epazote*'s use tends to be regional, with the South and Yucatán among its biggest champions. It is almost always cooked with black beans. Indeed, it acts as a carminative to reduce the gas in beans.

Sauces: Cooked Sauce

Mexico contributes a highly unusual, if not unique, technique to the cooking of sauces. Most Mexican cooked sauces—especially those based on dried, soaked, and blended chiles—are "fried." Fat such as lard or oil is heated in a deep skillet or pan. Onions and/or garlic may be sautéed before the addition of the blended chile mixture, which is quickly "fried" in the hot fat to combine and bond the flavors. This step is messy, and the chile mixture spatters with abandon. Broth frequently is added after the frying, and the sauce is then cooked over low heat until it thickens or reduces and all the ingredients are thoroughly cooked.

Uncooked Sauce

As essential in Mexico as salt and pepper is *salsa de molcajete* (stone-mortar sauce). This uncooked sauce or a variation of it is found on most tables throughout Mexico. The order of the grinding of the ingredients in the *molcajete* is essential to the flavor of the sauce. Garlic and salt are ground first. The chile is added and ground. Finally, roasted tomatoes or cooked *tomatillos* are added and ground into the other ingredients. Chopped cilantro is added for garnish and for flavor.

If a blender or food processor is used to prepare the sauce, all the ingredients are blended just briefly to retain some texture.

In some regions, knob onions and radishes are cut in the shapes of flowers to garnish the *salsas*.

Tomatillos

Tomatillos are an indispensable ingredient in Mexican cookery. Although they often are called "green tomatoes" (*tomates verdes*), they are not unripe tomatoes, and green tomatoes cannot be substituted for them. Indeed, there is no substitute. *Tomatillos* are sold both fresh and canned. The canned are a perfectly adequate substitute for the fresh.

The major use of *tomatillos*—blended or chopped, raw or cooked—is in sauces. Only occasionally is the *tomatillo* used raw, for salads. To prepare cooked *tomatillos*, first remove the papery husk. Wash the *tomatillos* thoroughly, because the skins tend to be sticky. Then roast them on a dry griddle or boil them slowly with some thick onion slices, *chiles serranos*, and whole garlic cloves until the skin begins to split, about 15 to 30 minutes. The *tomatillos* then are drained and usually blended with other ingredients for sauces. Cooking water is retained in case it is needed for thinning.

The most common *tomatillo*-based sauce is *salsa verde* (green sauce), which calls for cooked *tomatillos*, *chiles serranos*, white onion, garlic, salt, and cilantro.

A variety of Yucatecan liqueurs and sauces.

ALCOHOLIC BEVERAGES: FIRE FROM CACTUS AND CANE

Mexico produces innumerable fermented beverages, most of which are derived from fruits or cactuses. Many are esoteric and are not particularly appealing to foreign palates.

Tequila Without doubt, of course, tequila is the Mexican spirit best known outside the country's borders. It is a product of the *Agave tequilana* (blue) species of the agave plant and—by law—of those plants grown only in the states of Jalisco, Michoacán, and Nayarit. The juice of this agave species is both fermented and distilled in making tequila. White or silver tequila is the most common tequila, and it is the one used for the American-embraced Margarita. In Mexico, the Margarita is not a slushy, trendy, colorful affair served in an oversize brandy snifter. Far from it. It imposes precise standards, which make it a drink unsuited to the faint-hearted or dizziness-prone.

To make a Margarita, salt a stemmed cocktail glass (martini size) around the rim. In a shaker or blender (purists use only a shaker), mix a heaping spoonful of chipped ice with 1½ ounces tequila, 1 ounce fresh—and *only* fresh—lime juice and ½ ounce Triple Sec. Briefly mix the Margarita and pour into the prepared glass.

Tequila can also be gold, which implies that it was stored in oak barrels. Tequila *anejo* is caramel-colored and aged, by definition, for at least one year.

Pulque Another liquor from the agave—any number of species—is *pulque*, which is probably the oldest liquor in North America. It is fermented (not distilled) from the agave juice. A milky, sour substance, *pulque* is used in cooking primarily as a base for sauces. *Pulque*, when fresh, does not travel well and is not exported. Beer can be substituted for recipes that call for *pulque*.

Mezcal Mezcal, a distilled agave liquor, does not have to meet the rigid standards that govern the production of tequila. It is probably best known outside Mexico as the liquor with the worm in the bottle. Re-

Some of the most popular beverages are flavored with extracts of the vanilla bean, which is cultivated in Gutiérrez, Zamora, and Papantla.

search has not revealed any purpose for the worm, except perhaps as an informal, but highly recognizable, trademark.

Beer Mexican beer is excellent, as Americans already have discovered. Monterrey, in the North, is Mexico's second largest city and its beer capital, although other breweries are located throughout Mexico.

Aguardiente Still popular in Mexico is *aguardiente*, or "fire water"—really a homemade brandy. The Veracruz–Tabasco version comes from distilled sugar-cane sap. The sap is used to preserve fresh fruits. After the fruits have been macerated for two weeks, the brandy is poured off, and the fruits are served with ice cream.

UTENSILS AND COOKWARE

Clay   Mexican cooks rely extensively on clay cookware, bowls, and pitchers. Clay pieces must be treated before use. Rub the outside with cut garlic, and fill the inside with soapy water up to the rim. Place the piece on the stove over direct heat, and boil the water until it almost evaporates. Remove from heat, and let the pot stand for at least 20 minutes to seal the clay. If the pots are tiny, such as those used for coffee or for melting cheese, place them in a large pot filled with soapy water. Boil for 50 minutes. The clay pieces can be used for baking, broiling, or stove-top, direct-heat cooking.

Metate   The *metate*, one of the oldest kitchen utensils known to Mesoamerica, is a sloping, rectangular piece of volcanic stone supported on three legs. It is used with a *metlapil* (stone rolling pin). It must be tempered before being used for the first time. To temper, pour rice, dried chickpeas, or other grain onto the *metate*. Add a little salt. Grind the grain with the *metlapil*, repeating the procedure, changing the grain several times until the ground grain is pure in color and free of rock particles or dirt. The *metate* and *metlapil* are used principally to grind corn to make *masa* and to grind some sauces.

Molcajete   The *molcajete* is a mortar made from porous, volcanic stone. Its accompanying pestle is the *tejolote*. Both mortar and pestle must be tempered before being used for the first time. Temper them in the same way that the *metate* is tempered. Spices ground in a *molcajete*, rather than in a blender or food processor, are more finely pulverized; sauces blended in a *molcajete* have a better texture and more flavor.

MEALS IN MEXICO: THE RECURRENT FEAST

Meal times vary in Mexico, depending on the region and climate, which can range from desert to tropical forest. More respected than meal times as a gauge is one's appetite. Four or five meals are served daily in some regions.

Breakfast, served between 6:00 and 8:00 A.M., usually consists of coffee and bread or pastry or, alternatively, coffee and tamales.

Brunch is a heartier affair. Eggs, meat, or tortillas, accompanied by coffee and milk or fresh-fruit beverages, are served between 11:00 A.M. and noon.

Lunch is the heaviest and most traditional meal of the day. Served at about 3:00 P.M., the typical repast includes soup, rice or pasta, an entrée, usually refried beans or *frijoles de olla* (pot beans), tortillas or bread, dessert, and coffee.

Between 7:00 and 8:00 P.M., Mexicans enjoy *merienda*, a collation consisting of a cup of hot chocolate, coffee, or *atole* and some pastries or tamales.

The day's dining is completed with supper, prepared for between 9:00 and 10:00 P.M. It includes a main course, often leftovers from lunch, or a typical Mexican snack, such as *quesadillas*, tacos, or *tortas*. Coffee and milk are served as accompaniments.

The hectic rhythm of urban living is beginning to disrupt this traditional sequence of meals. Nowadays, it is common in cities to eat just three meals daily—breakfast, lunch, and dinner. The largest meal of the day is still lunch, with its leisurely pace rooted in Mexico's historical observance of siesta.

overleaf: *Mexicans shop daily for fresh produce at open markets.*

THE NORTH

The vast region that Mexicans call El Norte stretches for 1,800 miles from the rugged Pacific coast of Baja California to the lowlands of the Gulf of Mexico. Its sparsely populated landscape ranges from snow-capped sierras to scorching salt flats to lush citrus groves. The desolate mountain districts of El Norte are the most forbidding and remote in all Mexico.

Yet the North is also Mexico at its most modern, urban, and industrial. Monterrey, the pillar of the northern economy, exemplifies this prosperity with its booming iron, steel, cement, glass, and crystal plants, as well as its breweries, which date to the turn of the century.

The most singular of El Norte's several subregions is Baja California. Northwestern Baja's fog-moistened valleys nurture Mexico's finest vineyards, belying the peninsula's image as a harsh, infertile desert. Baja is Mexico's oldest continuously producing wine district; in the eighteenth century, Spanish friars in Baja California made altar wines for the California missions. In recent years, the region has earned a reputation for quality varietals. White wines, in particular, have improved dramatically. They are the perfect accompaniment to Baja's superb seafood, which includes lobster, shrimp, crab, and clams.

Amid the arid desert of Baja is Mulegé, an oasis covered with date palms. Dates are used in many dishes,

including a rich bread. The prototypal Norte, however, is the high-desert country of the states of Chihuahua and Sonora. A parched land of canyons and cattle ranches, this area has produced much of the culture and cuisine that non-Mexicans regard as "Mexican." Less Indian than the South and less European than central Mexico, the North is a uniquely Mexican hybrid, influenced by such unexpected groups as the Mennonites. Still in many ways a frontier society, it is the birthplace of the cowboy culture, which has left its indelible imprint on United States history. And in the industrialized cities of Hermosillo and Chihuahua, the working man's uniform is still characterized by cowboy boots, blue jeans, and a broad-brimmed straw hat.

Norteño food is rugged, hearty, and unpretentious. Fillet in oregano sauce, typical of Chihuahua, and *caldillo*, a hearty beef stew flavored with onions, tomatoes, and chiles are examples of this sturdy fare. Vegetarian dishes, such as melted cheese accented with Anaheim chiles, are also typical of this cuisine.

In the *norteño* heartland, on Mexico's side of the border, ranch-style, or hacienda, food predominates in even the most elegant homes and restaurants. Nowhere in the world is beef more expertly raised, deliciously seasoned, or enthusiastically consumed than in Sonora. To enhance the flavor of the beef, northerners eat it with

Tarahumaran Indians on one of the winding paths in the high-mountain country of Chihuahua.

tomato-based sauces, which tend to be less piquant in the North than in other regions of Mexico. The preferred chile of many *norteños* is the California, or Anaheim, variety—a long, slender chile that lacks the fire of a *jalapeño* or a *serrano*.

To some connoisseurs, however, *norteño* cooking is epitomized not by its beef, but by its spicy beans. They may be *frijoles charros* (literally, "cowboy beans")—boiled over an open fire with chiles, herbs, and bits of available meat. Just as likely are *frijoles borrachos* (literally, "drunken beans")—beans cooked with beer—or *frijoles maneados*—beans enriched by stringy cheese and rustic *chile ancho*.

Among the most important dishes of Nuevo León are scrambled eggs with *carne machacada*—pounded, shredded jerked beef—and *cabrito al pastor*, spit-roasted "shepherd-style" kid.

Accompanying every *norteño* meal is a basket of *tortillas de harina* (wheat-flour tortillas), a distinctive northern adaptation of the corn tortilla. As a practical matter, the doughy, elastic *tortilla de harina* is the perfect wrapper for *burritos* stuffed with such northern specialties as jerked beef, barbecued pork, and kid. The *tortilla de harina* is uniquely northern, a gastronomic declaration of a strong sense of regional identity.

Corn tortillas are common throughout Mexico, but tortillas made from wheat flour, like these Sonoran water tortillas, shown with, clockwise from top right, chiles gueros, chiles piquíns, *and* chiles anchos *are typical of the North.*

TORTILLAS DE HARINA
Flour Tortillas

4¼ cups unbleached flour
 1 teaspoon salt, or to taste
 3 heaping tablespoons vegetable shortening
 ½ cup water, approximately (varies depending on quality of flour), at room temperature

Put flour in a glass bowl. Add salt and vegetable shortening. Knead by hand until the mixture has a gritty texture. Add water a little at a time, and knead dough until it forms an elastic and shiny ball. If it is too greasy, add a little more flour and water.

Set dough aside, covered with a cloth, for 30 minutes. Pinch off a small ball of dough, and place between 2 sheets of waxed paper. With a rolling pin, roll the ball into a circle about 3 inches in diameter. The tortilla should be very thin. Pull edges with your fingertips, stretching the tortilla a little.

Cook tortilla on a hot thick griddle. Cook on each side for about 2 minutes or until light brown. The tortilla should puff slightly.

Repeat, using all the dough and making 20 tortillas.

To serve, place tortillas in a basket. Serve with cheese or ground meat.
Makes 20 tortillas.

preceding overleaf: *A Mulegé oasis in southern Baja California.*

QUESADILLITAS DE LA TIA
Auntie's Small Quesadillas

Flour tortillas play a key role in northern Mexican cuisine. They often are made small, folded over a variety of stuffings, and served as an appetizer.

FOR THE TORTILLAS
48 flour tortillas, 3 inches in diameter (see recipe on opposite page)

FOR THE CHEESE STUFFING
16 slices fresh Oaxaca, mozzarella, or Monterey Jack cheese, about ¾ inch by 2½ inches

FOR THE BEEF STUFFING
1 generous cup shredded beef (see recipe on page 46)

FOR THE EGG AND SAUSAGE STUFFING
⅓ cup vegetable oil
¾ cup fresh chorizo sausage, crumbled
¼ cup white onion, finely chopped
6 eggs, beaten with 1 teaspoon salt

Prepare the cheese quesadillitas: Put 1 cheese slice on each of 16 tortillas. Fold tortilla in half, pressing edges. Set aside.

Prepare the beef quesadillitas: Spoon 1 heaping tablespoon beef off-center on each of 16 tortillas. Fold tortilla in half, pressing edges. Set aside.

Prepare the egg and sausage quesadillitas: Heat oil in a frying pan. Brown chorizo in oil, and add onion. Continue frying for 10 minutes. Add egg. Stir with a spoon until mixture is creamy. Remove from heat. Spoon 1 tablespoon stuffing off-center on each of 16 tortillas. Fold tortilla in half, pressing edges.

Heat a comal or griddle. Toast all quesadillitas, in batches, on the comal, turning for even heating. Keep warm. Serve immediately.
Makes 48 quesadillitas.

GUACAMOLE
Avocado Dip

Guacamole is prepared differently in various regions of Mexico. In the city of Monterrey, it is garnished to reflect the colors of the Mexican flag.

FOR THE GUACAMOLE
6 ripe California avocados, peeled and pitted
1½ white onions, chopped
½ cup cilantro, chopped
   Juice of 2 limes, or to taste
1 very small zucchini, puréed
6 tablespoons olive oil
6 chiles serranos, finely chopped
   Salt to taste

FOR THE GARNISH
2 large tomatoes, chopped
1 green onion, finely chopped
2 chiles serranos, finely chopped
½ cup cilantro leaves
   Totopos (crisply fried tortilla wedges)

Put avocados in a glass bowl, and mash them with a fork. Add onion, cilantro, lime juice, zucchini, oil, chiles, and salt. Mix the ingredients thoroughly to form a purée.

Put the avocado pits in the guacamole to prevent darkening. To serve, spoon guacamole into a mortar, and decorate with tomato on one side and green onion, chiles, and cilantro leaves in the center. On the other side, place the totopos.
Makes 8 servings.

Although Baja California is the home of the finest vineyards in Mexico, wine is not the only beverage served here. Another popular drink is a daiquiri made with fresh, sweet mangoes.

DAIQUIRI DE MANGO
Mango Daiquiri

In Baja California, this drink is prepared with fresh mangoes from the region. Liquor enhances the strong, sweet flavor of this exquisite fruit.

12	large mangoes, peeled, pitted, and sliced
2	16-ounce cans sliced mangoes
4	quarts ice cubes
2½	cups light or dark rum, or to taste
	Sugar to taste

Blend fresh mangoes in a blender or food processor. Add canned mangoes. Blend. Add ice, and blend until the mixture is a frappé. (If necessary, mix in batches.) Add rum and sugar to taste. Stir.

To serve, pour daiquiris into 1½-cup goblets. Serve immediately.

Makes 8 servings.

SOPA DE MARISCOS ESTILO LA PAZ
Seafood Soup, La Paz Style

Baja California, with its thousands of miles of coastline, boasts exquisite seafood. Mussels, shrimp, crab, and fish dishes are local specialties.

½	cup olive oil
5⅓	tablespoons butter
8	cloves garlic, whole
6	large tomatoes, coarsely chopped
2	medium white onions, coarsely chopped
1½	tablespoons dried oregano
½	rib celery, with leaves
30	sprigs cilantro
1	teaspoon freshly ground pepper
	Salt to taste
2	fish heads, preferably grouper or perch
7	quarts water
4	crabs, whole, plus 4 crabs, chopped with shell
48	medium shrimp, unshelled
6	lobster tails, each cut in 3 pieces
10	fish fillets, 2 ounces each, cut in 2-inch squares

Heat oil and butter in a large saucepan. Brown 4 garlic cloves, and remove from oil. In a blender or food processor, blend tomato with 4 remaining garlic cloves and onion. Put these ingredients in the saucepan, seasoning with oregano, celery, cilantro, pepper, and salt.

Cook until fat begins to surface, about 30 minutes, and sauce begins to thicken.

Add fish heads and water to sauce, and simmer for 30 minutes. Add crabs, shrimp, and lobster tails, and continue cooking for 20 minutes. Correct seasoning, and remove celery, cilantro, and fish heads. Before serving, add fish fillets, and cook for 5 minutes.

To serve, pour soup into a tureen and spoon into individual soup bowls.

Makes 8 servings.

CARACOL MARINO ESTILO SAN LUCAS

Conch, San Lucas Style

FOR THE CONCH

12	conch, 5 to 6 ounces each, shelled, butterflied, and flattened
	Salt and pepper to taste
4	large eggs
4	cups fresh bread crumbs or crushed crackers
2	cups clarified butter

FOR THE SAUCE

1	quart fish stock (see recipe on page 214)
2	cups dry white wine
6	tablespoons butter, plus 7 tablespoons butter, in pieces
2	tablespoons olive oil
3	tablespoons white onion, grated
4	cups fresh crab meat, cleaned and shredded, or 4 cups canned crab meat, shredded
	Salt and pepper to taste
1	teaspoon corn starch, dissolved in ¾ cup fish stock

FOR THE GARNISH

¾	cup black olives
½	cup parsley, chopped
	Cilantro sprigs
4	carrots, cooked and sliced on the diagonal

Prepare the conch: Put conch in a large glass or ceramic dish. Salt and pepper lightly, and refrigerate for 25 minutes.

Beat eggs, and dip conch in egg, allowing excess to drip off. Put bread crumbs on a tray or waxed paper, and roll conch in the crumbs to coat. Arrange conch on a tray in a single layer, and refrigerate for 1 hour

Conch, or sea snails, are breaded, sautéed in butter, and served with crab sauce at Las Palmas restaurant in San Lucas.

or put in freezer for 25 minutes.

Heat 1 cup clarified butter, and fry conch until golden brown, turning once. Add more butter as needed. Keep conch hot in a warm oven.

Prepare the sauce: Put fish stock and wine in a saucepan, and reduce to 3 cups. Heat 6 tablespoons butter and oil in a frying pan. Add onion and crab, and sauté. Add reduced broth mixture, and season with salt and pepper. Add dissolved corn starch and, little by little, the pieces of butter. Stir well. Cook until mixture thickens slightly.

To serve, divide conch among 8 plates. Pour sauce over, and garnish with olives, parsley, cilantro, and carrots.

This recipe can also be prepared with fish fillets.

Makes 8 servings.

FILETE RELLENO DE CABRILLA
Stuffed Cabrilla

Cabrilla, a species of sea bass, is one of the many kinds of fish eaten in Baja California. In the Bismark Restaurant in La Paz, it is stuffed, giving it a savory flavor.

FOR THE FISH
- 8 cabrilla fillets, 7 to 8 ounces each, butterflied, or substitute red snapper, sea bass, or flounder fillets
  Salt and pepper to taste
- 8 teaspoons lime juice

Seafood-stuffed cabrilla fillets are served with local Baja wine.

FOR THE SAUCE
- ⅔ cup olive oil
- 1½ white onions, finely chopped
- 4 chiles serranos, finely chopped
- 4 tomatoes (2¾ pounds), finely chopped
  Salt to taste
- 1 tablespoon freshly ground pepper
- 1 teaspoon fresh oregano or ½ teaspoon dried oregano

FOR THE STUFFING
- 3 quarts water
  Salt to taste
- 2 sprigs thyme or ½ teaspoon dried thyme
- 2 bay leaves
- 1 teaspoon pepper
- 16 large shrimp, shelled and deveined
- 2 lobster tails

FOR THE BATTER
- 8 to 10 eggs, separated
- 1 teaspoon salt
- 2 to 3 tablespoons flour, plus flour to coat fillets
- 1 quart vegetable oil

FOR THE GARNISH
- 4 tomatoes, halved
- 4 carrots, peeled, sliced in 48 thin strips, and boiled in salted water until tender
- 48 canned chile jalapeño strips
- 8 limes, halved

Prepare the fish: Sprinkle cabrilla with salt, pepper, and lime juice. Set aside for 20 minutes.

Prepare the sauce: Heat oil in a saucepan. Lightly brown onion and chiles. Add tomatoes. Season with salt, pepper, and oregano. Simmer over low heat for 30 minutes or until the sauce thickens.

Prepare the stuffing: Put 1 quart water and salt in a saucepan. Add thyme, bay leaves, and pepper, and bring to a rolling boil. Add shrimp, and cook for 3 minutes. Remove from heat. Let stand for 3 minutes. Remove shrimp, and cut into ½-inch chunks or into 3 lengthwise strips.

Bring 2 quarts water and salt to a rolling boil in a large saucepan. Add lobster tails, and boil for 15 minutes. Remove from heat. Let stand for 5 minutes. Remove lobster, and cool. Shell, and slice into thin disks.

Prepare the batter: Beat half the egg whites with an electric mixer or by hand until stiff. Add ½ teaspoon salt, and beat for 2 seconds. Beat half the egg yolks lightly. Fold yolks and 1 to 1½ tablespoons flour into whites. Prepare more batter, using remaining ingredients, as necessary. Heat oil in a frying pan for 15 minutes or almost to smoking.

Put flour in a wide dish or on a sheet of waxed paper. Spoon some sauce, shrimp, and lobster onto open fillet. Fold over to close. Coat with flour, and dip in batter. Let excess batter drip off. Fry fish in oil on both sides until golden brown. Drain on paper towels. Repeat procedure with remaining 7 fillets.

To serve, place a tomato half on each of 8 plates. Arrange 6 carrot strips on top of tomato, overlapping. Garnish with 6 chile strips. Place cabrilla on the side, and cut open to expose stuffing. Garnish with limes.
Makes 8 servings.

A view of Bahía Concepción, located in southern Baja California.

ALMEJAS CHOCOLATAS
Chocolate Clams

This species of clam is gathered near the seashore and kept in mesh cages, delivered live to the marketplace.

48	chocolate clams or any small, fresh clams, in shells
16	limes, halved
	Tabasco sauce

Clean clams in sea water or fresh water. Open them, and rinse again. Detach each clam from the shell, and remove the stomach by making two incisions. Place clam in shell, and fold over the orange fringe of the clam.

To serve, divide clams among 8 plates. Squeeze fresh lime juice and sprinkle Tabasco sauce over clams to taste.
Makes 8 servings.

overleaf: *Fresh Chocolate Clams—which have nothing to do with chocolate but are simply known by this name—are eaten with a squirt of lime juice and a dash of Tabasco sauce.*

ENSALADA DE CHILES ESTILO SONORA
Chile Salad, Sonora Style

This salad, usually eaten in Sonora, is served as an appetizer. It also can be served as an entrée, accompanied with melted cheese and flour tortillas.

FOR THE SALAD

8	California (Anaheim) chiles
1½	heads romaine lettuce, shredded and chilled
24	tomatoes, peeled and sliced
24	thin slices white onion
	Freshly ground pepper

FOR THE VINAIGRETTE

1½	cups fruit vinegar (see recipe on page 128) or cider vinegar
1	cup olive oil
4	cloves garlic, chopped
16	thin slices white onion
¾	tablespoon salt
1	tablespoon sugar
1	tablespoon freshly ground pepper

Prepare the salad: Roast chiles, and let sweat for 6 minutes (see Basics). Peel and devein, if you choose. (Since these chiles are mild, they need not be deveined.) As an alternative to roasting, the chiles may be fried in oil until browned, and then peeled.

Prepare the vinaigrette: Whisk vinegar and oil in a bowl. Add garlic, onion, salt, sugar, and pepper. Let stand for 1 day.

To serve, place a bed of lettuce on each of 8 plates. Arrange the chiles and the tomato and onion slices on top. Pour vinaigrette over. Sprinkle with pepper.
Makes 8 servings.

preceding overleaf, left: Mild northern chiles are roasted for a chile salad, which is served on a glazed clay dish from Michoacán.
preceding overleaf, right: Norteños prepare seafood in a variety of ways. Rosarito Lobster may be garnished with fresh shrimp and fried fish fillets.

LANGOSTA ROSARITO
Rosarito Lobster

This dish can be prepared in two ways. The photo on page 41 shows the poached version. This recipe details the baked alternative.

1	cup butter
1	teaspoon dried oregano
1	tablespoon garlic salt, or to taste
1	tablespoon freshly ground pepper
4	large, fresh lobsters, halved

Preheat oven to 350 degrees, or heat a griddle or comal over medium heat for 25 minutes.

Cream butter with oregano, garlic salt, and pepper. Divide mixture into 1-tablespoon measures, and spread each over lobster half. Bake lobster in oven or on griddle for 20 minutes or until done and at its juiciest.

Serve with frijoles de olla, Pico de Gallo sauce, and freshly made flour tortillas.

Roll lobster into tacos.
Makes 8 servings.

Generally, the smaller the chile, the hotter it is.

FRIJOLES BORRACHOS
Drunken Beans

Drunken beans are a representative dish of the area around Monterrey, one of the first regions to enjoy beer.

FOR THE BEANS

1½ pounds dried pinto beans, cleaned, rinsed, and soaked overnight in water to cover
3 to 3½ quarts water
1 large white onion, halved
6 cloves garlic, whole
1 tablespoon lard or vegetable oil

FOR THE SAUCE

½ cup lard
1 large white onion, finely chopped
3 large tomatoes, finely chopped
4 chiles serranos or jalapeños, finely chopped
1½ cups cilantro, finely chopped
2 cups light or dark beer
Salt to taste

Prepare the beans: Put beans in a pressure cooker. Cover with water; then add onion, garlic, and lard. Cover and cook for about 45 minutes to 1 hour. If preparing in a regular pot, put the beans in a deep casserole, and add 3 times their volume in water. Add onion, garlic, and lard. Cook over low heat for 1½ to 2 hours or until beans are tender. If water evaporates, add more warm water.

Meanwhile, prepare the sauce: Heat lard in a heavy frying pan. Add onion, and fry until lightly browned. Add tomato, chiles, and cilantro. Add the beans. Salt to taste, and add beer. Correct seasoning, and continue to cook over low heat until mixture thickens, about 45 minutes.

To serve, pour hot beans into a clay or ceramic serving dish. Serve with roasted kid or other meat and corn or flour tortillas.
Makes 8 servings.

FRIJOLES MANEADOS
Tied-Up Beans

FOR THE BEANS

1½ pounds dried pinto or bayo beans, cleaned, rinsed, and soaked overnight in water to cover
1½ white onions
½ head garlic, unpeeled
Salt to taste

FOR THE SAUCE

¾ cup butter or lard
⅓ cup vegetable oil
6 chiles anchos, seeded, deveined, roasted, cleaned, soaked in water (see Basics), and blended
1 white onion, chopped
1 tablespoon ground chile or chile powder
Salt to taste
3 cups Chihuahua, Monterey Jack, or mozzarella cheese, shredded

Prepare the beans: Put beans, onion, and garlic in a large clay or ceramic pot, and add three times their volume in water. Bring to a boil. Reduce heat, and simmer for 1½ hours. If necessary, add more warm water during cooking. When beans are tender, salt to taste, and purée in a blender or food processor.

Prepare the sauce: Heat butter and oil in a heavy frying pan, and add chiles, onion, and ground chile. Fry until this mixture forms a thick sauce. Salt lightly. Gradually add puréed beans, stirring and cooking over medium heat until mixture thickens. Gradually add cheese, and cook over low heat until bean mixture is slightly thicker.

To serve, spoon beans onto a platter and accompany with freshly made flour tortillas.
Makes 8 servings.

Shredded meat and scrambled eggs—accompanied by Beans with Cheese, Northern Style.

FRIJOLES CON QUESO ESTILO NORTENO
Beans with Cheese, Northern Style

FOR THE BEANS

½ cup vegetable oil

4 slices white onion

1 generous pound dried pinto or bayo beans, cooked (see recipe on page 43)

2¼ pounds Oaxaca or mozzarella cheese, shredded

FOR THE GARNISH

¾ cup white onion, chopped

¾ cup cilantro, chopped

24 flour tortillas (see recipe on page 32)

Heat oil in a casserole. Add onion, and brown until al-most charred. Add cooked beans, and then gradually add cheese. Stir with a wooden spoon until cheese and beans are well mixed. Cook over low heat until mixture thickens.

To serve, spoon beans and cheese into a clay or an enamel casserole. Serve onion and cilantro in individual bowls on the side, along with freshly made tortillas. This dish usually accompanies meat or scrambled eggs. ***Makes 8 servings.***

CABRITO AL PASTOR
Broiled Kid

Kid has traditionally been savored in Nuevo León. Herbs growing in the northern state's saltpeter-rich soil give this meat an exquisite, unusual flavor.

Broiled kid is a celebrated dish in Monterrey, where the meat is roasted on an open spit.

FOR THE KID

2   kids, 6½ to 8½ pounds each, without heads
3   tablespoons salt
1   cup mild vinegar

FOR THE GARNISH

2   cups guacamole (see recipe on page 33)
3   tablespoons white onion, chopped
1   cup tomato, finely chopped
3   tablespoons cilantro, finely chopped
3   tablespoons chiles serranos, finely chopped
1   recipe frijoles de olla, mashed (see recipe on page 187)
1½ cups mozzarella or Monterey Jack cheese, freshly grated
16 totopos (crisply fried tortilla wedges)

Put kids in a large stock pot, and cover with water. Add salt and vinegar. Set aside for 2 hours. Meanwhile, build a pile of mesquite wood on the ground, and burn down to white coals. Remove kids from water, and thread on spits. Arrange over the hot coals, and roast for 2 to 3 hours, depending on the kids' weight, basting occasionally with a little salted water. Turn spits continuously so that the meat cooks evenly, or use a rotisserie. Add more white coals if necessary.

To serve, cut kid in pieces, and place on plates. Garnish with guacamole, onion, tomato, cilantro, and chiles. Serve with frijoles de olla sprinkled with cheese, totopos, and Pico de Gallo Sauce.

The kid may be shredded and used in fried tacos.
Makes 8 servings.

clockwise from top: Chile verde en bolita, chile piquín seco, chile de monte, *ripe* chiles serranos, *and* chile verde piquín.

CARNE SECA PARA BOTANA
Dried-Meat Appetizer

Dried meat served as an appetizer is one of the most popular dishes in the northern mountain range.

FOR THE BEEF

14	ounces dried beef, preferably from Monterrey, cut in 2-inch squares
	Vegetable oil

FOR THE GARNISH

2	large limes, sliced, plus 4 limes, quartered

Heat a comal or griddle. Lightly baste beef with oil, and roast on both sides.

To serve, place roasted beef on a platter. Garnish with limes. Serve with cold beer.
Makes 8 servings.

MACHACA CON HUEVO ESTILO SIENEGA
Shredded Beef with Egg, Siénega Style

Sun-dried meat is typical of Monterrey and of the entire state of Nuevo León, having originated in the town of Siénega. Once dried, the meat is rolled and sold as is.

FOR THE BEEF

1	cup vegetable oil
2½	cups white onion, finely chopped
2½	cups dried beef, finely shredded
2½	cups tomato, finely chopped
6	chiles serranos, piquines, or cambrayes, finely chopped
16	eggs, beaten
¾	teaspoon salt

FOR THE GARNISH

1	pound pinto beans, cooked, refried with chopped onion, and thickened (see recipe on page 43)
1	cup fresh cheese, such as feta, or dried ricotta, crumbled
12	sprigs cilantro

Heat ¾ cup oil in a saucepan. Add onion, and sauté until lightly browned. Add beef, tomato, and chiles. Continue cooking over low heat until sauce thickens. (The sauce can be made ahead to this point.)

Add ¼ cup oil. Reheat sauce, and return to boil. Add eggs and salt. Cook over high heat, occasionally stirring with a fork, until the eggs are spongy—do not allow them to dry.

To serve, spoon a layer of hot beans onto the center of a platter. Ring the beans with the shredded beef and egg mixture. Sprinkle with cheese. Decorate with cilantro. Serve with freshly made tortillas and coffee.
Makes 8 servings.

Shredded Meat with Egg, Siénega Style is prepared with ingredients basic to northern Mexican cuisine.

TAQUITOS DE TUETANO
Marrow Tacos

Marrow is served often in Mexican cuisine and plays a key role in hors d'oeuvres. It is mixed with masa to make sopecitos (miniature masa appetizers) and served with sauce and fresh, crumbled white cheese.

FOR THE MARROW
5	quarts water
32	marrowbones, each 4 inches long
	Salt to taste

FOR THE TACOS
Tortillas

In a saucepan, bring water to a boil. Add marrow-bones and salt. Reduce heat, and cook bones over low heat until the marrow is tender, about 1 hour.

To serve, place marrowbones on individual plates, and remove the marrow from the bones. Serve with freshly made tortillas, and roll into tacos, adding salt and sauce of your choice. Serve hot.

Makes 8 servings.

Beef stew and a glass of frosty cold beer.

CALDILLO
Stew

Caldillo, also called cazuela, is cooked by men, who compete to make the tastiest and hottest version. This is a prize-winning recipe for this northern regional stew.

½	cup olive oil or vegetable oil
2½	pounds beef steak, sirloin or fillet, ground
	Salt and pepper to taste
1	cup white onion, finely chopped
2	cups tomato, peeled, seeded, and chopped
4	teaspoons chile jalapeño or serrano, chopped
5	quarts hot beef stock

Heat a heavy saucepan for 10 minutes. Pour in oil, and heat.

Add beef, and fry until it begins to brown. Season with salt and pepper. Add onion, tomato, and chiles, and continue to fry until mixture begins to release its fat.

Pour beef stock into the mixture gradually. Cook stew until it thickens.

To serve, spoon stew into individual soup bowls. Serve with bread or freshly made corn tortillas.

This stew also can be prepared with dried beef.

Makes 8 servings.

Marrow Tacos are prepared with fresh corn tortillas.

above: *The ingredients for Chile with Melted Cheese; and* opposite, *the finished dish.*

CHILE CON ASADERO
Chile with Melted Cheese

The chiles used in Chihuahua are known as chilacas, or as California or Anaheim chiles, and are different from chilacas used elsewhere in Mexico. They are roasted, placed in a plastic bag for a few minutes to ease the peeling procedure, deveined, and sliced into thin strips. In the northern part of Mexico, asadero is one of the most popular dishes.

3⅓	cups vegetable oil
24	California (Anaheim) chiles
½	cup butter
3	red onions, finely chopped
8	cups asadero, soft Cheddar, Monterey Jack, or Mennonite cheese, cubed
2	cups milk
1½	cups heavy cream
1½	cups crème fraîche
	Salt and pepper to taste
2	large tomatoes, peeled, finely chopped, and well drained

Heat 3 cups oil in a frying pan, and fry chiles briefly, until skin begins to swell. Remove immediately. Place chiles in a plastic bag, and then peel and cut into thin strips (see Basics).

Heat butter and ⅓ cup oil in a frying pan, and sauté onions. Add chile strips, and sauté. Add cheese, and cook over low heat until cheese begins to melt. Add milk, heavy cream, and crème fraîche, and season with salt and pepper. Cook for 20 minutes or until a thick sauce is formed with the partially melted cheese.

Add tomatoes immediately before serving.

To serve, spoon into individual clay bowls or onto salad plates. Serve with freshly made corn tortillas.
Makes 8 servings.

TAMALITOS REGIOMONTANOS
Small Tamales, Monterrey Style

These small tamales are traditionally served at family reunions.

FOR THE HUSKS

120   dried corn husks, approximately

FOR THE STUFFING

2½   quarts water
6   cloves garlic, whole
1   large white onion, coarsely chopped
3   cloves
1   stick cinnamon, about 6 inches long
1¾   pounds pork leg or loin, in chunks
   Salt to taste

FOR THE SAUCE

¾   cup lard
2   thick slices white onion
8   chiles anchos, seeded, deveined, and soaked in water for 20 minutes (see Basics)
4   very dry chiles guajillos, lightly roasted, seeded, deveined, and soaked in water for 20 minutes (see Basics)
8   cloves garlic, whole
1   medium white onion, coarsely chopped
1   teaspoon freshly ground pepper
½   teaspoon freshly ground allspice
4   bay leaves
1   tablespoon cumin seeds
   Salt to taste
2   cups beef broth

FOR THE DOUGH

1½   pounds lard, prepared at least 1 day ahead
2   tablespoons salt, or to taste
3⅓   pounds masa or equivalent made with masa harina (see Basics)

The best tamales are prepared with homemade lard. Lard, chiles anchos, garlic, and pork are among the ingredients used to make Small Tamales, Monterrey Style.

Prepare the husks: Fill a stock pot with water, and soak husks overnight. Rinse husks well, and cut off the tip of each. Cut husks in half lengthwise. Dry well with paper towels. Set aside.

Prepare the stuffing: Bring water to a boil in a stock pot. Add garlic, onion, cloves, cinnamon, pork, and salt. Cook over low heat for 2½ hours or until meat is tender. Cool pork in broth for 2 hours. Shred or finely chop pork, and set aside.

Prepare the sauce: Heat lard in a heavy saucepan. Add onion slices, and sauté. Meanwhile, drain chiles, reserving soaking water. In a blender, purée chiles anchos and guajillos, garlic, onion, pepper, allspice, bay leaves, cumin, and ½ cup soaking water. Add chile mixture to lard, and simmer for 45 minutes. Salt, and continue cooking until the sauce thickens. Add shredded pork and beef broth. Continue cooking for 25 minutes.

Prepare the dough: Beat lard with an electric mixer or by hand until light and spongy. Add salt and masa. Beat or knead with a little water or stock until dough is light. The dough is light enough when a small amount floats when dropped in water.

Put 1½ teaspoons of dough in the center of a corn husk. With the back of a spoon, spread evenly almost to the edges. Line 1 teaspoon of stuffing down the center. Fold sides of husks toward the center, overlapping. Fold top and bottom toward the center. Tie with thin strips cut from corn husks.

Bring 3 cups water to a boil in a steamer base. Drop a coin into the water. When you can no longer hear the coin rattling, the water has evaporated. Add more water. Put rack in steamer, and cover with a layer of corn husks.

Place tamales on husks in steamer, standing upright. Cover with a layer of corn husks and a dish towel. Put lid on steamer, and steam for 1½ hours or until the husk can be easily peeled from the dough. If necessary, add more water to steamer, being careful it does not boil onto tamales.

To serve, arrange tamales, steaming hot, on a platter. Serve with black coffee, whipped hot chocolate, or atole.

Makes about 60 to 80 tamales.

FILETE AL CHIPOTLE
Fillet with Chipotle Chile

FOR THE SAUCE

¾   cup vegetable oil
3   to 6 dried, or 2 canned, chiles chipotles
1   chile ancho
1½   white onions, quartered
4   medium cloves garlic, whole
      Salt to taste
25   fresh or canned tomatillos, husked
½   cup cilantro, chopped
⅓   cup olive oil or corn oil
2   thick slices white onion

FOR THE BEEF

2   tablespoons butter
½   cup olive oil
8   beef fillets (filet mignon), 5 to 6 ounces each
      Salt to taste
¾   tablespoon freshly ground pepper
1½   cups beef broth

FOR THE GARNISH

8   tortillas, 4 inches in diameter, fried in oil
8   slices manchego or Monterey Jack cheese, 3
      ounces each
      Cilantro, chopped

Prepare the sauce: Heat vegetable oil in a frying pan. Fry chiles chipotles and ancho briefly. Remove, and drain. Add onion and garlic to oil, and brown. Salt to taste. Add more oil if necessary. Add tomatillos, and boil in 3 cups water for 15 minutes (or briefly if using canned). Remove from heat, and pour mixture into a blender. Add cilantro and blend.

Heat olive oil in a pan, and brown onion slices. Remove onion when brown, and discard. Add sauce, and cook over low heat for 40 minutes or until fat rises to the surface. Correct seasoning. Keep warm.

Prepare the beef: Heat a heavy, dry frying pan for 25 minutes. Add a little butter and oil. Heat. Brown 4 fillets, frying for 3 to 4 minutes on a side and turning once. When juice begins to rise to the surface, sprinkle with salt and pepper. Remove from skillet. Keep warm. Repeat procedure with remaining 4 fillets. Add chicken broth to pan juices. Boil until reduced by half. Add sauce, and simmer for 25 minutes. Put meat in sauce, and heat for 5 to 8 minutes.

To serve, place 1 tortilla on each plate. Place 1 fillet on the tortilla, and cover with 1 cheese slice. Slip under broiler to melt cheese. Cover with hot sauce, and sprinkle with cilantro. Serve with refried beans.
Makes 8 servings.

SALSA PICO DE GALLO (SALSA MEXICANA)
Pico de Gallo Sauce (Mexican Sauce)

Pico de Gallo *sauce is one of the most popular in Mexico. It is typically served from a clay bowl or stone mortar to accompany fresh tortillas and grilled meats, fowl, fish, or melted cheese.*

1½   white onions, finely chopped
4   tomatoes (generous 2 pounds), peeled, seeded, and finely chopped
2   to 4 chiles serranos, finely chopped
½   cup cilantro, finely chopped
      Salt to taste
      Juice of 1 lime
2   tablespoons olive oil

Put onion, tomato, chiles, and cilantro in a bowl. Season with salt, lime juice, and oil. Stir, and marinate for 1 hour before serving.

Serve with totopos (crisply fried tortilla wedges), cheese tacos, quesadillas, or empanadas.

Oregano or chopped avocado may be added to the sauce. Cilantro may be omitted, adding instead freshly ground pepper and chopping the ingredients more coarsely. This version is very popular in Baja California, where it is served wtih seafood and fried fish.
Makes 8 servings.

Mexican kitchenware and table linen are often excellent examples of Indian handicraft. The Tarahumaran jug complements a sarape on the chair, in a table setting for Fillet with Chipotle Chile.

The best beef in Mexico is raised and consumed in northern Mexico. It is used in innumerable dishes, such as this one for fillet tips garnished with cilantro and chiles jalapeños.

PUNTAS DE FILETE A LA NORTENA
Fillet, Northern Style

FOR THE SAUCE

½   cup butter
½   cup olive oil
4   medium white onions, sliced on the diagonal
15 chiles serranos, sliced in thin strips
6   tomatoes (2⅓ pounds), finely chopped
     Salt and freshly ground pepper to taste

FOR THE BEEF

24 slices bacon, finely chopped
½   cup olive oil
1   medium white onion, finely chopped
4   pounds beef fillet, cut in 2- by ½-inch pieces
     Salt and freshly ground pepper to taste

FOR THE GARNISH

4   chiles jalapeños, sliced in thin strips
¾   cup cilantro, finely chopped

Prepare the sauce: Heat a frying pan over medium-high heat for 6 minutes. Add butter and oil. Stir in onion and chiles. Cook onion until transparent and golden brown. Add tomatoes, and season lightly with salt and pepper. Stir. Bring to a boil, reduce heat, and simmer for 30 minutes or until the sauce thickens and the fat rises to the surface.

Prepare the beef: Heat a heavy frying pan over medium-high heat for 15 minutes. Fry bacon until crisp. Remove, and drain on paper towels. Add oil to frying pan. Stir in onion, and sauté until light brown. Add beef, and brown for 8 minutes. Season lightly with salt and pepper. Remove beef from frying pan. Keep warm.

Add sauce to frying pan used for cooking beef. Stir in bacon, and cook until the sauce thickens.

To serve, divide beef among 8 plates. Cover with sauce. Garnish each plate with chile strips, and sprinkle with cilantro. Serve with hot flour or corn tortillas.
Makes 8 servings.

COYOTAS DE DONA MARIA VILLA DE SERIS
Turnovers Courtesy of Doña María, Villa de Seris

The aroma of turnovers permeates the air of Villa de Seris, Sonora. No one can resist purchasing a few of these hot delicacies. The turnovers often are dipped in hot coffee with milk after dinner or served as a dessert.

FOR THE DOUGH
1	to 2 tablespoons butter
2½	pounds unbleached flour
1½	tablespoons salt
1¼	pounds vegetable shortening
	Cold water

FOR THE FILLING
4	cups unrefined brown sugar, grated, or dark brown sugar
¾	cup unbleached flour

Freshly baked Coyotas.

Preheat oven to 350 degrees. Butter 2 baking sheets, and set aside.

Prepare the dough: Put flour and salt on a pastry board. Mix in shortening, using fingertips, until a gritty consistency is obtained. Slowly add cold water, kneading until the dough is soft and elastic, about 40 minutes. Cover dough, and set aside for 4 hours. If dough is thin, let it sit twice as long. Reknead for 8 minutes. Form about 30 2-inch balls with the dough. Using a rolling pin, flatten balls into circles, about 4 inches in diameter. The dough will shrink, so turn and roll on both sides.

Prepare the filling: Combine sugar and flour. Put 1½ to 2 tablespoons of the filling in the center of a dough circle. Cover with another circle, and seal edges. Remove any excess dough with a knife. Continue until all the circles are filled. Place turnovers on prepared baking sheets, and bake for 35 minutes or until golden brown. Remove, and place in a basket. Serve warm.

The turnovers can be refrigerated in a plastic bag and reheated briefly in a warm oven (350 degrees). The turnover dough also can be filled with a pumpkin filling.
Makes 15 coyotas.

PAN DE DATIL MULEGE
Date Bread, Mulegé Style

FOR THE BATTER

8	egg yolks
¾	cup sugar
2	cups dates, chopped
1	cup butter, melted
10	egg whites
1	cup flour
½	teaspoon ground ginger
1	tablespoon ground cinnamon
1	tablespoon ground nutmeg
	Pinch of ground cloves
1½	cups pecans, coarsely chopped
¾	cup raisins

FOR THE GARNISH

	Powdered sugar
10	dates, whole

Preheat oven to 350 degrees. Grease an angel-food-cake pan or loaf pan. Line with waxed paper.

Beat egg yolks until thick and lemon-colored. Add sugar, and continue beating until mixture forms a thick ribbon when poured from a spoon. In another bowl, add dates to melted butter. Gradually beat in egg-yolk mixture. Set aside.

Beat egg whites until they form soft peaks. Fold half the egg-yolk mixture into whites. Set aside.

Sift flour with ginger, cinnamon, nutmeg, and cloves. Add to egg mixture. Stir in pecans and raisins. Fold in remaining egg-yolk mixture.

Pour batter into pan, and bake for 1 hour or until a toothpick inserted in bread comes out clean. Remove

Date bread, garnished with fresh dates from southern Baja California.

from oven, and allow to cool on a rack. Unmold onto a tray.

Decorate bread with sugar, and garnish tray with dates.

Serve alone or with vanilla or coconut ice cream.
Makes 1 10-inch loaf.

Pecan Brittle made from locally grown nuts.

PALANQUETA DE NUEZ
Pecan Brittle

In the state of Nuevo León, pecan trees grow in abundance on the mountainsides. Their nuts are used in many desserts and candies, including this nut brittle, which is very popular in northeastern Mexico.

4   cups sugar
½   cup water
3   cups pecans, halved and lightly toasted

Put sugar in a saucepan. Add water, and stir to dissolve. Without stirring, cook over low heat until sugar melts and begins to form a caramel, turning an amber color. Add nuts, and stir; pour immediately into a greased 7- to 8-inch round heat-resistant dish. Cool.

To serve, unmold nut brittle onto a round tray. Serve as a dessert.
Makes 8 servings.

LECHE CARAMELIZADA
Caramelized Milk

Caramelized milk has been a popular dessert in Mexico since the eighteenth century.

FOR THE PUDDING

8	egg yolks
1	cup sugar
⅓	cup corn starch, dissolved in a little milk
1	tablespoon flour
4½	cups milk, boiled for 8 minutes
1	tablespoon vanilla extract
¾	cup raw almonds, skinned and ground
4	tablespoons butter

FOR THE CARAMEL

½	cup sugar
1½	tablespoons butter, in small pieces

Beat egg yolks with an electric mixer, gradually adding sugar, until mixture is light-colored and airy. Add dissolved corn starch, flour, and milk, alternating, to egg-yolk mixture. Beat until all ingredients are well blended. Pour mixture into a saucepan, and heat over low heat for 20 minutes, stirring constantly with a wooden spoon. Add vanilla extract and almonds, cooking until mixture boils and thickens. Remove from heat. Add butter, mixing well. Cool by placing pan on a bed of ice, stirring constantly so top film does not form. Pour pudding into an ovenproof serving bowl. Sprinkle with sugar and butter.

Heat a comal for 25 minutes. Remove from heat. Place hot griddle on top of pudding until the sugar caramelizes. Alternatively, run pudding under a preheated broiler for 2 minutes or until the sugar caramelizes.

Makes 8 servings.

NARANJAS EN DULCE
Oranges in Syrup

This dessert is a typical dish of Montemorelos.

FOR THE ORANGES

20	Seville (bitter) or sweet oranges
	Salt to taste

FOR THE SYRUP

2	quarts water
6	quarts fresh orange juice
8	cups sugar
3	sticks cinnamon, each 8 inches long

FOR THE GARNISH

	Fresh cheese
	Yogurt or buttermilk
1	stick cinnamon
	Orange leaves (optional)

Prepare the oranges: Grate the peel from all the oranges, instead of peeling. Discard grated peel (or freeze and save for other recipes). Cut the oranges in quarters. Squeeze the juice from the oranges. Reserve. Using a needle and thread, thread orange quarters to form a long necklace.

Put oranges in a saucepan with water to cover and salt. Boil for 25 minutes. Remove from heat. Drain and rinse oranges. Soak. Change water throughout the day, until the water remains clear.

Prepare the syrup: Put water and reserved orange juice in a saucepan. Add sugar and cinnamon. Cook over medium heat until mixture forms a thick syrup, about 1½ to 2 hours. Add oranges, and continue cooking until oranges are golden and have absorbed some of the syrup.

To serve, spoon oranges in syrup onto a platter or into a clay pot. Garnish with fresh cheese, yogurt, a cinnamon stick, and orange leaves, if desired.

Makes 8 servings.

Candied oranges are garnished with orange leaves and cinnamon.

CHAPTER TWO

THE NORTH PACIFIC COAST

The states along the fertile northern stretch of Mexico's long Pacific shoreline—Sinaloa, Nayarit, Jalisco, and Colima—supply much of the country's staple grains, fruits, and vegetables as well as its freshest and widest selection of local cheeses, tomatoes, and chiles.

Mexico's northern Pacific coast is a spectacular succession of stately coconut plantations, sandy coves, and rocky, surf-battered headlands. The northernmost stretch of coast is washed by the clear, tranquil Gulf of California, a sheltered sea that opens to the south into the Pacific Ocean. The confluence of these two distinct marine environments yields a wide variety of fish; marlin, black sea bass, sailfish, and other valiant billfish are caught far offshore, while smaller species, such as porgy and amberjack, are abundant close to the beach. Aside from being masters of more traditional approaches to fish preparation, local cooks are wont to put aside the best marlin steaks for slow smoking. This technique is popular in the resort of Mazatlán, where swordfish is smoked over aromatic mesquite to give it a bold, rustic flavor. Gifted or thrifty cooks also smoke and shred various species of dogfish, which others might be tempted to

discard. Snook and tuna, among other species, are often served raw as a *ceviche*, following a brief marination in lime juice. Shrimp are also common and are prepared in *ceviche* or as a filling for tamales.

The state of Sinaloa is characterized primarily by vast fields of rice, sugar cane, and winter vegetables that dominate the landscape. Agribusiness gives Sinaloa its sense of identity; the state's professional baseball team, tellingly, is named the *Tomateros*—Tomato Growers.

Like Sinaloa, Nayarit, the next state to the south, is dedicated to commercial farming in the rich lowlands, with the brackish estuaries of the coast offering abundant shrimp and shellfish.

Bordering Nayarit is Jalisco, one of the most beautiful of Mexico's thirty-one states. Jalisco is the home of mariachi. Developed there a century ago as wedding-party entertainment, mariachi has evolved into the musical form that best symbolizes Mexico to Mexicans and foreigners alike. Jalisco also produced two of Mexico's greatest artists: the muralist José Clemente Orozco, a painter of dark and heroic vision, and Juan Rulfo, perhaps the greatest Spanish-language novelist of the first half of this century—a reputation earned from two slim volumes portraying peasant life in Jalisco's high, agave-studded plains.

Jalisco is also beaches. Puerto Vallarta pulsates with a tropical rhythm that draws both the famous and the not-so-famous tourist. The local specialty is a whole fish—usually a red snapper fresh from the ocean—skewered on a long wooden stick that is braced upright in the sand. The fish is grilled over a low fire and eaten *muy pronto*. It needs only a squirt of fresh lime juice to enhance its freshness to near perfection.

Inland lies Guadalajara, a city that most Americans find enchanting. The architecture is colonial at its best; the food is among Mexico's finest. The tortillas in this genteel city are very light in color and texture, almost delicate, but Guadalajara's two most famous culinary contributions are robust and hearty.

Pozole is the specialty of an endless variety of local restaurants. The stew, based on pork and hominy, is a meal in itself. Cooks prepare either white or red *pozole*. The red version is spiced with the rather mild *chile guajillo* and the fiery *chile de árbol*. The stew is served in earthenware bowls typical of the area and is garnished with a flourish of vegetables—radishes, onions, and cabbage—some oregano, and, of course, lime.

If *pozole* is the king of Jalisco cuisine, as the locals call it, then *birria* surely is a serious pretender to the throne. Its unmistakable bold flavor is unabashedly enjoyed throughout the city and countryside. Goat meat or mutton is spiced with chiles, cooked and shredded, and served in a tomato and meat broth. A sprinkle of raw onion and cilantro provides a final, contrasting garnish. This regional favorite is accompanied by Jalisco's gift to the world—tequila.

A generation before Mexico won its independence from Spain, the Cuervo family already was distilling the potent cactus drink in the small Jalisco town that gave the liquor its name. Jalisco also has provided the formula for a perfect tequila chaser, *sangrita*. While not intoxicating, it ignites the senses with its liberal ratio of *chile piquín* to fresh orange juice.

Bordering Jalisco to the south is Colima, the smallest of Mexico's coastal states. Manzanillo comes closest among Colima resorts to attracting the jet set, and restaurant specialties feature the bounty of both the sea—shrimp and fish dishes—and the land—creations like cold coconut soup.

In many ways, although no self-respecting native of Colima would admit it, Colima culture and cuisine are much like those of Jalisco—yet Colima's relative isolation has perhaps kept local traditions intact. Fittingly, when Juan Rulfo looked for a town to serve as a setting for *Pedro Páramo*, his classic portrait of Jalisco country life, he chose a town in Colima—Comala, which preserves its unhurried rural ways.

The essence of Colima flourishes inland—in the modest pueblos framed by snow-topped volcanoes; in the cantinas where Sunday snacks are served to big, hungry families; in the homes where the abundant Colima dinners are offered with their trademark components, such as thick soups and *tatemado*, a meat dish cooked with *chile pasilla*, tomatoes, cumin, ginger, pepper, and bay leaves. Accompanying these meals are such Colima creations as *tuba*—a mild, fermented beer-like drink made from palm sap—and *agua de granada*—a beverage made from local pomegranates. The state's renowned coconut brandy has a more potent kick. But Colima's most intoxicating specialty is its dense, balmy tropical air, which is suffused—as Rulfo wrote—with the fragrances "of alfalfa, of bread,...of the orange blossom in the warmth of the season."

SOPA VERDE
Green Soup

FOR THE SOUP

5	quarts water
2	fish heads, preferably red snapper, sea bass, or grouper, washed
1	fish backbone, washed
1	fish tail, washed
1	cup dry white wine
4	medium carrots, peeled
½	leek, in 4 pieces
1	small turnip
1	white onion, quartered
4	cloves garlic, whole
10	sprigs parsley
4	bay leaves
10	black peppercorns
2	tablespoons powdered chicken bouillon, or salt to taste

FOR THE SAUCE

6	chiles poblanos, seeded, deveined (see Basics), and chopped
2	cups parsley, chopped
1½	cups cilantro, chopped
½	cup epazote, or to taste
½	cup white onion, puréed
6	cloves garlic, whole
⅓	cup olive oil
5⅓	tablespoons butter
	Salt and pepper to taste
64	medium shrimp

FOR THE GARNISH

8	limes, halved

Prepare the soup: Bring water to a boil in a stock pot. Add fish heads, backbone, and tail. Stir in wine, carrots, leek, turnip, onion, garlic, parsley, bay leaves, peppercorns, and bouillon. Cook over low heat for 1¼ hours. Cool.

Strain broth, reserving vegetables. Blend about one-quarter of the vegetables in a blender or food processor. Add to broth, and stir. Heat to boiling point, and hold.

Prepare the sauce: Blend chiles, parsley, cilantro, epazote, onion, and garlic with 3 cups fish broth in a blender or food processor. Heat oil and butter in a saucepan. Add blended ingredients, and cook until thick. Salt and pepper to taste. Add shrimp, and heat for 10 minutes. Stir in boiling broth, correcting seasoning. Simmer for 25 minutes.

Serve green soup from a tureen, with lime halves on the side.

Makes 8 servings.

POZOLE JALISCIENSE
Pork and Hominy Soup, Jalisco Style

This hearty pork soup is enjoyed throughout Mexico. Jalisco has two versions: white and red soup. Since pozole contains meat, corn, and vegetables, it is considered a meal in itself and usually is served alone.

FOR THE CORN BASE

4½	quarts water
3	tablespoons ground limestone
2	white onions, halved
2¼	pounds dried hominy

preceding overleaf: Mexican cooks rely on clay cookware. Green Soup is served from a clay tureen from Michoacán.

FOR THE SOUP

10	quarts water
2	heads garlic, halved
2	white onions, halved
2¼	pounds pig's head, chopped
2	pork soup bones, preferably shoulder hocks
2	pig's feet, cleaned and halved
1	pound fatback
2¼	pounds boneless pork loin, in chunks
1	2¼-pound hen or frying chicken, in pieces
	Salt to taste

FOR THE GARNISH

1	head lettuce, shredded
1½	bunches large radishes, sliced or diced
3	large white onions, finely chopped
2½	to 3 ounces ground chile piquín
2½	to 3 ounces oregano, dried and crushed
48	stale corn tortillas, fried in oil until crisp
2	California avocados, peeled and sliced
16	limes, halved

Prepare the corn base: Bring water to a boil in a large saucepan. Add limestone, onions, and hominy, and cook over low heat until hominy is tender. Remove hominy, and cool. Wash, and remove skin from kernels.

Prepare the soup: Heat water in a large saucepan. Add hominy and garlic. Cook until hominy bursts open; then remove garlic, and discard. Add onion, pork meats, and hen. Salt. Cook over medium heat for 1½ hours or until meat is tender. If necessary, add more water.

To serve, ladle pozole into soup bowls. Serve lettuce, radishes, onion, chile, oregano, tortillas, avocado, and lime in bowls on the side.

To make red pozole: Soak 6 chiles anchos and 6 chiles guajillos in water for 20 minutes. Blend chiles in a blender or food processor with 8 garlic cloves, 1½ chopped white onions, 1 teaspoon oregano, and salt. Heat ½ cup vegetable oil or lard in a saucepan, and add blended ingredients. Cook for 35 minutes. Add to soup base along with meats.
Makes 16 servings.

CHARALES
Charales

Charales are small fish that are plentiful in Lake Cha-pala, near Guadalajara. Fried, the fish make an excellent appetizer. They often are sold by street vendors.

FOR THE CHARALES

2¼	pounds charales
4	eggs, beaten
¼	cup heavy cream
3	cups flour
3	cups vegetable oil
	Salt to taste

FOR THE GARNISH

16	limes, halved

Wash and drain fish well. Beat eggs with cream in a glass bowl. Spread flour on waxed paper. Dip charales in egg mixture, and coat with flour. Heat oil in a large frying pan, and fry charales until brown, about 8 to 10 minutes, turning once. Drain on paper towels, and salt.

To serve, place charales on a platter, and garnish with limes.
Makes 8 servings.

SOPA DE COCO
Cold Coconut Soup

Coconuts are native to the coastal state of Colima. This soup, created by Chef Gabriel Gambou at the restaurant Arrecife in Manzanillo, uses this abundant ingredient to make an unusual first course.

FOR THE SOUP

1	quart milk
2	cups fresh coconut, finely shredded
2	cups fresh coconut milk
2	cups canned coconut milk
½	cup sugar
	Salt to taste
1½	cups heavy cream

FOR THE GARNISH

Ground cinnamon

Bring milk to a boil in a medium saucepan. Cool a little, and stir in coconut. Simmer for 20 minutes.

Remove from heat, and blend in a blender or food processor. Add coconut water and coconut milk. Season with sugar and salt. Add cream, beating occasionally with a whisk. Cook for 25 minutes or until soup thickens slightly. If soup becomes too thick, add a little more cream. Cool soup on a bed of crushed ice, and refrigerate.

To serve, pour chilled soup into hollowed-out coconut shells. Sprinkle cinnamon on top.

Makes 8 servings.

PAN FRANCES
French Bread

2	generous ounces dry yeast
1	tablespoon salt
1	cup very warm water
1½	pounds unbleached flour
6	to 8 tablespoons lard, softened
3	banana leaves or 3 pieces aluminum foil (optional)

Dissolve yeast and salt in water. Allow to stand until it bubbles. Mix with flour, and knead until dough is soft and elastic. Divide into 2 or 3 balls, depending on desired length of loaves. Daub with lard, and cover with a dish towel. Set aside in a warm, draft-free place, and let rise until doubled in volume, about 45 minutes.

Knead each ball until elastic. Form into oblong loaves on a banana leaf, or put loaves on greased baking sheets, and cover with a dish towel. Let rise until doubled in volume, about 30 to 45 minutes. Slash tops of loaves with knife or razor.

Preheat oven to 350 degrees. Fill a shallow pan with water, and place on bottom oven rack. Bake bread on middle rack for 30 minutes, turning loaves after 15 minutes to brown evenly.

Makes 2 or 3 loaves.

Colima is famous for its coconut brandy, but coconuts are not only fermented. A delicious cold soup is prepared from shredded coconut, coconut milk, milk, cream, and sugar.

BIRRIA ESTILO JALISCO
Mutton Soup, Jalisco Style

This hearty soup, considered a remedy for hangovers, is served for brunch throughout Mexico, but it is especially popular in the state of Jalisco. Some restaurants, called birrerias, specialize in making this soup.

FOR THE MUTTON

1	6½-pound leg of mutton, in large chunks
½	cup lard
4	small maguey leaves, or 6 banana leaves, roasted (see Basics)
6½	pounds masa, kneaded with a little warm water and salt

FOR THE ADOBO PASTE

1	quart water
10	ounces chiles anchos, roasted, seeded, and deveined (see Basics)
7	ounces chiles guajillos, roasted, seeded, and deveined (see Basics)
14	cloves garlic, whole
2½	white onions, quartered
1	teaspoon cumin seeds
½	teaspoon ground ginger
1¼	tablespoons oregano, dried and crushed
8	cloves
15	whole allspice, ground
1	stick cinnamon, 3 inches long
3	sprigs thyme
4	bay leaves
	Salt to taste

FOR THE SOUP

5	large tomatoes (about 3 pounds), roasted (see Basics)
1½	white onions, coarsely chopped
4	cloves garlic, whole
1	teaspoon dried oregano

⅓	cup vegetable oil or lard
	Salt to taste
4	quarts chicken broth (see recipe on page 202)

FOR THE GARNISH

1½	white onions, finely chopped
1	cup cilantro, finely chopped
8	to 12 limes, halved

Prepare the mutton: Spread mutton with lard. Let stand for 30 minutes.

Preheat oven to 350 degrees.

Jalisco-style Birria, or Mutton Soup, is served with Charales (see recipe on p. 67).

Traditional garb of the Mexican cowboy.

Prepare the adobo paste: Heat water in a saucepan. Add chiles anchos and guajillos to water in saucepan, and simmer for 20 minutes. Drain chiles, and reserve water. In a blender or food processor, blend chiles with garlic, onion, cumin, ginger, oregano, cloves, allspice, cinnamon, thyme, bay leaves, and salt to form a thick paste. If paste becomes too thick, add a little cooking water. Spread paste over mutton, and let stand for 30 minutes.

To cook the mutton, line a large roasting pan with leaves. Place mutton on top of leaves, and fold leaves over meat. Line a pastry board with aluminum foil. Roll masa on foil to size of roasting pan. Place masa on top of leaves, peeling off aluminum foil. Put pan in a water bath (bain-marie), and bake for 3 to 4 hours or until mutton is tender. Cooking time will vary depend-

ing on the meat. Add water to water bath as necessary.

Prepare the soup: Blend tomatoes with onion, garlic, and oregano in a blender or food processor. Heat oil in a large saucepan, and add tomato mixture. Season with salt, and simmer for 25 minutes. Add chicken broth, and cook for 25 minutes.

Remove mutton from oven. Uncover and discard masa and leaves. Shred mutton with two forks while still hot. Drain pan juices, and add to soup.

To serve, place mutton in soup bowls, and ladle soup over. Garnish individually with onion, cilantro, and limes. This soup often is served with corn tortillas, tequila, and sangrita.
Makes 8 to 12 servings.

TACOS A LA CREMA
Tacos with Cream

When tacos are fried crisp and covered with cream and cheese, they are often called flautas, *which means "flutes."*

FOR THE TACOS

24	corn tortillas
3	or 4 large potatoes, peeled, cooked in salted water, drained, and mashed
2¼	pounds Oaxaca, mozzarella, or Monterey Jack cheese, sliced in thin strips
1	quart vegetable oil

FOR THE GREEN SAUCE

1½	quarts water
14	tomatillos, husked
1	white onion, halved
5	cloves garlic, whole
4	chiles serranos
1	cup cilantro
1	large California avocado
	Salt to taste

FOR THE RED SAUCE

1½	quarts water
3	tomatoes (1¾ pounds)
1	white onion, sliced
6	cloves garlic, whole
2	chiles chipotles, 4 chiles serranos, or 2 chiles jalapeños
	Salt to taste

FOR THE GARNISH

½	cup plus 2 tablespoons crème fraîche
1	cup sour cream
½	cup half-and-half
1½	cups feta or fresh cheese, crumbled

Prepare the tacos: Heat tortillas on a comal or griddle. Put some mashed potato and cheese strips off-center on tortillas. Roll, and secure with a toothpick. (The tacos can be prepared ahead of time to this point and stored in a plastic bag in the refrigerator.)

Prepare the green sauce: Bring water to a boil in a saucepan. Add tomatillos, ½ onion, 3 garlic cloves, and chiles. Boil for 30 minutes. Remove from heat, and cool. Drain, and reserve cooking water. Blend cooked ingredients with ½ onion, 2 garlic cloves, cilantro, and avocado in a blender or food processor. Salt. If sauce becomes too thick, add a little cooking water.

Prepare the red sauce: Bring water to a boil in a saucepan. Add tomatoes, half of the onion slices, 4 garlic cloves, and chiles. Boil for 25 minutes. Drain, and reserve cooking water. Blend cooked ingredients with reserved onion slices and 2 garlic cloves in a blender or food processor. Salt. Add a little cooking water to make a slightly thick sauce.

Heat oil in a frying pan to just under smoking point. Fry tacos until crisp, turning. Remove, and drain on paper towels.

To serve, place 3 tacos on each of 8 plates. Pour green sauce on one side and red sauce on the other. Mix crème fraîche, sour cream, and half-and-half, and pour over tacos. Sprinkle cheese on top. Serve with tequila.

Makes 24 tacos.

QUESO DERRETIDO
Melted Cheese

Cheeses native to Jalisco include panela, asadero, and Mennonite. They are served as an appetizer or as a main course when accompanied by a green salad.

preceding overleaf: Cream- and cheese-covered tacos, which have been stuffed, rolled, and fried, are served on a Tlaxcalteca ceramic dish. The rim of the glass of tequila has been dipped in coarse salt.

FOR THE SAUCE

1½	white onions, chopped
4	large tomatoes, finely chopped
5	chiles serranos, finely chopped
1	cup cilantro, finely chopped
½	teaspoon oregano, dried and crushed
¼	cup lime juice
	Salt to taste

FOR THE CHEESE

14	ounces Chihuahua or muenster cheese
14	ounces asadero or Monterey Jack cheese
14	ounces Oaxaca or mozzarella cheese

Prepare the sauce: Mix ingredients in a glass bowl. Macerate for 1 hour.

Preheat oven to 350 degrees. Grease 8 individual clay bowls or ramekins (about ¾-cup capacity).

Prepare the cheese: Grate Chihuahua, asadero, and Oaxaca cheeses, and mix. Divide cheese among the bowls. Bake until melted and bubbly.

Serve immediately with the sauce and warm corn or flour tortillas.

Makes 8 servings.

CHILES ROJOS RELLENOS DE QUESO BLANCO

Red Chiles Stuffed with White Cheese

FOR THE VINAIGRETTE

1⅓	cups mild cider vinegar or wine vinegar
3	cloves garlic, puréed
2	tablespoons sugar
	Salt to taste
1	teaspoon freshly ground pepper
1	teaspoon dried oregano
3	white onions, thinly sliced on the diagonal
2	bay leaves
½	cup vegetable oil
2	cups olive oil

FOR THE CHILES

16	chiles anchos, washed

FOR THE STUFFING

2	cups cottage cheese
2	cups fresh ricotta cheese, or 1½ cups feta cheese, crumbled
1½	cups white onion, finely chopped
3	tablespoons cream
1	teaspoon freshly ground pepper

FOR THE GARNISH

16	radishes, shaped like flowers
16	knob onions, shaped like flowers
1	white onion, sliced on the diagonal
1	cup feta cheese, crumbled

Prepare the vinaigrette: In a saucepan, mix vinegar, garlic, sugar, salt, pepper, oregano, bay leaves, and onion. Heat for 3 minutes over medium heat. Remove from heat, and add vegetable and olive oils, stirring with a whisk. Set aside.

Prepare the chiles: Toast chiles lightly on a hot griddle, seed and devein, and soak in vinaigrette. Cook vinaigrette over medium heat for 15 minutes.

Remove chiles, and cool. Shake off excess liquid, and drain on paper towels.

Prepare the stuffing: Mix cottage and ricotta cheeses, mashing with a fork. Add onion, cream, and pepper. Stir well. Fill chiles with cheese mixture.

To serve, place chiles on a platter, and pour vinaigrette over. Garnish with radish and onion flowers, onion slices, and cheese. Serve at room temperature or cold.

Makes 8 servings.

CHILES SALTEADOS ESTILO LOS ARCOS
Sautéed Chiles, Los Arcos Style

Chiles can be found on every Mexican table. This recipe comes from the chefs of Los Arcos restaurant, in the city of Culiacán.

¾	cup olive oil
24	chiles caribes or amarillos
24	small knob onions
	Salt to taste
I	tablespoon freshly ground pepper

Heat a griddle or heavy frying pan. Add a little oil, and sauté chiles and onions for 4 minutes or until light brown on both sides. Sprinkle with a little more oil, add salt and pepper, and remove from heat.

To serve, place 3 chiles and 3 onions on each of 8 plates.

This appetizer is best served with tequila. Rub the edge of 8 shot glasses with water. Dip glass in salt or in salt mixed with ground chile piquín. Fill with tequila. Serve with lime halves.

Makes 8 servings.

ARROZ BLANCO CON RAJAS A LA CREMA
White Rice with Chile and Cream Sauce

This recipe comes from the chefs at Las Palomas restaurant in the resort town of Puerto Vallarta.

FOR THE RICE

I	recipe white rice (see recipe on page 202)
2	cups carrots, peeled, finely chopped, and cooked in salted water for 8 minutes

FOR THE SAUCE

½	cup olive oil
5	tablespoons butter
4	medium white onions, sliced on the diagonal
14	chiles poblanos, roasted, peeled, seeded, deveined, soaked in water (see Basics), and sliced in thin strips
	Salt to taste
½	teaspoon freshly ground pepper
I	cup heavy cream
2	cups crème fraîche or sour cream
½	cup half-and-half

FOR THE GARNISH

½	cup parsley, chopped

Prepare the rice: Make rice according to the recipe. Add carrots. Stir.

Prepare the sauce: Heat oil and butter in a saucepan. Sauté onions until transparent. Add chiles, and sauté for 10 minutes. Season to taste with salt and pepper. Add heavy cream, crème fraîche, and half-and-half, and continue cooking over low heat for 15 to 20 minutes or until sauce thickens.

To serve, spoon rice onto a platter, and pour sauce over. Sprinkle with parsley.

Makes 8 servings.

Red Sangrita (see recipe on p. 98), an excellent tequila chaser, accompanies Sautéed Chiles, Los Arcos Style.

ENCHILADAS AL TIZOC
Enchiladas, Tizoc Style

FOR THE SAUCE

4	chiles anchos, washed
5	chiles guajillos, roasted, seeded, and deveined (see Basics)
2	chiles de árbol, washed
1	quart hot water
½	cup vinegar
6	cloves garlic, puréed
1	white onion, puréed
½	teaspoon cumin seeds
1	teaspoon freshly ground pepper
1	teaspoon dried oregano
	Salt to taste

FOR THE ENCHILADAS

1½	cups vegetable oil
24	thin corn tortillas

FOR THE GARNISH

½	cup sour cream or heavy cream
¾	cup half-and-half
2	cups feta cheese, crumbled, or ricotta cheese
1	cup green onion, finely chopped

Prepare the sauce: Soak chiles anchos, guajillos, and de árbol in mixture of hot water and vinegar for 1 hour. Drain, reserving water. Blend chiles in a blender or food processor with garlic, onion, cumin, pepper, oregano, and salt. Add enough water to blend to the consistency of a slightly thick sauce. Pour into a wide bowl.

Prepare the enchiladas: Preheat a frying pan. Heat a little of the oil. Dip tortilla in sauce, and fry immediately in hot oil on both sides. Work quickly; tortillas must not become crisp. Fold over, and roll. Remove from oil. Continue until all tortillas are fried, adding oil as necessary.

Place enchiladas on a serving platter, or place 3 on each of 8 plates. Mix together sour cream and half-and-half, and pour over enchiladas. Sprinkle with cheese and onion.

Serve immediately. Accompany with beans.
Makes 8 servings.

TACOS DE ESCUINAPA
Tacos from Escuinapa

The shrimpers of Escuinapa manage several shrimp-breeding grounds, which supply the village with this delicious crustacean. The harvest is at its peak in September.

FOR THE TORTILLAS

2¼	pounds fresh masa or equivalent made with masa harina (see Basics)
	Salt to taste
1	quart vegetable oil

FOR THE STUFFING

¾	cup vegetable oil
4	cloves garlic, whole
1½	white onions, finely chopped
4	chiles cuaresmeños or jalapeños, finely chopped
5	large tomatoes (2½ to 2¾ pounds), finely chopped
30	sprigs cilantro, tied in a bunch
1¾	pounds shrimp, shelled, deveined, and finely chopped
	Salt to taste

FOR THE SAUCE

4	tomatoes, quartered
1	large white onion, halved
5	cloves garlic, whole
⅓	cup vegetable oil
	Salt to taste
5	cups fish stock (see recipe on page 214)

FOR THE GARNISH

- 1 quart water
- ½ cup vinegar
- 2 sprigs thyme or pinch of dried thyme
- 3 bay leaves
- 2 sprigs marjoram or pinch of dried marjoram
- 1 teaspoon pepper
- 1 tablespoon sugar
  Salt to taste
- 10 carrots, peeled and sliced in thin strips
- 1½ white onions, sliced
- ½ head cabbage, shredded

Prepare the tortillas: Put masa in a bowl. Add a little water and salt to taste to form a pliable dough. Knead until masa forms a firm ball.

In a tortilla press, make tortillas 4½ inches in diameter (see Basics). Cook tortillas on a hot comal or griddle until they puff by pressing down on the tortilla with a dry dish cloth. Carefully remove the thin top layer with a sharp knife, being careful not to perforate the tortilla. Set aside this thin layer for making the tacos. (Save the thick bottom layer to make tostadas, tortilla soup, or machucas.)

Prepare the stuffing: Heat oil in a frying pan. Brown garlic, and discard. Brown onion, and add chile, tomato, cilantro, shrimp, and salt. Cook until mixture thickens.

Prepare the sauce: In a blender or food processor, blend tomatoes, onion, and garlic. Strain through a mesh strainer. Heat oil in a saucepan, and add tomato mixture. Fry, and salt to taste. Cook until sauce forms a thick purée. Add fish stock, and cook for 30 minutes. Correct salt. The sauce should have consistency of a light broth. Keep warm.

Prepare the garnish: Bring water to a boil in a saucepan. Add vinegar, thyme, bay leaves, marjoram, pepper, sugar, and salt. Cook carrots for 6 to 8 min-utes in boiling water. Drain, and set aside.

Heat oil in a large frying pan. If tortillas are cold, reheat on a comal so that they do not tear when folded. Spoon 1½ to 2 tablespoons of stuffing off-center on each tortilla. Fold tortilla in half, and fry in oil on both sides until crisp. Remove from oil, and drain on paper towels.

To serve, place tacos on individual plates, and cover generously with sauce, about ¾ cup per plate. Garnish with carrots, onion, and cabbage. Serve immediately.
Makes about 24 tacos.

Shrimp-stuffed Tacos from Escuinapa, garnished with onion, carrots, and cabbage, makes a delicious light supper.

ROMERITOS
Romeritos

Romeritos, *usually accompanied with shrimp patties in* mole *sauce, is served during two holiday seasons: Lent and Christmas.*

FOR THE SAUCE

2	cups lard
1½	white onions, sliced
6	cloves garlic, whole
4	chiles anchos, washed, seeded, and deveined (see Basics)
2	chiles mulatos, washed, seeded, and deveined (see Basics)
2	chiles pasillas, washed, seeded, and deveined (see Basics)
½	cup raisins
1	cup prunes, pitted
½	cup sesame seeds, lightly toasted
24	raw almonds, skinned
30	raw peanuts, skinned
4	cloves
6	black peppercorns
1	stick cinnamon, 2 inches long
2	cups chicken broth (see recipe on page 202)
½	ripe plantain, sliced and fried
½	cup crumbs from toast
2	slices white onion
	Salt to taste
20	sprigs cilantro

FOR THE SHRIMP PATTIES

2½	cups dried shrimp, heads and tails removed, lightly toasted in shell, and puréed
⅔	cup fine bread crumbs
⅔	cup añejo, Parmesan, or Romano cheese, grated
10	egg whites
10	egg yolks, lightly beaten
3	cups vegetable oil

FOR THE VEGETABLES

2¼	pounds fresh romeritos or spinach, finely chopped, cooked in salted water for 8 minutes, soaked in cold salted water for 2 minutes, and squeezed dry
24	new red potatoes, cooked in salted water for 8 minutes and peeled
2	cups nopales (cactus pads), boiled for 25 minutes in salted water with garlic, chopped, and soaked in cold water for 2 minutes, or substitute canned

Prepare the sauce: Heat a little lard in a stock pot or saucepan. Sauté onion and garlic. Remove, and set aside. Add chiles anchos, mulatos, and pasillas to lard. Brown lightly, and remove. Add more lard, and fry raisins, prunes, sesame seeds, almonds, and peanuts. Remove from lard, and drain. Add more lard, and lightly fry cloves, peppercorns, and cinnamon. In a blender or food processor, blend all fried ingredients with about ½ cup chicken broth. Add plantain and toast crumbs. Blend.

In a large saucepan, heat remaining lard, and brown onion slices. Slowly add blended sauce and salt. Simmer for 1 hour or until fat rises to the surface. Stir in remaining broth and cilantro. If sauce becomes too thick, add more broth or water. Cook over low heat for 1 hour.

Prepare the shrimp patties: Blend shrimp with bread crumbs in a blender or food processor. Add cheese. Mix. In a bowl, beat egg whites until they form stiff peaks. Fold in egg yolks and shrimp mixture.

Heat oil in a frying pan. Spoon 1-tablespoon portions of the mixture into the pan, and fry on both sides, about 8 minutes or until patties are golden brown. Do not crowd. Drain on paper towels, and repeat the procedure until entire mixture is used.

Add shrimp patties to hot mole sauce. Add romeritos, potatoes, and nopales. Cook for 25 minutes over low heat.

To serve, place shrimp patties and vegetables on a large platter. Serve with white rice.
Makes 8 servings.

Dried shrimp are used in a variety of preparations, including the patties that accompany romeritos.

ENSALADA DE SIERRA AHUMADA DE MAZATLAN

Smoked Swordfish Salad, Mazatlán Style

Mazatlán cuisine is characterized by the abundant use of spices and herbs with fish and seafood. Swordfish is prepared in two smoked versions. One method is oven smoking, which uses sawdust as a fuel. The other calls for basting the fish with a salty liquid and smoking it over mesquite wood. The techniques yield very different flavors.

FOR THE GREENS

- 1   pound fresh spinach, tough stems removed
- 1   head romaine or bibb lettuce

FOR THE VINAIGRETTE

- ¾   cup cider vinegar
- 3   cloves garlic, puréed
- 1   tablespoon freshly ground pepper
- Salt to taste
- 1   teaspoon sugar
- 1   California avocado, peeled
- 1½   cups olive oil
- 6   tablespoons green onion, finely chopped

FOR THE GARNISH

- 1   pound smoked swordfish or marlin, shredded
- 2   cups cherry tomatoes, halved
- 16   knob onions, halved and soaked in ice water for 2 hours

Prepare the greens: Wash spinach and lettuce. Shake dry, and squeeze with a dish towel. Cut into 2-inch pieces, and refrigerate for 3 hours or until crisp.

Prepare the vinaigrette: Blend vinegar, garlic, pepper, salt, sugar, avocado, and oil in a blender or food processor. Reseason, and stir in onion. Refrigerate for 2 hours.

Swordfish is one of many varieties of fish that are smoked and eaten as appetizers or in salads.

To serve, place lettuce and spinach on 8 plates. Garnish with fish, tomatoes, and onions. Pour vinaigrette over salad just before serving, or serve vinaigrette on the side.

Makes 8 servings.

CAMARONES RELLENOS CULIACAN
Stuffed Shrimp, Culiacán Style

The state of Sinaloa is famous for its shrimping industry. Several varieties are caught in the waters off this coastal state, ranging in size from baby to jumbo.

FOR THE SHRIMP

48	giant shrimp, shelled, deveined, and butterflied (but not cut through)
1	tablespoon freshly ground pepper
3	cups fresh mozzarella, Chihuahua, or mild Cheddar cheese, grated
96	slices bacon
½	cup clarified butter
⅓	cup olive oil

FOR THE SAUCE

2	cups sour cream
2	cloves garlic, puréed
2	canned, chiles chipotles or 7 ounces canned chiles jalapeños, finely chopped
	Salt to taste
1	teaspoon pepper

FOR THE GARNISH

4	small oranges, halved horizontally and pulp removed
8	sprigs parsley
8	baby shrimp, unshelled and cooked in salted water for 4 minutes
8	limes, halved

Prepare the shrimp: Sprinkle each shrimp with pepper and with 1 tablespoon cheese. Close shrimp by folding sides together. Wrap 2 bacon slices around each

Shrimp filled with a mild cheese and wrapped in bacon are ready to be fried for Stuffed Shrimp, Culiacán Style.

shrimp. Secure bacon in place with a toothpick. Refrigerate for 2 hours.

Prepare the sauce: Blend all ingredients in a blender or food processor. Refrigerate for 2 hours.

Preheat a griddle or large frying pan for 25 minutes. Add a little butter and oil, and put shrimp on griddle or in pan. (Cook in batches.) Fry on one side for 4 minutes. Turn, and baste with butter. Fry for 6 minutes. Do not overcook. Remove shrimp from heat, and drain on paper towels.

To serve, place an orange half on each of 8 plates. Fill with sauce, and sprinkle with parsley. Garnish with a baby shrimp. Line 6 stuffed shrimp on the plate, overlapping them. Garnish with limes.

Makes 8 servings.

Shrimp Ceviche, a variation on the marinated raw-fish cocktail.

CEVICHE DE CAMARON
Shrimp Ceviche

The shrimp caught in areas where fresh and salt water meet have an unusual flavor. This recipe comes from shrimpers who belong to a cooperative in Escuinapa.

FOR THE SHRIMP
160 barbón or fresh-water shrimp, shelled and deveined

FOR THE MARINADE
1½ quarts water
1 quart lime juice
3 cups red onion, chopped
Soy sauce to taste
Salt and freshly ground pepper to taste

FOR THE GARNISH
2 red onions, sliced on the diagonal
4 cucumbers, halved lengthwise, seeded, and sliced on the diagonal
Freshly ground pepper to taste
Tabasco or Guacamaya sauce to taste
8 limes, halved

Wash shrimp, and put in a glass bowl. Stir in water, lime juice, onion, soy sauce, salt, and pepper. Marinate for 3 minutes. (If frozen shrimp are used, marinate for 20 minutes.)

To serve, place red-onion and cucumber slices on individual plates. Spoon shrimp ceviche into the middle. Sprinkle with pepper and Tabasco sauce. Garnish with limes. Serve with tostadas and ice-cold beer.

Makes 8 servings.

Shrimp with Cheese, Peppers, and Onions.

CAMARONES AL QUESO CON PIMIENTOS Y CEBOLLA
Shrimp with Cheese, Peppers, and Onions

This dish is served in Mexico Lindo, a restaurant in the port of Manzanillo.

FOR THE SHRIMP

¾ cup olive oil
½ cup butter
3 large white onions, sliced on the diagonal
5 red bell peppers, roasted (see Basics) and sliced in strips
5 green bell peppers, roasted (see Basics) and sliced in strips
 Salt and pepper to taste
48 medium shrimp, shelled and deveined

FOR THE TOPPING

14 ounces Oaxaca, manchego, or mozzarella cheese, grated
14 ounces Monterey Jack cheese, grated

Preheat oven to 350 degrees. Grease 8 small clay bowls or ramekins.

Heat oil and butter in a frying pan. Brown onion. Add red and green peppers, and cook over low heat for 15 minutes. Season with salt and pepper.

Stir in shrimp, and cook for 5 minutes. Correct seasoning.

Divide shrimp mixture among the bowls. Cover with cheeses, and bake for 20 minutes or until mixture is hot and cheese has melted.

Makes 8 servings.

Shrimp Tamales, Barbón Style are wrapped in corn husks and then steamed for about an hour, until the husks peel away easily.

TAMAL DE CAMARON ESTILO BARBON

Shrimp Tamales, Barbón Style

FOR THE HUSKS

  2 packages corn husks (enough for 30 tamales)

FOR THE DOUGH

2¼ pounds fresh masa or equivalent made with masa harina (see Basics)

1½ to 2 tablespoons salt, or to taste

1½ cups fish stock (see recipe on page 214)

  1 pound, 2 ounces lard

FOR THE STUFFING

  1 cup olive oil or lard

  6 cloves garlic, minced

  2 white onions, finely chopped

  6 chiles anchos, roasted, seeded, deveined, and soaked in hot water for 15 minutes (see Basics)

  4 chiles guajillos, roasted, seeded, deveined, and soaked in hot water for 15 minutes (see Basics)

  6 tomatoes (about 3 pounds), finely chopped

1½ teaspoons ground cumin

1½ teaspoons freshly ground pepper

    Salt to taste

2¼ pounds small shrimp, shelled and deveined

Prepare the husks: Soak husks overnight in water to cover. Rinse husks well, and cut off the tip of each.

Prepare the dough: Put masa and salt in a bowl. Gradually add fish stock, and mix with hands until smooth. The dough should be a little salty.

Beat lard by hand or with an electric mixer until light and fluffy, about 10 minutes. Little by little, add dough to lard. Beat for 25 minutes or until a small amount floats when dropped in water.

Prepare the stuffing: Heat oil in a saucepan. Add garlic and onion, and brown. Drain chiles, and blend with a little soaking water in a blender or food processor. Add to saucepan. Stir in tomato. Season with cumin, pepper, and salt. Cook over medium heat for 40 minutes. Add shrimp, and cook for 10 minutes or until sauce thickens. Correct seasoning.

Overlap 2 corn husks, and spread 1½ tablespoons of dough almost to edges of husks. Spread a spoonful of stuffing with 2 or 3 shrimp over batter. Fold sides of husks toward the center. Fold top and bottom toward the center. Tie with string or thin strips cut from corn husks.

Put a rack in a steamer, and add 1½ quarts water. Bring to a boil. Drop a coin into the water. When you can no longer hear the coin rattling, the water has evaporated. Add more water. Cover rack with a layer of corn husks.

Place tamales on husks in steamer, standing upright. Cover with a layer of corn husks and a damp dish towel. Put lid on steamer, and steam for 1 hour or until the husk can be easily peeled from the dough.

To serve, arrange tamales, steaming hot, on a platter. Serve with hot coffee.

Makes about 30 tamales.

Flour tortillas are a good accompaniment to Shredded Shrimp, served on a hand-woven tablecloth from Chiapas.

MACHACA DE CAMARON
Shredded Shrimp

This tasty appetizer is generally unknown outside Sinaloa, although it is often prepared in that state.

1	cup olive oil
¾	cup butter
4½	cups white onion, finely chopped
12	chiles serranos, minced
20	medium tomatoes, diced
80	medium shrimp, shelled, deveined, and finely chopped
	Salt to taste
½	teaspoon freshly ground pepper

Heat oil and butter in a frying pan. Add onion, and brown lightly. Add chile and tomato, and simmer until the mixture begins to thicken and release its fat.

Add shrimp, and cook over low heat for about 25 to 30 minutes. Season with salt and pepper.

To serve, spoon shredded shrimp onto a large platter. Serve with hot tortillas for making tacos.

Makes 8 servings.

Sinaloan sea bass, fresh from the market.

CALLOS DE LOBINA ESTILO CULIACAN
Striped-Bass Scallops, Culiacán Style

FOR THE BASS

Coarse salt (kosher salt) to taste
6½ pounds striped bass, cut in 1-inch cubes
Crushed ice

FOR THE MARINADE

3 quarts water
1 quart lime juice
Ice cubes

FOR THE SAUCE

1 cup chiles piquíns
12 cloves garlic, whole
4 tomatoes, roasted (see Basics)
1 tablespoon oregano, dried and crushed
1 teaspoon pepper
1 teaspoon cumin seeds
1 teaspoon ground ginger
Salt to taste
1 to 1½ quarts fish stock (see recipe on page 214) or water

FOR THE GARNISH

4 red onions, sliced on the diagonal
4 cucumbers, halved lengthwise, seeded, and sliced on the diagonal
Soy sauce to taste
Tabasco or Guacamaya sauce to taste
Salt and freshly ground pepper to taste
8 limes, halved

Prepare the bass: The day before serving, line a glass bowl with cheesecloth. Add a layer of salt, a layer of fish, and a layer of ice. Repeat layers until all the fish is used. Bring ends of cheesecloth over, and tie. Refrigerate overnight.

Prepare the marinade: Mix water and lime juice in a glass bowl. Put ice in a large bowl, and chill marinade on a bed of ice for 1½ hours.

Prepare the sauce: Heat a frying pan. Roast chiles for 1½ minutes or until charred. Remove from pan, and grind in a molcajete, blender, or food processor. Add garlic, tomatoes, oregano, pepper, cumin, ginger, and salt. Blend well. Add fish stock, and correct seasoning.

Drain bass, and rinse in ice-cold water. Drain well.

To serve, on individual plates, prepare a bed of onion and cucumber slices. Put 16 pieces of bass in marinade, and let stand for 2 to 3 minutes. Remove, and drain. Arrange bass on onion and cucumber bed, and pour a little marinade and chile sauce on top. Sprinkle with soy sauce, Tabasco sauce, salt, and pepper. Repeat procedure for remaining bass. Garnish with limes, and serve immediately.
Makes 8 servings.

Colorful red onion and cucumber and pungent Tabasco sauce garnish Striped-Bass Scallops, Culiacán Style.

LOMO DE PUERCO EN SALSA DE CIRUELA

Pork Loin in Prune Sauce

FOR THE PORK

1½	white onions
6	cloves garlic, whole
	Salt to taste
1	teaspoon pepper
3¼	pounds pork loin, in 1 piece

FOR THE SAUCE

8	chiles anchos, roasted, seeded, deveined, and soaked in water for 20 minutes (see Basics)
4	chiles pasillas, roasted, seeded, deveined, and soaked in water for 20 minutes (see Basics)
4	chiles mulatos, roasted, seeded, deveined, and soaked in water for 20 minutes (see Basics)
2	white onions, halved and roasted (see Basics)
6	cloves garlic, roasted (see Basics)
1	tomato, roasted (see Basics) and chopped
2¼	to 2¾ cups lard
8	tomatillos, husked
½	cup raw almonds, skinned
½	cup raw peanuts, skinned
3	tablespoons sesame seeds
3	cups prunes, pitted
8	cloves
14	black peppercorns
1	stick cinnamon, 2½ inches long
½	croissant
½	cup cider vinegar
2	slices white onion
	Salt to taste
1	quart chicken broth (see recipe on page 202)

FOR THE GARNISH

8	knob onions, shaped like flowers
8	radishes, shaped like flowers

Prepare the pork: Purée onions, garlic, salt, and pepper in a blender or food processor. Put pork in a glass bowl, and pour mixture over. Marinate for 2 hours in the refrigerator.

Meanwhile, prepare the sauce: Drain chiles, and reserve soaking water. Purée chiles, onions, garlic, and tomato in a blender or food processor. Add a little soaking water, and reblend. Set aside.

Heat a little lard in a frying pan or saucepan, and fry tomatillos. Remove tomatillos, and add more lard. Fry almonds, peanuts, sesame seeds, prunes, cloves, peppercorns, cinnamon, and croissant until golden. Drain. In a blender or food processor, blend fried ingredients with vinegar and a little water until they form a thick paste. Heat remaining lard, and add onion slices and tomatillo mixture. Cook until mixture begins to release its fat. Add chile mixture, and cook over low heat for 1 hour. Salt to taste, and gradually add 2 cups chicken broth.

Preheat oven to 350 degrees.

Put pork in a roasting pan. Pour 4 cups sauce and ½ cup chicken broth over pork, and bake for 1½ hours or until meat is done, basting regularly. Remove from oven. Let cool for 30 minutes before thinly slicing. Reserve pan juices.

Mix together pan juices, remaining sauce, and 1½ cups chicken broth. The gravy should be thin. If necessary, add more broth.

To serve, place pork slices on a platter. Pour some gravy over, and garnish with onion and radish flowers. Serve remaining gravy in a gravy bowl.

The prune sauce also can be served with chicken enchiladas.

Makes 12 servings.

MANITAS DE CERDO EN VINAGRETA LOS CAZADORES

Pig's Feet In Vinaigrette, Hunters' Style

Pig's feet, a common appetizer in Mexico, are prepared in different marinades in different regions. This recipe is Jalisco style.

FOR THE PIG'S FEET

- 6 quarts water
- 2 white onions, halved
- 2 heads garlic, halved
- 16 pig's feet, lightly roasted on a griddle, peeled, washed, and halved or quartered
- 6 bay leaves
- 4 sprigs thyme or ¼ teaspoon dried thyme
- 4 sprigs marjoram or ¼ teaspoon dried marjoram
- 1 tablespoon whole allspice
  Salt and pepper to taste

FOR THE VINAIGRETTE

- 1 cup olive oil
- 12 cloves garlic, whole, plus 4 heads garlic, halved
- 3 white onions, sliced
- 8 large knob onions
- 16 carrots, peeled, sliced in 30 slices, and boiled in salted water for 12 minutes
- 2¼ pounds new potatoes, boiled and peeled
- 1 head cauliflower, in pieces, boiled in salted water for 6 minutes (optional)
- 16 zucchini, each in three pieces, boiled in salted water for 6 minutes (optional)
- 1 pound chiles caribes or amarillos
- 1 tablespoon freshly ground pepper
- 1 tablespoon ground allspice
- 1 teaspoon dried oregano
- 20 bay leaves
- 12 sprigs thyme or 1 tablespoon dried thyme
- 12 sprigs marjoram or 1 tablespoon dried marjoram
- 2 quarts cider vinegar
- 1½ quarts water
  Salt to taste

Prepare the pig's feet: Heat water in a saucepan. Add onions, garlic, pig's feet, bay leaves, thyme, marjoram, allspice, salt, and pepper. Boil over medium heat for 45 minutes or until pig's feet are tender. Remove from heat, and cool in broth. Remove pig's feet.

Pig's Feet in Vinaigrette, Hunters' Style is offered in the restaurants of Jalisco.

Prepare the vinaigrette: Heat oil in a frying pan or saucepan. Brown garlic cloves, and discard. Brown garlic heads and white and knob onions. Add carrots and potatoes. Stir. Add cauliflower and zucchini. Add chiles, pepper, allspice, oregano, bay leaves, thyme, and marjoram. Sauté for 10 minutes. Add vinegar and water, and salt to taste.

Add pig's feet, and cook for 30 minutes. Remove from heat, and cool in marinade. Let stand overnight.

To serve, place pig's feet on a platter, and garnish with vinaigrette. Serve at room temperature. Store in the refrigerator.

Makes 16 servings.

Roasted squab is served with an individual masa casserole (see recipe on p. 97).

PICHONES JALICIENCES
Squab, Jalisco Style

Hunting is popular in Jalisco, where squab and quail are abundant.

FOR THE SAUCE

½   cup olive oil
16   chiles anchos, seeded, deveined, washed, and dried (see Basics)
1   quart water
⅓   cup red-wine vinegar
6   cloves garlic, whole
1   medium white onion
1   teaspoon oregano, dried and crushed
1   teaspoon ground cumin
1   teaspoon black peppercorns
     Salt to taste

FOR THE SQUAB

8   squab or quail, 3 to 3½ ounces each, cleaned and singed
½   cup olive oil
8   teaspoons butter, in pieces, plus ½ cup butter
     Dried oregano to taste

FOR THE GARNISH

8   masa casseroles (see recipe on page 97)
8   sprigs parsley

Prepare the sauce: Heat oil in a frying pan. Lightly fry chiles. Remove. Mix water and vinegar. Soak chiles in this mixture for 40 minutes. Remove chiles, and reserve soaking water.

In a blender or food processor, purée chiles with garlic, onion, oregano, cumin, peppercorns, salt, and a little soaking water.

Prepare the squab: Put squab in a baking dish, and pour sauce over. Sprinkle with a little oil, 8 teaspoons butter, and oregano, and let stand for 1 hour. Remove birds from sauce. Preheat a heavy skillet for 25 minutes. Heat ⅓ cup oil and ½ cup butter. Fry squab for 8 to 10 minutes or until done, turning and basting continually with sauce. Remove birds.

Cook sauce a little longer, until thick. Halve squab. To serve, place a masa casserole on each of 8 plates. Cover with cream sauce. Place 2 squab halves on plate. Pour sauce over squab, and garnish with parsley. **Makes 8 servings.**

LENGUA ENTOMATADA
Tongue in Tomato Sauce

FOR THE TONGUE

6	quarts water
2	beef tongues, about 3⅓ pounds each, pounded
2	white onions
1	head garlic, unpeeled
1	tablespoon freshly ground pepper
6	bay leaves
2	sprigs thyme or ½ teaspoon dried thyme
¾	tablespoon dried oregano
	Salt to taste

FOR THE SAUCE

½	cup vegetable oil
2	white onions, finely chopped
3	chiles jalapeños or 4 chiles serranos, sliced or chopped
10	medium tomatoes
	Salt to taste

FOR THE GARNISH

2	tablespoons cilantro or parsley, chopped

Prepare the tongue: Bring water to a boil in a stock pot. Add tongues, onions, garlic, pepper, bay leaves,

The Cabañas orphanage in Guadalajara is notable for the murals that José Orozco painted on its walls.

thyme, oregano, and salt. Cover, and simmer over medium heat for 2½ hours or until meat is tender. Cool tongues in broth. Remove from broth, and peel. Cut in slices ¼ inch thick. Reduce 1 cup broth to ½ cup, and reserve for sauce.

Prepare the sauce: Heat oil in a large skillet. Add onion, and lightly brown. Add chiles and tomatoes, and continue cooking over low heat until sauce thickens, about 35 to 40 minutes. Add reduced broth and salt.

Add tongue slices, and simmer for 20 minutes.

To serve, place hot slices of tongue on a platter. Pour tomato sauce over, and sprinkle with cilantro. **Makes 8 servings.**

BROCHETA DE FILETE ESTILO EL ARRECIFE
Fillet Kabobs, Arrecife Style

Chef Gabriel Gambou at the Arrecife restaurant in Co-lima adds chiles cascabeles to beef kabobs to give them a special flavor.

FOR THE KABOBS

4½	pounds beef fillet, cubed
4	green bell peppers, sliced in squares
2	red onions, sliced in triangles
	Freshly ground pepper to taste
¾	cup olive oil
I	cup clarified butter

FOR THE SAUCE

8	chiles cascabeles
½	cup vegetable oil
½	white onion
I	tomato, roasted (see Basics)
4	cloves garlic, whole
I	teaspoon cumin seeds
2	bay leaves
I	teaspoon freshly ground pepper
	Salt to taste

Prepare the kabobs: On 8 skewers, 8 to 8½ inches long, alternate beef, peppers, and onions. Brush with ¼ cup oil, and season with pepper. Refrigerate for 40 minutes.

Meanwhile, prepare the sauce: Fry chiles in oil for 2 minutes. Drain, and soak in hot water for 20 minutes. Drain, reserving soaking water, and seed. In a blender or food processor, blend chiles with onion, tomato, garlic, cumin, bay leaves, and pepper. Add a little soaking water, and reblend. Salt.

Heat a griddle. Brush kabobs with a little oil and butter. Grill, turning skewers every 3 minutes and basting with oil and butter until brown.

To serve, place a skewer on each of 8 plates. Serve with chile sauce and freshly made corn tortillas.
Makes 8 servings.

opposite: The ingredients for Fillet Kabobs, Arrecife Style; and above, the beef is skewered, grilled, and served with chile cascabel sauce.

SOPITOS
Little Sopes

Sopes are prepared throughout Mexico. This is Colima's version.

FOR THE TOPPING

5	quarts water
14	ounces boneless round rump roast, in chunks
2	white onions, halved
2	heads garlic, unpeeled and halved
2	bay leaves
2	carrots, coarsely chopped
1	leek, split
2	turnips, halved

Little Sopes are prepared and served like tacos.

1	stick cinnamon, 2 inches long
1	teaspoon pepper
4	cloves
	Salt to taste
1	chicken breast, halved

FOR THE SAUCE

4	tomatoes (about 2¾ pounds)
1	white onion, thickly sliced
3	cloves garlic, whole
4	chiles serranos, coarsely chopped
1	cup cilantro, chopped
	Salt to taste

FOR THE SOPES

24	tortillas, 3 inches in diameter
2	cups lard

FOR THE GARNISH

2	cups cabbage, shredded
1	cup white onion, finely chopped
1½	cups fresh feta or ricotta cheese, crumbled

Prepare the topping: Bring water to a boil in a stock pot. Add beef, onions, garlic, bay leaves, carrots, leek, turnips, cinnamon, pepper, cloves, and salt. Reduce heat, and cook over medium heat for 2½ hours or until meat is tender. If necessary, add more water during cooking. Add chicken when beef is tender, and cook until done, 20 to 30 minutes. Cool meats in broth. Remove meats, and grind in food processor or meat grinder. Strain broth. Set aside ground meats.

Prepare the sauce: In a blender or food processor, purée tomatoes with onion, garlic, chile, cilantro, and salt. Set aside.

Prepare the sopes: Heat a comal or griddle. Add a little lard. Lightly fry 12 tortillas on both sides. Heat a little more lard. Fry remaining 12 tortillas, and keep hot.

To serve, arrange tortillas on a platter. Cover with ground meats. Cover with sauce, and garnish with cabbage, onion, and cheese. Serve immediately.

Makes 8 servings.

TORTA DE MASA A LA TAPATIA
Individual Masa Casseroles, Tapatía Style

Although casseroles are common in Jalisco, this dish is distinctive because of its raw-chile flavoring.

FOR THE STUFFING

3¾	quarts water
1	pound pork loin, in chunks
1	white onion, halved, plus 1 large white onion, finely chopped
½	head garlic, plus 4 cloves garlic, finely chopped
4	bay leaves
2	sprigs thyme
2	sprigs marjoram
	Salt to taste
2	teaspoons freshly ground pepper
½	cup olive oil
4	tomatoes (2½ pounds), roasted (see Basics) and puréed
⅔	cup green olives, minced
⅔	cup raisins
½	cup almonds, skinned and finely chopped
1	teaspoon ground cumin
½	cup beef broth

FOR THE DOUGH

1	cup plus 2 tablespoons butter, at room temperature
⅔	cup sugar
8	eggs, separated
2	teaspoons baking powder
1¾	pounds fresh masa or equivalent made with masa harina (see Basics)
⅓	cup water
1½	teaspoons salt

FOR THE SAUCE

5	chiles poblanos, seeded (See Basics) and finely chopped
1	cup heavy cream
1	cup half-and-half

Salt to taste

FOR THE GARNISH

1	bunch cilantro

Prepare the stuffing: Heat water in a large saucepan. Add pork, halved onion, garlic head, bay leaves, thyme, marjoram, salt, and 1 teaspoon pepper. Cook over medium heat for 1½ hours. If necessary, add more water. Remove from heat, and cool. Remove pork from broth, and shred. Reserve broth.

In a separate saucepan, heat oil. Brown chopped onion and garlic. Stir in tomatoes, olives, raisins, almonds, cumin, 1 teaspoon pepper, beef broth, pork, and salt. Cook over low heat until mixture thickens, about 40 minutes.

Preheat oven to 350 degrees.

Prepare the dough: Beat butter with an electric mixer for 10 minutes or until light and fluffy. Add sugar, and beat for 5 minutes. Add egg yolks and baking powder. Mix.

Knead masa with water, 1⅓ cups reserved pork broth, and salt. Gradually add dough to butter mixture, mixing thoroughly. In a separate bowl, beat egg whites until stiff. Add to dough, and knead.

Grease and flour 8 ¾-cup molds. Line molds with waxed paper, and grease again. Fill each with ¼ cup dough, covering bottom and sides. Place 1½ tablespoons of stuffing on top of dough, and top with another layer of dough. Seal to first layer. The molds will be about three-quarters full. Bake casseroles for 35 minutes or until the crust is golden brown and a toothpick inserted in center comes out clean. Keep hot.

Prepare the sauce: Mix chiles, heavy cream, half-and-half, and salt.

To serve, turn casseroles out onto plates. Cover with sauce, and garnish with cilantro.

One large casserole can be made from this recipe, using an 8- or 9-inch ring mold. Bake the casserole for 45 minutes or until done.
Makes 8 servings.

SANGRITA ESTILO JALISCO
Sangrita Chaser, Jalisco Style

Sangrita *is the perfect chaser for Mexico's number-one spirit—tequila. In Jalisco, the home of tequila, this strong drink is served with such appetizers as* charalitos *or melted cheese.*

3   cups fresh orange juice
¼   cup grenadine
¾   teaspoon ground chile piquín
1   tablespoon salt

Mix all ingredients in a blender or food processor for 1 minute. Refrigerate for 2 hours. Serve sangrita cold in shot glasses with separate shot glasses of tequila.
Makes 3¼ cups.

AGUA DE GRANADA
Pomegranate Beverage

Pomegranates grow on the Colima mountainside, where the Mexican author Juan Rulfo was inspired to write his classic novel Pedro Paramo.

20   pomegranates, peeled
6   quarts water

Fresh pomegranate seeds are puréed with water and sugar for a refreshing drink.

2   cups sugar, or to taste
1½   quarts crushed ice

Set aside 2 cups of pomegranate seeds. In a blender or food processor, blend remaining seeds with water and sugar. Strain. Pour into a pitcher over ice. Garnish with the reserved seeds.

Pomegranate beverage traditionally is served from a large glass jar.
Makes 8 servings.

CHIQUITA BANANA
Banana Beverage

This refreshing banana beverage is served in the Camino Real Hotel in Mazatlán.

FOR THE GARNISH
8   wedges fresh or canned pineapple
8   slices lime
8   melon balls

FOR THE BEVERAGE
1   quart canned pineapple juice
2   cups canned coconut cream
3   large bananas, peeled and chopped
16   1½-inch chunks fresh or canned pineapple
1   cup grenadine
1½   cups light rum
1   cup dark rum
1   quart ice cubes

Spear pineapple, lime, and melon on a toothpick. Put beverage ingredients in a bowl. Purée in a blender or food processor in batches.

To serve, pour banana beverage into 1½-cup goblets, and place fruit on rim of goblet. Serve immediately.
Makes 8 servings.

opposite, clockwise from top: Colorful coconut sweets are sold throughout Mexico. Pinturitas are a popular candy made from sweetened corn meal and lard. A frosted strawberry daiquiri makes a festive apéritif.

Jericalla, a rich, custardlike dessert, is served in a Tlaxcalteca ceramic dish.

JERICALLA
Jericalla

This dessert originated in Jalisco. It is sold in the local Guadalajara market, San Juan de Dios, from early morning throughout the day.

1½	quarts milk
2	sticks cinnamon, each 2½ inches long
1	teaspoon pure vanilla extract

1½	cups sugar
4	egg yolks

Preheat oven to 350 degrees.

Bring milk, cinnamon, and vanilla extract to a boil. Reduce heat, and simmer for 10 minutes. Remove from heat, and cool. Stir in sugar, and cook over low heat, stirring occasionally, for 40 minutes. Remove from heat, and cool. Meanwhile, beat egg yolks. Add to cool milk. Divide mixture among 8 heat-resistant dessert dishes or ramekins. Bake in a water bath (bain-marie) for 30 to 35 minutes or until a toothpick inserted in center of custard comes out clean.

Brown under broiler for 3 to 5 minutes or until tops are golden. Refrigerate for 2 hours. Unmold onto dessert plates.
Makes 8 servings.

PASTEL DE TRES LECHES
Three-Milk Cake

This unusual cake is served for special occasions in Mexico, particularly in Sinaloa, where it originated.

FOR THE BATTER

¾	cup plus 2 tablespoons butter
1¾	cups sugar
8	egg yolks
2½	cups flour, sifted
2½	teaspoons baking powder
½	teaspoon salt
1	teaspoon vanilla extract
1	cup milk
6	egg whites

FOR THE MILKS

2	cups evaporated milk

1½ cups sweetened condensed milk
3½ cups evaporated cream
6 egg yolks

FOR THE MERINGUE

6 egg whites
2 cups sugar
1¾ cups light corn syrup
Juice of 2 limes

FOR THE GARNISH

10 strawberries, halved

Preheat oven to 350 degrees. Grease and flour a 12-by 8-inch cake pan.

Prepare the batter: Cream butter. Gradually mix in sugar, and continue beating until mixture is light and creamy. Add egg yolks. Slowly mix in flour, baking powder, and salt. Add vanilla extract, and slowly mix in milk until batter is thick.

In another bowl, beat egg whites until stiff. Fold into batter. Pour batter into cake pan.

Bake for 40 minutes or until edges are golden brown. Remove from oven, and cool on rack.

Prepare the milks: Blend evaporated and condensed milks and evaporated cream with egg yolks in a blender or food processor. Bring half this mixture to a boil in a saucepan, stirring constantly. Remove from heat, and stir in remaining mixture. Pour over cake.

Prepare the meringue: In a double boiler, mix egg whites and sugar. Beat until stiff. Slowly add corn syrup, and continue beating until stiff peaks form. Add lime juice, and continue beating until shiny. Remove from heat. Invert cake on a deep dish or platter. Spread meringue over cake, and decorate with strawberries. Serve at room temperature.

Makes 8 servings.

Pears in Wine, flavored with cinnamon, is an elegant dessert, yet easy to prepare.

PERAS AL VINO DEL BRASS
Pears in Wine, Brass Style

Alejandro Avalos, chef of the Brass restaurant in Guadalajara, created this recipe using brown sugar and pears, a bountiful fruit.

3 quarts water
2 quarts red wine
1 to 1½ pounds piloncillo (unrefined brown sugar), or dark brown sugar to taste
2 sticks cinnamon, each 3½ inches long
1 tablespoon pure vanilla extract
16 small pears, peeled

Bring water, wine, sugar, cinnamon, and vanilla extract to a boil in a medium saucepan. Reduce heat, and cook over low heat for 1 hour or until syrup is reduced by half. Add pears, and cook for 15 to 20 minutes or until pears are tender, but not mushy. Remove from heat, and cool.

Serve cold or at room temperature in individual bowls, drenching pears with syrup.

Makes 8 servings.

THE SOUTH PACIFIC COAST

The highlands of Guerrero, Oaxaca, and Chiapas are a succession of deep valleys separated from one another by cool, craggy peaks. For centuries, each valley has been a world unto itself, its inhabitants preserving the local dress, dialect, food, and folklore. Along with the Yucatán, the states of the southern Pacific coast compose Mexico's most purely Indian region and boast what is arguably the most indigenous of Mexico's provincial cuisines.

Although modern urban civilization increasingly influences the region's Indian heritage, much of the culture remains defiantly alive, even within the cities to which farming families migrate to escape rural poverty. In Oaxaca, briefcase-toting lawyers still speak Zapotec at home, eat traditional foods, and interrupt work routines for feast days. Nearby, in corn fields that mark the city limits, farmers quietly murmur prayers as they sow their precious seed.

The highlands are only one feature of the states of Mexico's southern Pacific coast. With a vibrant culture that seems to have more in common with the Caribbean than with Mexico's mountainous interior, the south-

ern Pacific coast is a region of sheltered caves and dramatic shorelines, of contagious fiestas and pulsating music. Skilled fishermen transform a motley catch of octopus, shrimp, and shark into an exquisite seafood stew. Children dig pink-shelled clams from estuary flats, knowing that before being eaten, their quarry should be tested with a squirt of fresh lime juice. If the raw clam does not recoil, it is dead and must be discarded.

Not all of southern Mexico is Indian, however. Acapulco, exuberantly Latin, contemporary, and tropical, is the biggest city in the region and Mexico's first world-class resort. Not surprisingly, its food can be sophisticated. *Ceviche*, the cocktail of raw fish marinated in lime juice, is said to have originated in Acapulco.

For centuries before its metamorphosis into a mecca for tourists, Acapulco was the New World's principal link to the Orient. In colonial days, Spain's Manila galleons carried East Asian silks and spices to Acapulco, and this Oriental influence can be detected in the dishes of this part of Mexico. A dish that reflects this impact is *arroz con pulpo al curry* (octopus and rice with curry). *Chiles jalapeños* spice the rice base, and curry powder seasons a wine and fish-broth sauce. The Guerrero shoreline to the south of Acapulco, known as the *costa chica*, is the only area of Mexico where African blood and culture dominate the local ethnic mix. Farther down the coast, in southern Chiapas, descendants of German settlers grow coffee and cotton.

The principal ingredient in southern Mexican cooking—as in Mexican life in general—is corn. Virtually every tillable slope is planted with *milpa* (literally, "corn field," but also, tellingly, the generic term for a farm plot). Maize harvest cycles determine the traditional fiesta calendar. Rural meals are still based on the Mesoamerican "holy trinity" of corn, beans, and squash.

In Chiapas, more than anywhere else, Mexican Indian food is reduced to its essentials. For example, in a soup prepared by the native Zoque Indians, vegetables and chicken broth are flavored by the addition of fresh corn *masa* balls.

Chile—as is typical in indigenous cuisine—usually accompanies meals as a condiment in Chiapas, rather than being cooked into the dish. And perhaps for good reason: Chiapas chiles are among Mexico's most fiery. The best known is the small *chile de siete caldos*, so called because one is enough to season seven pots of stew. Natives of Chiapas seem to prefer a savory sweetness to their foods or the contrast of sweet and salty tastes. Thus, for special occasions—a baptism, wedding, or holy day—a succulent pork roast is stuffed with a cinnamon-flavored mincemeat.

The marketplaces of Chiapas consistently boast the country's most abundant selection of herbs and greens, many of which are unavailable elsewhere and are known only by their local names. Although some are used primarily for seasoning, most are eaten as a vegetable supplement to corn and beans. It is not unusual for a woman preparing a meal in an Indian household to duck out back, uproot from her yard what would look like weeds to the uninitiated, and dump them into the pot. Flowers are also commonly eaten; *tamales de puchulu*, a Chiapas specialty, are stuffed with fresh petals similar to orange blossoms. Another tamale common to Chiapas is the *tamale juacane*, which is filled with a mixture of beans, dried shrimp, and pumpkin seeds. The tamales are wrapped in the leaves of *hierba santa*, an indigenous plant, instead of in corn husks.

Oaxaca, the center of the southern highland region, is considered by some to offer the most outstanding regional dishes in Mexico. Here, traditional Indian cooking has been tempered and elevated to a complex cuisine unrivaled in variety and invention. Oaxaca's refined meat dishes are of southern Spanish provenance, yet are wholly Mexican in their use of dozens of mixed nuts and spices. The cuisine's native exoticism is epitomized by its extensive use of insects—living and dead, fried and fresh. Where else in the world could one order grasshopper or ant tacos? In the better bars of the capital, cocktail glasses are often rimmed with *sal de gusano*—a mixture of salt, crushed chile, and dried maguey worms—and filled with *mezcal*.

There is no better place to eat in southern Mexico than Oaxaca, known as the "Land of the Seven *Moles*." The most famous *moles* are the *colorado* (red), *amarillo* (yellow), and *negro* (black), but there is also a *mole* made with avocado leaves and one that contains pineapple and banana. The Oaxacans are unrestrained when it comes to food combinations.

The market is a showplace for the local cheese, which is white and stringy. It is rolled into balls of varying sizes or is braided into rounds. A delicious specialty is *quesillo asado en salsa verde*—sliced cheese grilled until it begins to melt and then topped with a green sauce made of *tomatillos* and *chiles serranos*.

The ideal place to eat Oaxacan food is in one of the many hospitable restaurants that ring the capital city's lovely Zocalo, complete with a bandstand. If you are lucky, a concert will be in progress. Enclosed by fine colonial buildings, its sidewalk cafés bustling, Oaxaca's central square is one of those magical places where time slows and dusk is a spectacle to be savored. Dine here on guacamole, Mixtec style, and on savory *mole negro* with chicken or pork, chased by a fiery shot of *mezcal*. This is what life is all about, Oaxacans will tell you, and they are right.

GUACAMOLE DE LA MIXTECA
Guacamole, Mixtec Style

Avocado is a fruit rich in vitamins and believed to have extraordinary medicinal powers. The Oaxaca–Mixteca region is famous for its abundant yields of this fruit.

FOR THE GUACAMOLE

4	large California avocados, purchased ahead of time to allow for ripening, if necessary
	Salt to taste
1	cup white onion, minced
4	chiles serranos, minced
½	cup cilantro, finely chopped

FOR THE GARNISH

½	tomato, diced
¼	cup white onion, minced
4	to 6 sprigs cilantro, with leaves and a bit of stem

Peel and pit avocados. Mash pulp in a bowl or molcajeté, and salt to taste. Add onion, chile, and cilantro. Continue mashing until guacamole is thick and lumpy.

Garnish with tomato, onion, and cilantro. Serve with corn tortillas or totopos (crisply fried tortilla wedges).

Serve immediately.

Makes about 3 cups.

SALSA VERDE
Green Sauce

Green sauce is a classic Mexican hot sauce. It can accompany anything from a tortilla to a cut of broiled meat. In the state of Oaxaca, green sauce is served with pork rind or barbequed meat.

FOR THE SAUCE

1	quart water
12	tomatillos, husked
7	medium cloves garlic, whole
4	to 8 chiles serranos (vary according to preference for piquancy)
3	tablespoons white onion, coarsely chopped
	Salt to taste
¾	cup cilantro leaves, with a bit of stem

FOR THE GARNISH

¼	cup white onion, chopped
¼	cup cilantro, chopped

Bring water to a boil in a saucepan. Add tomatillos, 4 garlic cloves, 4 or more chiles, and onion. Cook over medium heat for 20 minutes, and remove from heat. Drain, and reserve cooking water. Cool.

Meanwhile, purée 3 garlic cloves in a molcajete or food processor, adding salt to taste. Add cilantro, and blend. Add tomatillo mixture. Add a little cooking water, and blend. The sauce should have a slightly thick consistency. Correct seasoning.

To serve, pour green sauce into a molcajete, and garnish with onion and cilantro.

Makes about 2 cups.

In Oaxaca, traditional cooking makes use of the rich variety of local chiles.

A fourteenth-century Mixtecan lintel is an appropriate backdrop for Green Sauce, Guacamole Mixtec Style, and Green Sauce with Chiles Cascabels and Guajillos.

SALSA DE TOMATILLO CON CHILES CASCABELES Y CHILES GUAJILLOS

Green Sauce with Chiles Cascabeles and Guajillos

FOR THE SAUCE

1	quart water
32	tomatillos, husked
6	cloves garlic, whole
¼	white onion, plus 2 tablespoons white onion, minced
4	chiles cascabeles or de árbol, lightly fried
3	chiles guajillos, seeded, deveined (see Basics), and lightly fried
	Salt to taste

FOR THE GARNISH

2   tablespoons cilantro, chopped

Bring water to a boil in a large saucepan. Add tomatillos, 4 garlic cloves, and ¼ onion. Add chiles cascabeles and guajillos. Boil for 20 minutes. Set aside to cool. Drain, discard garlic and onion, and reserve cooking water. Set aside tomatillos and chiles.

Meanwhile, grind 2 garlic cloves in a molcajete, or put through a press. Add minced onion, and salt to taste. Mix.

Gradually add tomatillos and chiles, and grind well in a molcajete or food processor. Add a bit of the cooking water to form a fairly thick sauce, and season to taste.

To serve, pour green sauce into a molcajete or bowl, and sprinkle with cilantro.

Makes about 1 quart.

FOR THE SAUCE

2	quarts water
3	to 3½ pounds tomatillos, husked
1½	white onions, coarsely sliced, plus ½ white onion
9	chiles serranos
9	cloves garlic, whole
20	sprigs cilantro
¾	cup corn oil
1	slice onion
	Salt to taste

FOR THE CHEESE

4	pounds very fresh Oaxaca, asadero, or mozzarella cheese, sliced in 16 slices
	Oil

Mexican Indians believed that chiles possess nutritive and medicinal properties. To ensure good health by including chiles in the daily diet, they created numerous recipes, such as Green Sauce, which can be served with a host of dishes, including Roasted Cheese.

QUESILLO ASADO EN SALSA VERDE
Roasted Cheese in Green Sauce

Oaxaca cheese, or quesillo, *is a light, stringy cheese often served as an appetizer. It is sold in many sizes, ranging from miniature to large balls. Broiled in green sauce, this cheese is a favorite at the restaurant of the Presidente Hotel, the former convent of Santa Catalina, in Oaxaca.*

Prepare the sauce: Bring water to a boil in a heavy saucepan. Add tomatillos, sliced onion, 6 chiles, and 6 garlic cloves. Cook for about 30 minutes or until tomatillos are tender. Cool slightly. Drain, and reserve cooking water. In a blender or food processor, blend tomatillo mixture with ½ onion, 3 chiles, 3 garlic cloves, cilantro, and a little cooking water. Set aside.

Heat oil in a heavy saucepan. Add onion slice, and fry until golden. Remove. Pour tomatillo mixture into the hot oil. Salt, and continue cooking over medium heat until fat begins to rise to the surface. Add 2 cups cooking water; the sauce should be slightly thick. Correct salt.

Preheat oven to warm.

Prepare the cheese: Heat a griddle or heavy frying pan. Brush each cheese slice with a little oil. Grill slices briefly on griddle, and place 2 slices on each of 8 plates. Keep warm in oven, but do not let the cheese melt.

To serve, cover cheese slices with hot sauce, and accompany with freshly made, hot corn tortillas.

If you like, add freshly chopped cilantro and chopped onion to sauce before serving.
Makes 8 servings.

Oaxacan cheeses rest on the stone laundry sinks of the former convent of Santa Catalina, which is now a hotel.

SOPA DE CHIPILIN CON BOLITAS
Zoque Indian Soup

Chipilín *soup has been made since pre-Hispanic times.*

FOR THE SOUP

3   quarts water or chicken broth (see recipe on page 202), skimmed of fat

4   large knob onions or 20 green onions, with tops, halved lengthwise

1   chile chamborate or serrano
     Kernels from 4 ears corn
     Salt to taste

2   cups chipilín or watercress or spinach leaves, chopped

¼   cup masa harina, dissolved in ½ cup water

FOR THE BOLITAS

1   pound fresh masa or equivalent made with masa harina (see Basics)

½   cup lard, preferably homemade
     Pinch of salt

1   cup fresh cheese, such as feta, crumbled

FOR THE GARNISH

1   cup chipilín, watercress, or spinach, chopped

2   cups heavy cream

2   cups fresh cheese, such as feta, diced

Prepare the soup: Put water in a stock pot with onions, chile, and corn. Bring to a boil, and salt. When the corn is cooked, about 20 minutes, add chipilín and dissolved masa harina. Bring to a boil. Reduce heat to simmer.

Prepare the bolitas: Put masa in a bowl, and add a little warm water, lard, salt, and cheese. Knead until smooth. Make little balls, about the size of walnuts, and drop into the simmering soup. Cook for 20 minutes or until soup has the consistency of a light porridge. If soup becomes too thick, add water or broth.

To serve, ladle soup into 8 soup bowls. Garnish each bowl with chipilín, cream, and cheese.
Makes 8 servings.

PAN INTEGRAL
Whole-Wheat Bread

This recipe comes from Na Bolon, where a balanced diet is the rule. Whole-wheat bread is a nutritious substitute for the traditional tortilla.

¼   cup dry yeast

2   quarts warm water

6   cups white flour

2   cups whole-wheat flour

1   cup ground or whole bran

2   tablespoons sugar

1   tablespoon salt

Dissolve yeast in warm water in a glass bowl. Set aside for 15 minutes.

Meanwhile, sift white and whole-wheat flours, and add bran, sugar, and salt. Stir in dissolved yeast. Knead dough until smooth and elastic.

Grease 2 bread loaf pans, and sprinkle with flour. Divide dough into 2 loaves, and place in prepared pans. Set aside, and let rise for 1 hour.

Preheat oven to 350 degrees. Bake bread for 40 minutes or until crust is golden.

This bread is excellent served with Ocotzingo cheese or spread with fresh butter.
Makes 2 loaves.

Zoque Indian Soup, served in an Oaxacan tureen.

SOPA DE PAN NA BOLON
Bread Soup from Na Bolon

This hearty "soup" is a representative dish of the San Cristobal de las Casas region in Chiapas. It is the specialty of Gertrude Duby de Blom, proprietor of the well-known Casa de Na Balom.

FOR THE SOUP

1	cup lard
1	tablespoon annatto seeds
2	white onions, sliced
4	or 5 large tomatoes, thinly sliced, plus 1 large tomato, chopped
2	ripe plantains, thinly sliced
1½	to 2 quarts chicken broth (see recipe on page 202), skimmed of fat
1	teaspoon pepper
½	teaspoon ground cinnamon
½	teaspoon dried thyme
¼	teaspoon ground cloves
½	teaspoon ground saffron
1½	tablespoons sugar
	Salt to taste
16	slices French or sourdough bread, about 1½ by 3 inches
6	zucchini, chopped or sliced and cooked in water for 8 to 10 minutes
1	cup green beans, chopped and cooked in water for 8 to 10 minutes
5	small potatoes, boiled for 15 minutes and chopped
¾	cup raw almonds, skinned
¾	cup raisins

FOR THE GARNISH

6	small hard-cooked eggs, halved lengthwise

Preheat oven to 375 degrees. Grease a deep glass or ceramic dish, approximately 9 by 13½ inches, with lard.

Heat a little lard in a medium frying pan. Add annatto seeds, and fry until lard turns red. Remove annatto, and discard. Add a little more lard, and fry

above and opposite: *Bread Soup from Na Bolon is hearty enough to be served as a main course.*

onion. Remove and reserve onion. Add a little more lard, and fry sliced tomato. Remove and reserve tomato. Add plantain, and fry until golden. Remove plantain, drain, and reserve.

Simmer broth with chopped tomato, ½ teaspoon pepper, pinch of cinnamon, and thyme for 30 minutes. Add ½ teaspoon pepper, cinnamon, cloves, and saffron. Stir in sugar and salt.

To assemble the soup, layer 8 slices of bread and half of the onion, tomato, plantain, zucchini, beans, and potatoes in the prepared dish. Sprinkle with half the almonds and raisins. Repeat layers, reserving some plantains for the top. Pour broth over. Bake for 30 minutes. Remove from oven, and garnish with eggs. ***Makes 12 servings.***

Ceviche can be made with one type of fish fillet or shellfish or with a combination of several varieties.

CEVICHE
Ceviche

Ceviche is one of the most popular dishes in the state of Guerrero. This recipe was created by Susana Palazuelos, a caterer to the rich and famous in the port of Acapulco.

FOR THE FISH

1½ pounds red snapper or sierra fillets, cut in 1- by ½-inch pieces

Juice of 12 limes
Salt to taste

FOR THE MARINADE

1½ white onions, finely chopped
 4 chiles serranos, chopped
 3 large tomatoes, finely chopped
1½ cups pimento-stuffed green olives, finely chopped
 ¾ cup parsley, finely chopped
 1 cup cilantro, finely chopped
 4 cups catsup
1½ cups olive oil
 1 4-ounce can chile jalapeño strips, finely chopped, with juice
 ¼ cup Worcestershire sauce
 1 tablespoon oregano, dried and crushed
    Salt to taste

FOR THE GARNISH

 2 tablespoons cilantro, chopped
    Soda crackers

Prepare the fish: Put fish in a glass bowl. Cover with lime juice, salt to taste, and macerate for 15 minutes. Rinse fish, and drain. Return fish to bowl.

Prepare the marinade: Mix onion, chiles serranos, tomato, olives, parsley, and cilantro. Stir in catsup, oil, chile jalapeño, Worcestershire sauce, oregano, and salt. Pour sauce over fish, and marinate for 1 day in the refrigerator.

Fill serving cups with ceviche, garnishing with cilantro and crackers.

The ceviche can be refrigerated for up to 5 days.
Makes 8 servings.

Chefs in popular tourist cities compete with one another to create tastier renditions of traditional recipes, such as this Lobster Ceviche invented in the restaurant of an Acapulco hotel.

CEVICHE DE LANGOSTA LAS BRISAS

Lobster Ceviche, Las Brisas Style

Lobster ceviche is a new version of the Mexican favorite. This idea comes from the chefs at the Brisas Hotel in the resort town of Acapulco.

FOR THE LOBSTER

2 to 3 quarts water
   Salt to taste
6 fresh lobster tails

FOR THE MARINADE

2 quarts fresh orange juice
½ cup fresh lime juice
⅓ cup tequila
½ cup chives, finely chopped
   Salt to taste

FOR THE GARNISH

2 tablespoons chives, chopped

Prepare the lobster: Bring water and salt to a boil in a saucepan. Add lobster tails, and boil for 15 minutes. Cool slightly in cooking water, remove, and shell tails. Shred meat.

Prepare the marinade: Mix orange juice, lime juice, tequila, chives, and salt. Pour over lobster meat, and refrigerate for 2 hours.

To serve, spoon lobster ceviche into individual bowls, garnishing with chives. Serve with sesame bread sticks.

Makes 8 servings.

CEVICHE DE CAMARON LAS FUENTES

Shrimp Ceviche, Las Fuentes Style

This seafood hors d'oeuvre is a specialty of Susana Palazuelos, a well-known Acapulco caterer.

FOR THE SHRIMP

5 quarts water
   Salt to taste
32 large shrimp, deveined and unshelled
½ recipe marinade (see recipe on page 112)

FOR THE GARNISH

2 tablespoons cilantro, chopped
16 slices lime
   Soda crackers

Bring water and salt to a boil in a stock pot. Add shrimp, and cook for 5 minutes. Remove from heat, and cool shrimp in cold water. Shell. Cut 8 shrimp in half, and reserve for garnish.

Prepare marinade, and marinate shrimp in it for 6 hours in the refrigerator.

To serve, divide shrimp among 8 glass bowls, decorating with halved shrimp and cilantro. Garnish with lime slices and crackers.

Makes 8 servings.

HUACHINANGO AL AJO ESTILO BETO
Red Snapper in Garlic, Beto Style

FOR THE RED SNAPPER

8   red snappers, about 1¾ pounds each, cleaned
6   cloves garlic, puréed, plus 8 cloves garlic, finely chopped
     Salt and pepper to taste
     Juice of 6 limes
1½   cups clarified butter
1   cup olive oil
1   to 2 cups flour

FOR THE GARNISH

8   small potatoes, washed and brushed with oil
½   cup butter, softened
3   tablespoons parsley, chopped

6   limes, sliced

Put fish in a large baking dish. Do not stack (use 2 dishes if necessary). Spread with puréed garlic, and sprinkle with salt, pepper, and lime juice. Marinate for 2 hours in the refrigerator.

Preheat the oven to 375 degrees.

Wrap oil-brushed potatoes in aluminum foil, and bake for 45 minutes to 1 hour or until done.

Heat butter in a frying pan until foaming. Add oil and chopped garlic. Season with salt and pepper to taste, and sauté over low heat for 10 minutes. Strain, dividing butter in half. Put half aside.

Spoon flour onto waxed paper. Roll fish in flour to coat. Preheat broiler. Broil fish, basting with prepared butter, 10 minutes on one side. Turn. Broil for 10 minutes or until fish is tender, basting frequently with prepared butter.

To serve, place 1 fish on each of 8 plates. Cover

Red Snapper in Garlic, Beto Style is served at Beach Condesa in Acapulco.

with a portion of reserved prepared butter. Serve 1 potato on each plate, garnishing with 1 tablespoon butter and parsley. Garnish plate with limes.

Makes 8 servings.

CAMARONES EN SALSA DE CHIPOTLE ESTILO BARRA VIEJA
Shrimp in Chipotle Sauce, Barra Vieja Style

This recipe is treasured by the townspeople of Barra Vieja and is rarely shared with strangers.

8	chiles guajillos, washed, roasted, seeded, de-veined, and soaked in salted water for 20 minutes (see Basics)
6	chiles chipotles, washed, fried in oil, seeded, de-veined, soaked in salted water for 20 minutes (see Basics), and ground in a blender
2	white onions, roasted (see Basics)
10	cloves garlic, roasted (see Basics), plus 13 cloves garlic, whole
5	tomatoes, roasted (see Basics) and thickly sliced
1	teaspoon pepper
4	cloves, ground
1	stick cinnamon, 2 inches long
6	bay leaves
1	teaspoon cumin seeds
1	teaspcon thyme
1	teaspoon marjoram
	Salt to taste
4½	cups fish stock (see recipe on page 214)
1	cup lard
80	small shrimp, unshelled and heads removed

Put chiles guajillos and chipotles, onions, roasted garlic, 5 garlic cloves, tomatoes, pepper, cloves, cinnamon, bay leaves, cumin, thyme, marjoram, and salt in a blender or food processor. Add 3 cups fish stock, and purée very well.

Most Mexican recipes that include chiles guajillos *call for the moderately hot, dried variety. In Shrimp in Chipotle Sauce, Barra Vieja Style, however, these chiles are used fresh.*

Heat lard in a frying pan. Add 8 garlic cloves, and brown. Remove garlic, and discard. Add shrimp, and sauté until the shells begin to brown. Remove. Add blended sauce, and cook over low heat for 1½ hours or until sauce begins to release its fat. Correct seasoning. Add remaining fish stock and shrimp. Simmer for 25 minutes. (If necessary, add more fish stock.)

Serve shrimp as an appetizer, with freshly made, warm corn tortillas. Serve with fresh coconut water or ice-cold beer.

Makes 8 servings.

RELLENITOS DE PLATANO MACHO
Stuffed Plantain Patties

FOR THE PLANTAINS
4   plantains, partially ripe, peeled and thickly sliced
     Salt to taste
2   large eggs
¼   cup flour
2½   cups vegetable oil

FOR THE STUFFING
1½   cups refried beans (see recipe on page 187)

FOR THE GARNISH
⅔   cup sour cream
⅓   cup crème fraîche
16   romaine lettuce leaves

Boil plantains in salted water to cover until fork tender. Drain, and set aside to cool. Purée plantains in a blender or food processor.

Beat eggs, and add flour. Add egg mixture to puréed plantains. Form patties, and stuff with 1 tablespoon beans, shaping batter to enclose. Heat oil until almost smoking, and fry patties, turning once. Drain on paper towels.

Before serving, mix sour cream and crème fraîche. Serve 2 to 3 patties on individual plates. Place lettuce leaf and mixed creams on the side. Serve hot.
Makes 24 patties.

TOSTADITAS TURULAS
Tostaditas Turulas

FOR THE DOUGH
1¼   pounds fresh masa or equivalent made with masa harina (see Basics)

preceding overleaf left: Plantain patties may be stuffed with beans and garnished with a dollop of cream.
preceding overleaf right: For a light lunch or an appetizer, dried shrimp are placed on tortillas and covered with tomato sauce.

⅓   cup warm water
½   cup vegetable oil or lard
½   teaspoon salt

FOR THE SHRIMP
32   small dried shrimp, shelled, or 32 fresh baby shrimp

FOR THE SAUCE
1   small white onion, finely chopped
2   tomatoes, peeled and finely chopped
2   or 3 chiles serranos, finely chopped
2   tablespoons cilantro, finely chopped
¼   cup fresh oregano, chopped, or ¾ tablespoon dried oregano
     Salt to taste
     Juice of 1 lime

Prepare the dough: Put masa in a bowl, and add water, oil, and salt. Knead for a maximum of 3 minutes.

Heat a comal or griddle for 20 minutes, and prepare a tortilla press (see Basics). Form 24 balls, 1½ inches in diameter, from the masa, and make tortillas. Cook on the comal until crisp. Keep warm.

Prepare the shrimp: If dried shrimp are salty, soak in cold water for 10 minutes. Drain well. Set aside.

Prepare the sauce: Put onion, tomato, chiles, and cilantro in a bowl. Mix, and season with oregano and salt. Add lime juice.

To assemble tostaditas, place shrimp on top of tortillas, and cover with tomato sauce. Serve 3 tostaditas on each of 8 plates.
Makes 24 tostaditas.

BOMBA DE PESCADO
Fish Bombe

This recipe was created by the author for the first Mexican Cooking Festival, held in December 1984 in Acapulco. Most of Mexico's top chefs cooked for that event, which was attended by prominent food editors from the United States.

FOR THE STUFFING

½   cup vinegar
½   cup olive oil
3   cloves garlic, puréed
    Salt to taste
1   teaspoon freshly ground pepper
8   chiles anchos, seeded, deveined, and lightly
    roasted (see Basics)

FOR THE FISH

8   red snapper, grouper, or flounder fillets, 6 to 8
    ounces each
2   tablespoons garlic, finely chopped
1   tablespoon freshly ground pepper
    Salt to taste

FOR THE SAUCE

1   quart fish stock (see recipe on page 214)
4   chiles anchos, lightly roasted, seeded, deveined,
    and soaked in water for 20 minutes (see Basics)
1   medium white onion
4   cloves garlic, whole
5⅓ tablespoons butter
    Salt to taste
1   quart crème fraîche
2   cups half-and-half
1½ tablespoons corn starch, dissolved in 1 cup
    water
1   cup Parmesan cheese, freshly grated

FOR THE DOUGH

2½ pounds puff-pastry dough, cold

FOR THE GLAZE

2   egg yolks
1   egg
2   tablespoons half-and-half

Prepare the stuffing: Put vinegar, oil, garlic, salt, and pepper in a glass bowl. Mix, and add chiles. Macerate for 2 hours.

Prepare the fish: Put fillets in a baking dish. Do not stack. Sprinkle with garlic, pepper, and salt. Fold over to enclose seasonings. Refrigerate for 1 hour.

Mexican fish dishes may be intricate preparations, such as Fish Bombe, which was created for a cooking festival.

Prepare the sauce: Reduce fish stock to 1½ cups. Blend chiles in a blender or food processor with onion and garlic. Heat butter in a frying pan. Fry chile mixture until thick, seasoning with salt. Add reduced fish stock, crème fraîche, half-and-half, dissolved corn starch, and salt. Simmer for 25 minutes or until sauce thickens slightly. If it becomes too thick, add a little half-and-half. Stir in cheese.

Preheat oven to 375 degrees. Grease 3 baking sheets, and wet lightly.

Prepare the dough: On a floured surface, roll dough in a sheet ⅛-inch thick. Cut 8 3½- to 4-inch circles and 8 4- to 4½-inch circles.

Place small circles on baking sheets. Spread with chile stuffing, and place fish on top. Cover with large circles, and press circles together to seal edges.

Beat egg yolks with egg and half-and-half. Brush top of bombes with egg mixture to glaze. Bake for 40 minutes or until golden brown. Remove from oven.

To serve, spoon sauce to cover a platter. Arrange fish bombes on sauce. Pass extra sauce in a bowl.
Makes 8 servings.

Whole-Wheat Bread (see recipe on p. 109) often accompanies Ocotzingo cheeses.

ENCHILADAS DE OCOTZINGO
Enchiladas, Ocotzingo Style

FOR THE SAUCE

15	chiles anchos, roasted, seeded, deveined, and soaked in water (see Basics)
1½	white onions, roasted (see Basics)
6	cloves garlic, roasted (see Basics)
1½	ripe plantains, sliced
1¼	cups vegetable oil
10	prunes, pitted and puréed
2	tortillas, toasted or fried and sliced in strips or squares
2	tomatoes, roasted (see Basics)
1	tablespoon reserved chile seeds, roasted (see Basics)
1	teaspoon pepper
1	teaspoon whole allspice
1	stick cinnamon, 3 inches long
2	thick slices white onion
2	sprigs thyme or ½ teaspoon dried thyme
3	small tablets (6 ounces) Mexican chocolate (containing ground almonds and cinnamon)
	Salt to taste

FOR THE ENCHILADAS

1	cup vegetable oil
24	thin tortillas
1	recipe mole sauce (see recipe on page 122)
3	chicken breasts, cooked and shredded

FOR THE GARNISH

2	cups fresh enchilado, Ocotzingo, or farmer cheese, crumbled
1	cup white onion, finely chopped
¾	cup parsley, chopped

Prepare the sauce: In a blender or food processor, blend chiles, and set aside. Blend onion and garlic, and set aside. Fry plantain in ¼ cup oil, and add prunes, tortilla strips, tomatoes, chile seeds, pepper, allspice, and cinnamon. Fry lightly. Blend together fried and blended ingredients, adding water if necessary.

In a heavy skillet, heat 1 cup oil, and brown onion slices. Remove, and set aside. Strain blended sauce, and add to oil. Season with thyme, chocolate, and salt. Fry until sauce is slightly thick.

Prepare the enchiladas: Heat oil. Quickly fry tortillas, turning once. Do not let tortillas become crisp. One by one, dip in mole sauce, and put chicken in center of tortilla. Roll into a taco.

To serve, place hot enchiladas on a platter. Pour remaining mole sauce over. Sprinkle with cheese, onion, and parsley. Serve with refried beans.

The tortillas also can be stuffed with fresh cheese, chopped onion, and parsley, and covered with mole sauce.

Makes 24 enchiladas.

The ingredients for preparing Enchiladas, Ocotzingo Style include chiles anchos, plantains, prunes, and corn tortillas.

MOLE NEGRO OAXAQUENO
Black Mole from Oaxaca

Oaxaca is famous for its many mole sauces. The nick-name for this state, in fact, is the "Land of the Seven Moles." Black mole—a king among moles—is tradition-ally used in making enmoladas, two fried tortillas that are folded into a triangle and soaked in the sauce, then garnished with onion rings and fresh Oaxaca cheese. This recipe is from Vazquez Colmenars.

2   cups lard, preferably homemade, or vegetable oil
1   small sweet roll or croissant
3   ounces raw almonds, skinned
3   ounces raw peanuts or walnuts

4   ounces sesame seeds
1   medium plantain, sliced in 1/2-inch slices
1 1/2   white onions, roasted (see Basics)
10   cloves garlic, roasted (see Basics)
10   chiles chihuacles or mulatos, roasted, seeded, deveined, and soaked in water (see Basics)
10   chiles pasillas, preferably black pasillas, roasted, seeded, deveined, and soaked in water (see Basics)
2   chiles chipotles, roasted, seeded, deveined, and soaked in water (see Basics)
2   to 3 tablespoons mixed seeds from above chiles, roasted (see Basics)
6   avocado leaves (optional) or 1/4 teaspoon dried anise, roasted (see Basics)
1   tablespoon whole allspice, roasted (see Basics)
1/2   teaspoon black peppercorns, roasted (see Basics)
4   large plum tomatoes, roasted (see Basics)
4   tortillas, charred
1 1/2   to 2 quarts chicken broth (see recipe on page 202), skimmed of fat
4   onion slices
     Salt to taste
3   to 4 ounces Mexican chocolate tablets (containing cinnamon), in pieces

Heat a little lard in a skillet. Fry sweet roll until brown, and remove. Drain on paper towels. Add almonds, peanuts, and sesame seeds, and fry. Remove and drain. Add a little more lard, and fry plantain. Remove and drain.

In a blender or food processor, blend onions, garlic, and chiles chihuacles, pasillas, and chipotles. Add enough water in which chiles were soaked to facilitate blending. Set chile mixture aside. In a blender or food processor, blend roll, almonds, peanuts, sesame seeds, plantain, chile seeds, avocado leaves, allspice, pepper-corns, tomatoes, and tortillas with enough broth (about 1 to 2 cups) to blend smoothly. (Blend in batches, if necessary.) Strain and reserve.

Put remaining lard in a heavy saucepan. Sauté onion slices until brown, and remove. Pour in nut–spice mix-ture, and fry over low heat until fat begins to rise to the surface. Add chile mixture. Continue cooking over

Black Mole is as common to Oaxacan tables as is the characteristic black pottery.

low heat until fat rises to the surface. Salt to taste. Add chocolate and as much of the remaining broth as necessary to make a mole the consistency of thick cream.

Serve mole sauce with tortillas or with turkey, chicken, or pork that has been stewed and then cooked in the mole to flavor. The mole also makes an excellent sauce for squab.

Makes 8 servings.

HUEVOS A LA OAXAQUENA
Eggs, Oaxaca Style

This light vegetarian dish is served for either breakfast or lunch.

FOR THE SAUCE

2½	quarts water
8	large tomatoes
2½	white onions
12	cloves garlic, whole
3	chiles de agua or 6 chiles serranos or California (Anaheim) chiles
¾	cup vegetable oil
2	slices white onion
	Salt to taste
3	sprigs epazote or cilantro

FOR THE EGGS

¾	cup vegetable oil
24	fresh eggs
	Salt to taste
8	epazote or cilantro leaves

FOR THE GARNISH

8	epazote or cilantro leaves

Prepare the sauce: Put water in saucepan. Add tomatoes, 2 onions, 8 garlic cloves, and chiles, and boil over medium heat for 40 minutes. Drain, and reserve cooking water. Cool, and blend cooked ingredients with ½ onion, 4 garlic cloves, and a little cooking water in a blender or food processor.

Put oil in a frying pan, and brown onion slices. Remove. Add sauce (without straining), and season with salt and epazote. Cook over low heat until fat begins to rise to the surface, about 20 minutes.

Prepare the eggs: Heat a 12- to 16-inch frying pan for 15 minutes. Add oil, and heat. Beat eggs with a fork, and season with salt and epazote. Mix. Pour into frying pan, and cook until eggs set on underside. Turn, and cook until firm. Cut omelet into pieces, and add sauce. Cook over low heat for 20 to 30 minutes. Correct seasoning. Add a little water if the sauce becomes too thick.

To serve, pour eggs and sauce onto a deep platter. Garnish with epazote. Serve with freshly made tortillas and frijoles de olla.

Makes 8 servings.

Eggs, Oaxaca Style is served in the kitchen of the former convent of Santa Catalina.

CHILAPITAS
Chilapitas

The chilapita *is named after an important city in Guerrero. The Nahuatl Indian word means "river near the chile field." This dish can be served with bean, chicken, sausage, or other stuffings.*

FOR THE DOUGH

2¼ pounds masa made with masa harina (see Basics)
2 tablespoons flour
½ teaspoon baking powder
1 teaspoon salt
1½ cups lard
1½ cups vegetable oil

FOR THE STUFFING

2 chicken breasts, poached and finely shredded
1½ cups crème fraîche
1 cup avocado, finely chopped
24 canned chile chipotle strips
48 slices white onion, thinly sliced on the diagonal

Prepare masa, and add flour, baking powder, and salt. Knead until the dough is smooth. Divide masa into 24 balls, measuring about 2 inches in diameter. With your fingers, shape into little baskets or bowls, using a greased bowl as a mold. Fry dough in lard and oil until dark yellow. Remove, and drain on paper towels.

Serve hot, filling with chicken and garnishing with cream, avocado, chile strips, and onion.

Makes 24 chilapitas.

above: *A partial view of the ruins of the Temple of the Inscriptions at Palanque.*

opposite: *Chilapitas are served with green pozole in Guerrero pottery.*

In Chiapas, herbs and greens are used not only for seasoning, but also as vegetable supplements in meals such as Chicken Stew, Diego de Masariego Style.

POLLO EN ESTOFADO DIEGO DE MASARIEGO

Chicken Stew, Diego de Masariego Style

Chiapas cuisine is less spicy than that of other areas and often combines sweet and salty tastes.

FOR THE CHICKEN

1	white onion, grated
6	cloves garlic, puréed
¼	teaspoon ground cloves
1	stick cinnamon, ground
1	teaspoon salt
2	chickens, in pieces
½	cup vegetable oil
6	tablespoons butter

3	cups dry white wine
1	quart water or chicken broth (see recipe on page 202)
4	bay leaves
2	sprigs thyme or ½ teaspoon dried thyme
1½	cups prunes, pitted
	Salt to taste
1½	tablespoons corn starch, dissolved in ¾ cup water

FOR THE VEGETABLES

2	quarts salted water
2	cups zucchini, sliced
2	cups small carrots, sliced
2	cups new potatoes, peeled

Prepare the chicken: Mix onion, garlic, cloves, cinnamon, and salt. Spoon over chicken, and marinate for 2 hours.

Heat oil and butter in a heavy, deep skillet, and brown chicken. Add wine, water, bay leaves, and thyme. Cook over low heat, uncovered, for 25 minutes. Add prunes and salt. Add dissolved corn starch, and continue cooking over low heat for 20 minutes.

Prepare the vegetables: Bring water to a boil. Cook zucchini for 6 minutes. Remove, and plunge in cold water. Add carrots to boiling water, and cook for 10 minutes. Remove, and plunge in cold water. Add potatoes to boiling water, and cook for 20 minutes. Cool, and slice. Add vegetables to chicken, and cook for 10 minutes before serving.

To serve, spoon chicken stew onto a platter.

Makes 8 servings.

AJOS Y CHILES CHIPOTLES A LA OAXAQUENA
Garlic and Chiles Chipotles, Oaxaca Style

The smoked flavor of Oaxacan chiles chipotles makes this accompaniment special.

Oaxaca is known for its spicy dishes, many of which require a prodigious amount of garlic.

2¼	pounds chiles pasillas or chipotles, washed, pierced with a needle, and soaked in water for 2 hours (see Basics)
6	white onions, quartered
60	cloves garlic, whole
8	sprigs thyme or 1 teaspoon dried thyme
1	teaspoon whole cloves
2	tablespoons black peppercorns
	Salt to taste
3	quarts mild fruit vinegar (see recipe on page 128)

Layer chiles, onion, garlic, thyme, cloves, peppercorns, and salt in a 1½-gallon glass jar. Repeat layers until all ingredients are used. Pour vinegar over layers, and macerate for 4 to 5 days, covered tightly, to pickle thoroughly.

Serve 2 or 3 chiles on a small plate with onion, garlic, and vinegar as an appetizer, or stuff pickled chiles with gefilte fish or fish croquettes. They also can be used in table sauces.

Makes about 1 gallon.

Poultry is often the basic ingredient of nonvegetarian recipes in southwestern Mexico.

VINAGRE DE FRUTAS
Fruit Vinegar

This fruit vinegar is lighter than alcohol or wine vinegar and gives pickled dishes a less acidic flavor.

1	quart pulque or beer
2	quarts water
	Peel of 1 large pineapple
1	banana
2	apples
1	cup unrefined brown sugar or dark brown sugar

Mix all ingredients, and pour into a 1-gallon glass jar. Let stand at room temperature for 5 days or until fermented.

The vinegar may be varied by using green plums, onions, chile pasilla, and chile de árbol instead of fruits listed.

Another variation is to use quinces or mangoes for the fruit. Add roasted chiles chipotles, pasillas, or Oaxaqueños, and garlic.

Makes 1 gallon.

LOMO DE PUERCO RELLENO ESTILO CHIAPANECO
Stuffed Pork Loin, Chiapas Style

Stuffed pork loin is one of the most important specialty dishes of this region, prepared for holidays, celebrations, weddings, and baptisms.

FOR THE PORK

- 3   to 3½ pounds boneless pork loin, butterflied
  Salt and pepper to taste

FOR THE STUFFING

- 1   pound pork, cubed
- 1   white onion, studded with cloves, plus 1½ white onions, chopped
- 1   head garlic, plus 5 cloves garlic, minced
- 1   stick cinnamon
- 2   quarts water
- ½   cup olive oil
- 2   tomatoes, roasted (see Basics) and chopped
- ½   cup raisins
- ½   cup raw almonds, skinned and finely chopped
- 1½ cups dry white wine
- 1   tablespoon coarsely ground pepper
  Salt to taste

FOR THE SAUCE

- 8   chiles anchos, roasted, seeded, deveined, soaked in water (see Basics), and puréed
- 1   white onion, roasted (see Basics), plus ½ white onion
- 8   cloves garlic, roasted (see Basics) and peeled, plus 10 cloves garlic, whole
- 1   teaspoon coarsely ground pepper
- 4   cloves, ground
- ½   stick cinnamon, ground
- ¾   cup unrefined brown sugar or dark brown sugar
- ⅓   cup fruit vinegar (see recipe on page 128) or other mild vinegar
- ¾   cup lard
- 4   sprigs thyme or ½ teaspoon dried thyme
  Salt to taste

FOR THE GARNISH

- 8   romaine lettuce leaves, washed
- 16 radishes, shaped like flowers
- 6   green onions, cut like brushes

Preheat oven to 350 degrees.

Prepare the pork: Spread pork loin flat, and season with salt and pepper.

Prepare the stuffing: Simmer pork, clove-studded onion, garlic head, and cinnamon in water for 1½ hours or until done. Cool pork in broth. Remove pork, and chop finely by hand or in a food processor. Reserve broth.

Meanwhile, put oil in a clay casserole or heavy saucepan, and brown chopped onion and minced garlic. Add tomatoes, raisins, almonds, and wine. Cook over low heat until sauce reduces and thickens. Add chopped pork, pepper, and salt to taste. Cook stuffing until thick and flavors are well blended. Spread the stuffing on the loin. Roll loin, and tie with string so it retains shape.

Prepare the sauce: In the blender, blend chiles with roasted onion, ½ onion, roasted garlic, 4 garlic cloves, pepper, cloves, cinnamon, sugar, and vinegar. Set aside. Heat lard in a saucepan. Brown 6 garlic cloves, and remove. Add chile mixture. Fry briefly, and cook sauce over low heat until thickened and fat begins to rise to the surface. Stir in thyme and salt. If sauce is too thick, add a little broth or water. Generously baste the pork roll with the sauce. Reserve some sauce. Roast for 2 hours or until tender, basting frequently with sauce. If too dry, add a little broth or water.

To serve, slice pork in thin or thick slices, as preferred. Line a platter with lettuce leaves, radishes, and onions. Place meat slices in center. Combine hot meat juices with a little broth or water, and add to remaining sauce. Serve on the side. Serve hot or at room temperature with fried plantain slices.

Makes 8 servings.

TAXCALATE
Taxcalate

This is one of the most popular beverages served in Chiapas, dating to pre-Hispanic times.

2¼ pounds hominy, cleaned and dried
¾ cup cocoa beans
1½ tortillas
2½ cups sugar, or to taste
1 teaspoon annatto seeds

The ingredients for two popular regional drinks, Taxcalate and Pozol.

1 stick cinnamon, 3 inches long
Ice cubes

Preheat oven to 350 degrees.

Put hominy on a baking sheet, and bake in oven. Alternatively, the corn can be toasted on a preheated comal. Set aside. Repeat procedure with cocoa beans. Peel cocoa beans. Toast tortillas, and cut into small pieces. Mix all ingredients, and blend in a food processor in small quantities. Or grind ingredients in a meat grinder. Store paste in a glass jar.

To prepare taxcalate, mix 2 heaping tablespoons paste with 1 cup water and sugar to taste. Add ice, and serve cold.

Makes 8 servings.

POZOL DE CACAO
Cold Chocolate Drink

Pozol is a refreshing drink enjoyed at noon in the hottest areas of Chiapas.

1¾ pounds cooked corn kernels, skins removed (see Basics)
10 cocoa beans, roasted (see Basics) and peeled
Sugar to taste
Water to taste
Ice cubes

Put corn and cocoa beans in a blender or food processor, and purée until consistency of a thick paste. Add sugar and water to make a slightly thick beverage. Add ice, and serve cold.

This drink traditionally is served in hollowed-out gourds called jícaras.

Makes 8 servings.

AGUA FRESCA DE LIMON VERDE
Fresh Lime Beverage

Refreshing fresh-fruit beverages are characteristic of Oaxaca. In the central market, Indian women grind lime peels in molcajetes to carefully extract green oils that color the popular limeade they sell.

2   quarts water
1   cup sugar, or to taste
    Peel of 10 limes, finely grated
    Juice of 10 limes (approximately 1 cup)
2   cups ice cubes

Put water and sugar in a 1-gallon glass jug or pitcher. Stir to dissolve. Add grated lime peel, and stir. Add lime juice and ice cubes, and stir. Serve in tall glasses.
Makes about 3 quarts.

AGUA DE SANDIA
Watermelon Beverage

4½   pounds red or yellow watermelon, whole, plus 3 cups watermelon, finely chopped
3   quarts water, or to taste
2   cups sugar, or to taste
1½   quarts ice cubes

Remove rind from watermelon, and cut in chunks. In batches, blend with water and sugar in a blender or food processor. In a large pot, mix beverage with ice and chopped watermelon.

Pour watermelon beverage into a large jug or pitcher, and serve immediately.
Makes about 1½ gallons.

Merchants peddle their produce in the main square of Oaxaca.

POSTRE DEL VIRREINATO
Viceroy's Cake

Desserts served during the colonial period were rich and usually liqueur-based. Several of these desserts were the creations of convent kitchens to please royalty.

FOR THE BATTER

12	eggs, separated
¾	cup sugar
4½	ounces potato starch or corn starch, sifted twice
4½	ounces (generous 1 cup) flour, sifted
½	teaspoon baking powder

FOR THE CUSTARD

1	cup water
3⅓	cups sugar
16	egg yolks
1	tablespoon ground cinnamon
½	cup sweet sherry, or to taste

FOR THE FILLING

½	cup figs, chopped
½	cup orange, chopped
½	cup candied citron, chopped
⅓	cup lime, chopped
1	cup dry sherry

FOR THE FROSTING

4	egg whites
2½	cups heavy cream, chilled in freezer for 1 hour
1	cup powdered sugar

FOR THE GARNISH

½	cup sweet sherry, approximately
3	figs, sliced in strips
1	orange, sliced in strips
2	limes, sliced in strips
12	almonds, toasted
¼	cup pink or blond pine nuts

Preheat oven to 350 degrees. Grease and flour 2 8-inch round cake pans.

Prepare the batter: Beat egg yolks with an electric mixer until thick. Gradually add sugar. Continue beating until very thick and sugar is completely dissolved. Combine potato starch, flour, and baking powder. Gradually add to egg-yolk mixture. Set aside.

Beat egg whites in large bowl until stiff. Carefully fold into egg-yolk mixture. Fill cake pans equally with batter. Bake for 30 minutes or until cake springs back when gently pressed with fingertip. Cool for 10 minutes in pans. Invert on cake racks. Cool cakes.

Prepare the custard: Heat water and sugar in a heavy saucepan, stirring until sugar dissolves. Boil without stirring until syrup forms a hard ball (260 degrees on a candy thermometer). Remove from heat. Cool slightly. Beat egg yolks in a bowl until creamy, and slowly add syrup, beating until mixture thickens a little. Add cinnamon. In a double boiler, cook custard over simmering water for 20 to 30 minutes, until thick and creamy. Stir constantly. Remove from heat, and stir in sherry. Cool. Refrigerate for several hours.

Prepare the filling: Put figs, orange, citron, and lime in a glass bowl, and macerate in sherry for 1 hour.

Prepare the frosting: Beat egg whites until stiff. In another bowl, beat chilled heavy cream until it thickens. Add sugar, and beat until soft peaks form. Carefully fold in egg whites, and refrigerate until serving time.

To assemble cake, place a layer of cake on a buttered cake plate, and sprinkle with about ¼ cup sherry. Cover with a layer of custard. Layer macerated fruit over custard. Top with second cake layer. Sprinkle with sherry. Repeat custard and fruit layers. Frost top and sides with frosting, and garnish with figs, orange, limes, almonds, and pine nuts.

Refrigerate cake for 2 hours before serving.

Makes 8 to 12 servings.

Viceroy's Cake is a rich layering of cake, custard, and macerated fruit.

CHAPTER FOUR
THE BAJIO

I n the Bajio, the area of Mexico most steeped in pious, Old World Spanish tradition, midday meals last until dusk. Young boys taunt imaginary bulls, while *rebozo*-wrapped women search the streets for their husbands, who are ensconced on park benches and engaged in debates over politics and religion. An immense, fertile plateau bordered by rugged mountains, the Bajio—including the states of San Luis Potosí, Querétaro, Guanajuato, and Michoacán—even resembles the central Spanish plains, homeland of its first colonists. Roman-style aqueducts frame views of vineyards and steeples that date back almost to the conquest. The Bajio's flowering trees and rolling hills, green and cool in summer, give the region a pastoral beauty quite unlike the forbidding grandeur of the Mexican sierra. Unlike Indian farmers, who labor with hoes and pointed planting sticks, Bajio peasants use Mediterranean agricultural tools: donkeys, oxen, and plows. Many of the region's characteristic dishes are also clearly Spanish in origin: *lengua rellena* (stuffed tongue), *puchero* (a rich stew), and *fiambre* (cold meat) are among the best.

Its Iberian heritage notwithstanding, the Bajio was the birthplace of Mexicans' struggle for independence. Troops were led into battle by priests and aristocrats

The entrance to the Museo Regional de Querétaro.

from the old Bajio towns that now bear their names: Dolores Hidalgo, San Miguel de Allende, Morelia. Guanajuato, the crown jewel of the Bajio colonial gems and rich in revolutionary history, is also the hometown of such twentieth-century Mexican cultural luminaries as the balladeer and movie star Jorge Negrete and the painter Diego Rivera. In Querétaro, where Maximilian, the French-imposed emperor of Mexico, was captured and executed in 1867, and where, fifty years later, key revolutionary clauses of the Mexican constitution were drafted, tourists on Mexico's independence trail can find exotic culinary rewards. The town's famed *pichones en lodo*, for instance, is quail stuffed with herbs and garlic and roasted in a casing of mud.

Beneath its Spanish colonial surface, the Bajio has never lost touch with its pre-Columbian past. The Indian foundation is most visible in marketplaces, where food vendors offer such delicacies as *cabuche*-cactus blossoms and *nopal*-cactus pads. Cactuses of all kinds are part of the Bajio daily diet. Multicolored prickly-pear fruits—*tunas*, in Aztec-derived Spanish—are a favored dessert, served raw, cooked in syrup, or made into a paste called *queso de tuna*. *Pulque*, the beer-like fermented cactus drink, is not only a convivial beverage, but also an essential ingredient of sauces and stews.

The dominant local *mestizo* culture has been forged

The cathedral of Morelia at night.

over centuries from a tough blend of the Otomi Indians and the highland Spanish peasants who became Mexico's *gambusinos*—free-lance miners eking out a meager but independent livelihood digging for precious and semi-precious gems. Scores of tiny *gambusino* towns, with their bulky Spanish churches, still surround the great colonial mining centers. While some still thrive, others are almost deserted. The region is renowned for its sweet desserts, such as *cajeta* (goat's milk caramel), *chongos* (curds in syrup), *arroz con leche* (rice pudding), and *buñuelos* (fritters).

The decay of the Bajio's mining centers is offset by newly affluent towns, such as San Luis Potosí and Querétaro. Wealth keeps the young from emigrating, and restaurants, too, have improved with affluence, locals say. San Miguel de Allende, a charming colonial town with a busy foreign artists' colony, is emerging as a center of modern Mexican cuisine. Hotels serve sophisticated fare, such as pork loin in almond sauce.

In Morelia, rivaled only by Guanajuato in architectural splendor, discerning travelers will forgo the "international" dishes offered at fancy hostelries for a platter of unpretentious *pollo de plaza* (plaza-style chicken). This specialty is cooked in and sold from stands within view of Morelia's verdant central square and impressive cathedral. Served with enchiladas and a robust *chile ancho* sauce, *pollo de plaza* can perfect a sunny Michoacán afternoon.

Another of this region's best-known culinary contributions can be savored within a short drive into the mountains. The whitefish of Patzcuaro are caught from the local lake by fishermen who gracefully manipulate butterfly nets. The fish are coated in batter, fried, and served with a garnish of fresh limes.

Patzcuaro and the lake island Janitzio are famous for their inhabitants' ritualistic observance of All Souls' Day (November 2), when food offerings are placed on the graves of deceased relatives. Elaborate sugar skeletons or skulls immortalize the loved ones by carrying their names, and local bakers pay great homage by making *pan de muerto* (bread for the dead). The egg-rich, orange-flavored bread is also a fine treat for the living.

San Diego Temple in Guanajuato.

ENCHILADAS POTOSINAS
Enchiladas, Potosí Style

In the Tangamanga market in San Luis Potosí, local cooks prepare this typical dish on braziers while hungry market-goers huddle around them eagerly awaiting the fresh enchiladas.

FOR THE STUFFING
¼ cup vegetable oil
½ cup white onion, chopped
1 cup green sauce (see recipe on page 104)
  Salt to taste (use sparingly if cheese is salty)
2½ cups ricotta or feta cheese

FOR THE DOUGH
6 ounces chiles anchos, lightly roasted, seeded, and deveined (see Basics)
2 cloves garlic, whole
1 teaspoon salt
2¼ pounds fresh masa or equivalent made with masa harina (see Basics)
3 cups vegetable oil

FOR THE GARNISH
1 cup ricotta or feta cheese, crumbled
1 cup white onion, finely chopped
2 cups guacamole (see recipe on page 33)

Prepare the stuffing: Heat oil in a frying pan. Sauté onion until soft. Add green sauce. Salt, and cook over medium heat for 10 minutes. Remove from heat, and cool. Stir in cheese.

Prepare the dough: Soak chiles in water to cover for 25 minutes. Drain, and reserve soaking water. Blend chiles in a metate, blender, or food processor with garlic, salt, and a little soaking water. Add chile mixture to masa, and knead until dough is smooth and not sticky. If necessary, add more soaking water.

Divide dough into 24 balls, 2 inches in circumference. Make tortillas, using a tortilla press (see Basics). Heat tortillas on a hot comal or griddle, turning once. Immediately place 1 teaspoon of stuffing in the center of tortilla, and fold over, like a turnover. Repeat, using

all tortillas. Keep hot.

Heat oil in a saucepan for 10 minutes. Fry enchiladas in oil over low heat for 3 to 4 minutes. They should remain soft. Drain on paper towels.

To serve, place enchiladas on a platter. Garnish with cheese and onion. Serve with guacamole.

The enchiladas can be made ahead through filling and folding. Freeze, and thaw at room temperature until partially thawed. Fry immediately.
Makes 24 enchiladas.

TARTARA ESTILO GUANAJUATO
Tartar Steak, Guanajuato Style

Tartar steak, or raw ground-beef patties, is eaten throughout the world. Guanajuato, a town that boasts advanced cultural development, despite its relatively small size and remote location, has adapted many international dishes and accented them with local flavor.

FOR THE TARTAR STEAK
2½ pounds beef fillet, very fresh and finely ground

FOR THE GARNISH
3½ cups white onion, finely chopped
½ cup chile serrano, finely chopped
3 cups tomato, finely chopped
1 cup cilantro, finely chopped
  Salt and freshly ground pepper to taste
32 limes, halved
  Worcestershire sauce
  Olive oil

Place 5 ounces ground fillet on individual plates. Flatten into patties, and garnish with onion, chile, tomato, cilantro, salt, pepper, and limes. Allow diners to season with Worcestershire sauce and olive oil. Serve with totopos (crisply fried tortilla wedges).
Makes 8 servings.

Natives of Guanajuato have adapted the international recipe for steak tartare to suit their tastes.

SOPA TARASCA ESTILO PATZCUARO
Tarascan Soup, Patzcuaro Style

This soup comes from Patzcuaro, the heart of Tarascan Indian country.

FOR THE SOUP

12	to 13 ounces dried bayo, pinto, or other light-colored beans, soaked overnight in water to cover (about 3 quarts)
1½	white onions, quartered, plus 1 medium white onion
8	cloves garlic, whole
	Salt to taste
3	small tomatoes, roasted (see Basics)
1	chile ancho, seeded, deveined (see Basics), and lightly fried in a little oil
4	tablespoons lard
2	slices white onion
1	to 1¼ quarts hot chicken broth (see recipe on page 202)

FOR THE GARNISH

1½	cups crème fraîche or sour cream
6	tablespoons half-and-half or heavy cream
2	cups panela, ricotta, feta, or mozzarella cheese, cubed
16	tortillas, sliced in 1- by 4-inch strips, fried in oil until crisp, and drained
4	chiles pasillas or anchos, fried in a little oil and sliced in strips
1	chile chipotle, dried or canned
1	avocado, sliced (optional)

Cook beans in water in which they soaked, with quartered onion, 4 garlic cloves, and salt in a pressure cooker for 45 minutes to 1 hour or in a bean pot for 1½ hours or until tender. Salt to taste. Remove beans from heat, and cool. Put beans and their liquid in a

Tortillas, sliced in strips and fried in oil, make a crisp addition to Tarascan Soup, Patzcuaro Style, which is served in ceramic bowls from Michoacán.

Calla lilies are abundant in San Miguel de Allende.

blender or food processor, and purée. Strain through a sieve twice. Set aside.

Blend onion, 4 garlic cloves, tomatoes, and chile in a blender or food processor. Heat lard in a large saucepan, and fry onion slices until brown. Remove onion, and pour tomato mixture into fat in pan. Cook over low heat until mixture thickens, about 20 minutes. Add bean purée, and simmer until the ingredients thicken. Add chicken broth, and salt to taste. Stir and heat through.

Before serving, mix créme fraîche and half-and-half. Ladle hot soup from a clay tureen. Serve garnishes in individual bowls, allowing diners to add cream, cheese, tortillas, chiles, and avocado to taste.

Makes 8 servings.

UCHEPOS DE LECHE
Fresh Corn Tamales with Milk

This is Carmen Arriaga de Zaraleta's version of these tiny, sweet tamales.

FOR THE STUFFING

Kernels from 12 ears corn
1¼ cups scalded milk
1½ to 2 cups sugar
½ teaspoon salt
2 sticks cinnamon, each 3 inches long

FOR THE HUSKS

20 fresh corn husks, approximately, tips removed

Blend corn with milk in a blender or food processor. Strain mixture through a mesh sieve, and pour into a medium saucepan. Add sugar, salt, and cinnamon. Cook over low heat for 45 minutes, stirring often until mixture thickens and separates to reveal bottom of the pan. Cool, and remove cinnamon sticks.

Place 2 tablespoons of mixture on a corn husk, and fold edges of husk over the mixture to form a rectangle.

To serve, arrange uchepos on a platter, and serve either hot or cold. Uchepos may be served with cream, pickled chile strips, onion, and butter, or as a filling for chiles poblanos, served with sour cream.
Makes about 20 uchepos.

ENSALADA DE CABUCHES Y PALMITOS
Cabuche and Hearts of Palm Salad

Cabuches are the little-known blossoms of the biznaga cactus, which grows wild in the state of San Luis Potosí. One of their uses is as a salad ingredient, along with hearts of palm.

FOR THE VINAIGRETTE

2 white onions, finely chopped
4 large tomatoes, finely chopped
1 cup hard-cooked eggs, whites only, finely chopped
1 cup green olives, finely chopped
1 cup parsley, finely chopped
Salt and pepper to taste
1½ cups cider vinegar
1½ cups vegetable oil

FOR THE SALAD

32 slices canned hearts of palm
8 cups canned cabuches, or cooked baby artichoke hearts

FOR THE GARNISH

¼ cup cilantro, chopped

Prepare the vinaigrette: Put onion, tomato, egg whites, olives, parsley, salt, pepper, and vinegar in a glass bowl. Slowly add oil, stirring with a fork, until incorporated. Refrigerate for 2 to 3 hours.

Prepare the salad: Place 4 hearts of palm slices on one side of an individual salad plate, and 1 cup cabuches on the other side of plate. Spoon vinaigrette down center of plate. Sprinkle with cilantro.
Makes 8 servings.

An unusual salad is prepared from cactus blossoms and hearts of palm.

BLANCO DE PATZCUARO
Whitefish from Patzcuaro

This variety of fresh-water whitefish can be found only in the state of Michoacán.

FOR THE WHITEFISH

8 whitefish, preferably from Patzcuaro, 10 ounces each, deboned, or 8 red snapper, sole, or flounder fillets, 5 ounces each
   Juice of 3 limes
   Salt and pepper to taste
2 cups flour
1½ quarts vegetable oil

Whitefish from Patzcuaro are coated with an egg-white batter and are deep fried.

FOR THE BATTER

10 medium egg whites
    Salt to taste
5   medium egg yolks
2   tablespoons flour

FOR THE GARNISH

6 plum tomatoes, sliced lengthwise
8 long romaine lettuce leaves
8 slices lime
4 limes, halved

Prepare the whitefish: Wash the fish well, and dry. Sprinkle with lime juice, salt, and pepper. Let sit for 45 minutes. Dredge fish in flour, shaking off excess. Heat oil.

Preheat oven to 350 degrees.

Meanwhile, prepare the batter: Beat the egg whites with a pinch of salt until stiff. Beat egg yolks lightly. Gently fold yolks into whites; then gradually fold in flour.

Dip fish in batter, and fry in hot oil, turning once. Remove from oil, and drain on paper towels. Repeat until all fish are fried. Keep hot in the oven.

To serve, place whitefish on a platter, decorating edges with tomato and lettuce. Garnish with lime slices, and serve lime halves on the side.
Makes 8 servings.

PICHONES EN LODO
Squab Baked in Mud

FOR COOKING

    Firewood
8¾ pounds mud or clay

FOR THE SQUAB

8   squab with feathers, freshly killed
16 cloves garlic, whole

½ teaspoon salt
1½ tablespoons dried oregano
8 bay leaves
8 teaspoons lard or butter

Ignite firewood, and allow to burn down for 2 to 3 hours. Mix mud with water to form a thick paste.

Remove innards of squab, and wash and rinse squab well. Mix garlic, salt, oregano, bay leaves, and lard. Fill squab cavities with this seasoning. Spread prepared mud over squab against the grain of the feathers, covering with a thick layer. Set aside until mud hardens, about 45 minutes. Place squab directly on hot coals, and cook for about 1 hour, turning occasionally. Cooking time will vary depending on the kind of mud or clay used.

To serve, break hardened clay with a hammer or knife. The skin and feathers of the bird will detach with the clay. Place squab on individual plates, and serve with green sauce or pickled chiles and hot tortillas.

Makes 8 servings.

ENCHILADAS VERDES ESTILO MESÓN SANTA ROSA
Green Enchiladas, Mesón Santa Rosa Style

FOR THE SAUCE

3 quarts water
25 tomatillos, husked
1 white onion, halved, plus ½ white onion
10 cloves garlic, whole
6 to 11 chiles serranos
30 sprigs cilantro
⅔ cup vegetable oil
2 slices white onion
Salt to taste

FOR THE TORTILLAS

24 tortillas, 5 inches in diameter
1½ cups vegetable oil

FOR THE STUFFING

2 quarts water
3 chicken breasts, halved
1 white onion, coarsely sliced
4 cloves garlic, whole
Salt to taste

FOR THE GARNISH

1 quart crème fraîche
4 cups manchego, Chihuahua, Oaxaca, mozzarella, or Monterey jack cheese, grated

Prepare the sauce: Bring water to a boil in a saucepan. Add tomatillos, halved onion, 6 garlic cloves, and 6 to 8 chiles. Simmer for 30 minutes. Cool slightly. Drain, and reserve cooking water. Blend ingredients in a blender or food processor with ½ onion, 4 garlic cloves, 3 chiles, cilantro, and a little cooking water. Heat oil in a saucepan, and brown onion slices. Add blended sauce and salt. Simmer sauce for 45 minutes or until it thickens slightly. If it becomes too thick, add more cooking water.

Prepare the tortillas: Dip tortillas in hot oil in a frying pan just until pliable. Do not crisp. Remove from oil, and drain on paper towels.

Prepare the stuffing: Bring water to a boil in a saucepan, and add chicken, onion, garlic, and salt. Cook over low heat for 30 minutes or until chicken is cooked. Cool, and remove chicken; shred.

Preheat oven to 350 degrees. Grease 8 individual rectangular baking dishes.

Fill tortillas with shredded chicken, and roll to form enchiladas. Place 3 enchiladas on each dish, and pour green sauce over. Cover with 2 tablespoons crème fraîche, and sprinkle with cheese. Bake in oven for 25 minutes, and then place under broiler until top is brown. Serve hot with frijoles de olla.

Makes 24 enchiladas.

POLLO DE PLAZA ESTILO MORELIA
Plaza Chicken, Morelia Style

This chicken dish can be savored in Morelia. Every day at 6:00 P.M., a tantalizing aroma emanates from the stands in San Francisco Plaza, advertising this chicken specialty.

FOR THE CHICKEN

1½ quarts water
1½ white onions, halved
6   cloves garlic, whole
2   bay leaves
1   sprig thyme or ¼ teaspoon dried thyme
1   teaspoon freshly ground pepper
    Salt to taste
4   chicken breasts, halved, bone-in

FOR THE ENCHILADAS

½   cup vinegar
3   cups water
6   chiles anchos or pasillas, roasted, slit, seeded, deveined (see Basics), and washed
4   cloves garlic, whole
½   white onion, coarsely chopped
1   teaspoon oregano, dried and crushed
    Pinch of ground cumin
½   teaspoon freshly ground pepper
    Salt to taste
1   cup vegetable oil or lard
24 medium tortillas

FOR THE GARNISH

16 romaine lettuce leaves
1½ cups white onion, finely chopped and mixed
    with 1 teaspoon salt and 1 teaspoon dried oregano
3   cups homemade tomato sauce
2   cups feta cheese, grated
8   chiles jalapeños
6   cups carrots, chopped and cooked
6   cups potatoes, peeled, chopped, and cooked

Prepare the chicken: Bring water to a boil in a medium saucepan. Add onion, garlic, bay leaves, thyme, pepper, salt, and chicken. Simmer for 25 minutes. Remove from heat, and cool chicken in broth. Remove chicken.

Prepare the enchiladas: Mix vinegar and water. Soak chiles in this solution for 30 minutes. Drain, reserving liquid. In a blender or food processor, purée chiles, garlic, onion, oregano, cumin, pepper, salt, and ½ to 1 cup soaking solution. Pour sauce into a wide bowl or pan.

Heat a deep frying pan. Add oil. Briefly dip tortillas, one by one, into chile sauce. Let excess sauce drip off. Quickly fry tortillas, one by one, in frying pan. Fold tortillas in half as they fry, turning over to fry well but not until crisp. They will spatter as they fry. Remove tortillas from pan, and place in a baking dish. Keep warm in oven. Add more oil, if necessary, and repeat procedure for all tortillas.

In same oil, fry chicken, browning on all sides.

To serve, place 2 lettuce leaves on each of 8 plates. Place 3 enchiladas on lettuce bed, and top enchiladas with a piece of chicken. Garnish with onion, tomato sauce, cheese, and chiles. Serve hot with freshly cooked carrots and potatoes.

Makes 24 enchiladas.

Fried tortillas topped with seasoned chicken and garnishes make a savory meal of Plaza Chicken, Morelia Style.

above: *The Museo Regional de Querétaro.*
left: *The escutcheon at the former home of the count of Ecala.*

PIERNA DE VENADO MARINADA EN VINO TINTO

Leg of Venison in Red Wine Dough

FOR THE MARINADE

1½	cups olive oil
8	cloves garlic, chopped
1	cup shallots, minced
3	white onions, thinly sliced
8	carrots, peeled and sliced in strips
2	cups celery, chopped
20	sprigs parsley
2	tablespoons sugar
1	tablespoon salt
10	black peppercorns
1	tablespoon fresh ginger root, peeled and chopped

6   sprigs thyme or 1 teaspoon dried thyme
1   tablespoon dried sweet basil
1   teaspoon whole cloves
1   teaspoon whole allspice, crushed

FOR THE VENISON

1   6½- to 8½-pound venison or mutton leg, boned
     and pounded

FOR THE DOUGH

2¼   pounds flour
1   tablespoon salt
1   to 1½ bottles dry red wine, approximately

FOR THE GARNISH

1   quart water
2   cups sugar
2   sticks cinnamon, each 2½ inches long
8   red apples, peeled and cored
1   bunch cilantro

FOR THE GRAVY

1   cup sweet sherry
7   tablespoons butter
2   teaspoons corn starch, dissolved in a little of the
     sherry

The ingredients for Leg of Venison in Red Wine Dough.

Prepare the marinade: Heat oil in a saucepan. Brown garlic, shallots, and onion. Add carrots, celery, parsley, sugar, salt, peppercorns, ginger root, thyme, basil, cloves, and allspice. Bring to a boil; reduce heat, and simmer for 25 minutes.

Prepare the venison: Put venison in an enamel baking dish, and pour marinade over. Refrigerate for 2 to 3 days, turning meat regularly. Just before baking, remove venison from marinade, and dry. Reserve marinade.

Preheat oven to 350 degrees. Grease a baking tray.

Prepare the dough: Mix flour and salt together. Slowly add wine, and knead to form a stiff dough. (The amount of wine varies, depending on the flour and humidity.) Roll out dough to roughly the size of the venison leg. Place leg on baking tray, and cover with dough. Bake for 4 hours or until done.

Remove venison leg from oven. Discard dough, and reserve pan juices.

Prepare the garnish: Bring water to a boil in a saucepan. Add sugar and cinnamon. Boil for 25 minutes. Add apples, and cover saucepan with lid. Cook for 20 minutes or until apples are tender.

Prepare the gravy: Mix pan juices and marinade. Heat mixture over low heat for 20 minutes. Add sherry, butter, and corn starch. Cook and stir gravy for 10 minutes. Strain through a mesh sieve.

To serve, place roasted leg of venison on a platter. Let rest for 20 minutes before slicing. Garnish with cooked apples and cilantro. Pass gravy.

Makes 12 servings.

FIAMBRE POTOSINO
Cold Meat from Potosí

Cold meat is one of the most typical dishes of the city of San Luis Potosí. Its preparation dates to the baroque era, the late seventeenth and early eighteenth centuries, a time reflected in the city's architecture.

FOR THE MEATS

6	quarts water
I	large beef tongue
4	pig's feet, cleaned and halved
2	heads garlic, halved
2	white onions or 4 green onions
3	carrots, peeled
2	turnips
6	bay leaves
20	sprigs parsley
2	sprigs marjoram or ½ teaspoon dried marjoram
2	sprigs thyme or ½ teaspoon dried thyme
½	tablespoon whole allspice
	Salt to taste
4	medium chicken breasts

FOR THE VINAIGRETTE

6	cloves garlic, puréed
I	tablespoon dried oregano
I	tablespoon dried marjoram
I	tablespoon dried thyme
I	teaspoon pepper
½	teaspoon whole allspice
	Salt to taste
¼	cup Dijon mustard
I½	cups cider vinegar
I	quart vegetable oil

FOR THE GARNISH

6	red potatoes, peeled and sliced with curly potato cutter
8	large carrots, peeled and sliced with curly potato cutter
I	head lettuce, thinly sliced
I	cup canned chiles güeros or jalapeños
2	tablespoons chives, chopped

Prepare the meats: Heat water in a stock pot. Add tongue, pig's feet, garlic, onions, carrots, turnips, bay leaves, parsley, marjoram, thyme, allspice, and salt. Bring to a boil. Lower heat, and cook for 2½ hours or until tongue is tender and pig's feet are cooked.

Add chicken breasts, and continue cooking for 30 minutes. Remove meat from heat. Remove vegetables, and set aside. Cool meats in broth, and then remove. Refrigerate tongue; then peel and thinly slice. Debone the chicken breasts, and slice them on the diagonal.

Prepare the vinaigrette: In an electric blender, blend garlic, oregano, marjoram, thyme, pepper, allspice, salt, mustard, and vinegar for 3 minutes. Slowly add oil in a steady stream. Correct seasoning. Put tongue, chicken, pig's feet, and reserved vegetables in a bowl, and cover with vinaigrette. Mix gently. Refrigerate for 24 hours.

Prepare the garnish: In a casserole, bring salted water to a boil. Cook the potatoes and carrots until tender, being careful not to overcook. Drain vegetables, and add to meat in vinaigrette. Refrigerate for 24 hours.

To serve, place piles of thinly sliced lettuce on a large platter. Arrange potato and carrot slices on top, overlapping them. Place tongue in the center, surrounded by sliced chicken and pig's feet. Garnish with chiles, and sprinkle with chives.
Makes 8 to 12 servings.

TOSTADAS MINERAS
Miners' Tostadas

Tostadas are sold in Guanajuato outside the local Hidalgo market. This version of the Mexican classic pays homage to regional miners.

FOR THE TOSTADAS

3	cups vegetable oil
I6	tortillas, 4 inches in diameter

FOR THE TOPPING

3	cups pinto beans (see recipe on page 43)

1½   quarts water
 3   chicken breasts, halved
 1   white onion, quartered, plus 1½ white onions,
     minced
 6   cloves garlic, whole
 2   bay leaves
 1   sprig thyme
     Salt to taste
 ½   cup olive oil or vegetable oil
 4   ripe tomatoes (about 2¾ pounds), finely chopped
 4   chiles serranos, minced
 ½   cup cilantro; finely chopped
 1   teaspoon freshly ground pepper

FOR THE GARNISH

 4   cups lettuce, shredded
16   slices tomato
16   slices avocado, ¼-inch thick
 1   cup sour cream
16   slices chiles jalapeños (see Basics)

Prepare the tostadas: Heat oil in a frying pan almost to
the smoking point. Fry tortillas until crisp, and drain on
paper towels.

   Prepare the topping: Prepare the beans, allowing
them to thicken until they form a spreadable paste.
Keep warm.

   Heat water in a medium saucepan, and simmer
chicken, quartered onion, garlic, bay leaves, thyme,
and salt for 40 minutes. Cool in chicken broth. Remove and shred chicken.

   Heat oil in a frying pan, and brown minced onion.
Add tomato, chile, cilantro, salt, and pepper. Cook
over low heat for 30 minutes. Add shredded chicken,
and cook for 25 minutes. Remove from heat. Set
aside, and cool.

   To serve, spread tostadas (the fried tortillas) with
warm bean paste. Spoon chicken mixture on top, and
cover with lettuce. Garnish each tostada with 1 tomato and avocado slice and 1 tablespoon sour cream.
Top each with 1 chile slice. Serve immediately.
Makes 16 tostadas.

above: *Cold Meat from Potosí.*
right: *Miners' Tostadas.*

PUCHERO ESTILO EX-HACIENDA DE SANTIAGO
Stew, in the Style of the Former Hacienda of Santiago

Stew is a traditional dish in the region where the former hacienda of Santiago is located, on a high plateau in the state of San Luis Potosí. Surrounded by prickly pear cactus, Indian figs, and pirul trees, the hacienda is a site where bulls are tested for their ferocity.

FOR THE BROTH

6½	quarts water
4	sprigs mint or ½ teaspoon dried mint
30	sprigs cilantro
6	bay leaves
20	sprigs parsley
4	sprigs thyme or 1 teaspoon dried thyme
4	sprigs marjoram or 1 teaspoon dried marjoram
2	turnips, peeled
2	white onions, sliced
2	heads garlic, unpeeled and halved
6	green onions, with tops
3	ears corn, cleaned and each cut in 3 pieces
2¼	pounds beef soup bones
2¼	pounds beef hind shank
3¼	pounds beef chuck, cut in 2-inch cubes
	Salt or powdered beef bouillon to taste
6	carrots, peeled and sliced
2	large chayote squash, peeled and quartered
6	zucchini, sliced

FOR THE SAUCE

15	tomatillos, husked
	Salt to taste
4	cloves garlic, whole
8	chiles de árbol or small dried red chiles, fried lightly in oil

FOR THE GARNISH

½	cup green onions, with tops
4	cups long-grain white rice, cooked (see recipe on page 202)
2	cups chickpeas, cooked

The ingredients for beef stew in front of the San Francisco Plaza.

The beef broth is served separately from the stew.

½   cup chiles poblanos or serranos or California
     (Anaheim) chiles, chopped
¾   cup cilantro, chopped

Prepare the broth: Bring water to a boil in a large
saucepan. Tie fresh herbs together, and add to water.
If using dried herbs, add with turnips, white onions,
garlic, green onions, and corn. Return to a boil.

Add soup bones, beef shank and chuck, and salt.
Bring to a boil over medium heat. Turn heat to low,
and simmer broth for 2½ hours. Remove from heat,
skimming off foam and fat. Remove vegetables, and
cool beef in broth. Cook the broth 1 day ahead, so it
can be skimmed easily.

Prepare the sauce: In a saucepan, boil tomatillos in
water to cover until tender, about 10 minutes. Drain,
and reserve cooking water. Add salt to tomatillos. In a
molcajete or blender, grind salt, garlic, and chiles to a
paste. Gradually add tomatillos, grinding after each addition. Make a thin sauce, adding cooking water if necessary. Set aside.

Add carrots and chayote squash to broth, and cook
for 25 minutes. Eight minutes before serving, add zucchini. Remove vegetables from broth. Remove beef.

To serve, pour broth into a soup tureen. Place beef
in the center of a platter, and garnish with cooked
vegetables and green onions. Serve rice, chickpeas,
chiles, cilantro, and sauce in bowls on the side. Allow
diners to garnish stew to taste. Serve with freshly
made tortillas.

Makes 8 servings.

FILETE ESTILO SAN MIGUEL DE ALLENDE
Fillet, San Miguel de Allende Style

*Ranches in the San Miguel de Allende area provide
markets with fresh produce, including chiles, tomatoes,
corn, and broccoli.*

FOR THE SAUCE

2½   quarts water

20   tomatillos, husked
14   small chiles anchos, seeded, deveined (see Ba-
      sics), and fried
 7   long chiles pasillas, seeded, deveined (see Basics),
      and fried
 1   medium white onion, halved, plus ½ white
      onion, halved
10   cloves garlic, whole
½   cup vegetable oil
 2   slices white onion
      Salt to taste

FOR THE BEEF

3½   pounds beef fillet, in 1 piece
 3   cloves garlic, puréed
½   teaspoon pepper
½   cup olive oil
½   cup butter, melted and cooled
      Salt to taste

FOR THE GARNISH

 6   chiles amarillos or caribes, sliced

Prepare the sauce: Bring water to a boil in a saucepan.
Boil tomatillos, 10 chiles anchos, 5 chiles pasillas, halved
onion, and 6 garlic cloves for 30 minutes. Cool. Drain,
reserving cooking water. Blend boiled ingredients with
4 chiles anchos, 2 chiles pasillas, ½ onion, and 4 garlic
cloves in a blender or food processor. Add 2 cups
cooking water, and blend again until the sauce is thick
and flavors are well blended. Heat oil in a saucepan,
and sauté onion slices. Add blended sauce, and salt to
taste. Simmer sauce for 40 minutes or until thick.

Prepare the beef: Put the beef in a bowl. Mix garlic,
pepper, oil, and butter in a food processor or blender.
Pour over meat. Marinate for 30 minutes. Preheat a
thick griddle or cast-iron frying pan. Grill beef on the
griddle for 35 minutes, basting with marinade and
turning every 5 minutes to avoid over-browning. Remove from heat, and salt. Cover with aluminum foil,
and let stand for 15 minutes before slicing.

To serve, place fillet on a platter, and garnish with
chiles. Serve with sauce on the side.

Makes 8 servings.

Stuffed Tortillas, San Luis Style are garnished with lettuce, tomatoes, and cheese.

GORDITAS DE SAN LUIS
Stuffed Tortillas, San Luis Style

The San Luis stuffed tortillas are a favorite breakfast dish, especially on Sundays, of people who gather in Morales Park. The park area is filled with food stands in which vendors prepare the stuffed tortillas, serving them with strong, hot black coffee.

FOR THE DOUGH

2¼ pounds fresh masa or equivalent made with masa harina (see Basics), or substitute dough from Enchiladas, Potosi Style (see recipe on page 138)
Salt to taste

FOR THE BEAN STUFFING

3 cups pinto beans, cooked and puréed (see rec-ipe on page 43)

FOR THE NOPAL STUFFING

½ cup vegetable oil
4 cloves garlic, whole, plus 1 tablespoon garlic, finely chopped
4 to 6 chiles de árbol, finely chopped
2 cups tender nopales (cactus pads), sliced in thin strips
Salt and pepper to taste

FOR THE CHILE STRIPS

½ cup olive oil
1½ green onions, finely chopped
6 chiles poblanos, roasted, peeled, seeded, de-veined, soaked in salted water, and sliced in thin strips or cubed (see Basics)
Salt and pepper to taste

FOR THE BEEF

½   cup vegetable oil
1   cup green onion, chopped
10   to 11 ounces beef skirt steak, cooked with 1 onion, 6 garlic cloves, and salt for 1½ hours or until tender, and shredded
3   medium tomatoes, puréed
4   cloves garlic, puréed
½   cup red potato, boiled and finely chopped
½   cup pickled or canned chile jalapeño strips

Prepare the dough: Put masa in a glass bowl. Add a little water and salt, and knead until dough is smooth but not sticky. Set aside.

Prepare the bean stuffing: Heat beans and mash them, using the back of a spoon, to form a thick purée. Keep purée hot.

Prepare the nopal stuffing: Heat oil in a saucepan. Add garlic cloves, and brown. Remove garlic; add chopped garlic, and cook until golden. Add chiles and nopal strips. Sauté for 8 to 10 minutes. Season with salt and pepper. Keep stuffing hot.

Prepare the chile strips: Heat oil in a saucepan. Add onion, and sauté. Add chile strips, and sauté for 8 minutes. Season with salt and pepper.

Prepare the beef: Heat oil in a casserole. Sauté onion. Add beef, tomato purée, and garlic. Cook over low heat, stirring with a spoon, until mixture begins to thicken. Add potatoes and chile strips. Continue cooking until sauce is thick.

Heat a comal or griddle. Make small tortillas, about 2 inches in diameter (see Basics). Heat on comal, and press centers with a dry dish cloth to encourage puffing. Remove tortillas from heat, and slit tortilla puff, lifting top layer with a knife. Daub inside with bean purée, and then stuff with a little nopal mixture, chile strips, and shredded meat. Reheat stuffed tortilla before serving, or keep warm on the edge of the comal.

To serve, place tortillas on a platter, and serve while hot.

Makes 24 tortillas.

CARNITAS AL ESTILO SANTA ROSA DE JAUREGUI
Pork, Santa Rosa de Jauregui Style

The fame of Querétaro pork can be traced to the town of Santa Rosa de Jauregui. The pork can be savored in the local taco stands throughout the state.

FOR THE PORK

7   cups lard
    Salt to taste
1   teaspoon pepper
4½   pounds pork leg, in large chunks
3¼   pounds pork loin, in large chunks
6   sprigs thyme or 1 teaspoon dried thyme
2   bay leaves
6   sprigs marjoram or 1 teaspoon dried marjoram
3   heads garlic, halved
3   white onions, halved
2   quarts water

FOR THE GARNISH

3   cups cilantro, chopped
2   cups white onion, finely chopped

With an electric mixer, beat 3 cups lard with salt and pepper for 20 minutes. Spread on pork pieces. Spread half the thyme, bay leaves, marjoram, garlic, and onion on a baking sheet. Put pork on top, and cover with remaining herbs, garlic, and onion. Refrigerate for 2 hours.

Heat a deep enamel, clay, or copper pot for 20 minutes. Add ½ cup lard, and brown pork over low heat. Add remaining lard and water. Add herbs, garlic, and onion from baking sheet, and cook over medium heat for 1½ to 2 hours or until pork is done.

Remove from heat, cover with aluminum foil, and let pork cool in broth for 10 minutes.

Chop pork. Serve from a clay bowl garnished with cilantro and onion. Accompany with green and red sauces and freshly made tortillas. Diners can prepare their own tacos.

Makes 16 servings.

ALMENDRADO CON LOMO DE PUERCO A LAS BUGAMBILIAS
Pork Loin Amandine, Bugambilia Style

The cuisine of San Miguel de Allende, a picturesque mountain city in Guanajuato, is strongly influenced by tradition. This recipe is served at the Bugambilia restaurant in that quaint pueblo.

FOR THE PORK

3	pounds pork loin
½	white onion
4	cloves garlic, whole
1	teaspoon pepper
6	bay leaves
½	cup olive oil
	Salt to taste
1½	quarts water

FOR THE SAUCE

3	cups lard
14	ounces chiles anchos, slit open, seeded, and deveined (see Basics)
3	to 4 ounces chiles pasillas, slit open, seeded, and deveined (see Basics)
1½	large white onions, halved
6	cloves garlic, whole
1	stick cinnamon, 6 inches long
1	teaspoon pepper
¼	teaspoon ground cloves
3	to 4 ounces sesame seeds
10	ounces raw almonds, skinned
½	croissant
3	bay leaves
4	ripe tomatoes (about 2¾ pounds)
4	slices white onion
	Salt to taste
1½	to 2 quarts chicken broth (see recipe on page 202)

FOR THE GARNISH

8	sprigs broccoli, cooked in salted water for 4 minutes
8	knob onions, shaped like flowers
8	carrots, scored and sliced
½	cup raw almonds, sautéed in butter

Preheat oven to 350 degrees.

Prepare the pork: Put pork loin in a baking dish. Blend onion, garlic, pepper, and bay leaves in a blender or food processor. Mix in oil and salt, and pour over pork. Marinate for 1 hour.

Bake pork for 30 minutes. Pour water over, and bake for 1½ hours or until meat is done. Do not overcook. Remove pork from oven, and cover with aluminum foil. Cool for 40 minutes before slicing pork.

Prepare the sauce: Heat a little lard in a saucepan, and fry chiles anchos and pasillas until crisp. Remove, and drain on paper towels. Add more lard, and sauté onions, garlic, cinnamon, pepper, cloves, sesame seeds, and almonds. Remove, and drain. Add a little more lard, and fry croissant and bay leaves until well browned. Remove, and drain. Add more lard, and fry tomatoes. Remove, and drain. Blend thoroughly chiles and all fried ingredients in a blender or food processor. Strain mixture through a mesh sieve.

Heat 1 cup lard in a saucepan. Fry onion slices until brown. Remove onion slices, and discard. Slowly add strained sauce. Salt to taste, and simmer for about 1 hour or until bottom of pan shows when mixture is pushed aside with a spoon. Add chicken broth, and continue cooking until sauce thickens slightly, about 45 minutes.

To serve, place 4 slices of pork loin on each of 8 plates. Cover with amandine sauce. Garnish with broccoli, onions, and carrots. Sprinkle almonds over pork. Serve with freshly made corn tortillas.
Makes 8 servings.

CORUNDAS
Ash Tamales, Michoacán Style

Corundas are an unusual version of tamales, since they are shaped in triangles. They also are steamed differently from traditional tamales. Corundas are sold on almost every street corner in Patzcuaro, where they originated. They usually are accompanied by hot atole or black coffee.

FOR THE DOUGH

2¾   pounds dry corn and 3 quarts water, or 2¼ pounds prepared flour for tamales (see Basics) and 4½ cups water

2   cups ashes, from burned firewood

¼   cup ground limestone

1   tablespoon salt, plus salt to taste

2   cups lard

1   cup water

¾   teaspoon baking soda

1   teaspoon baking powder

1   cup crème fraîche

9   ounces panela or ricotta cheese, crumbled

2   white onions, sliced on the diagonal

6   large chiles poblanos or 10 chiles chilacas, roasted, peeled, seeded, deveined (see Basics), and sliced in strips

FOR THE SAUCE

1½   quarts water

20   tomatillos, husked

3   tomatoes (3½ ounces each)

8   chiles serranos

1   white onion, quartered

6   cloves garlic, whole

    Salt to taste

FOR THE LEAVES

80   fresh corn leaves (*not* husks)

FOR THE GARNISH

3   cups crème fraîche, or 1½ cups sour cream mixed with 1½ cups light cream

Prepare the dough: Put corn, water, ashes, limestone, and salt in a large saucepan. Boil over high heat for 45 minutes. The corn is ready when the kernel skin can be easily removed. Remove from heat, and cool.

Rub kernels between palms of hands to loosen skins. Wash in water, and remove skins. Discard skins. Grind kernels in a blender or food processor. (Or mix tamal flour with boiling water until soft.)

Beat 1½ cups lard with an electric mixer or by hand until light and fluffy. Add water, baking soda, and bak-

ing powder. Continue beating until well incorporated. Add crème fraîche and cheese. Beat mixture until fluffy.

Heat ½ cup lard in a saucepan. Sauté onion and chile. Salt to taste. Cook over medium heat for 20 minutes. Mix with the tamale dough.

Prepare the sauce: Bring water to a boil, and add tomatillos, tomatoes, chiles, onion, and garlic. Boil for 25 minutes. Drain, reserving cooking water. Blend ingredients in a blender or food processor. Salt to taste. If sauce becomes too thick, add a little cooking water. Keep warm.

Spoon 2 tablespoons of dough in the center of a corn leaf. Fold leaf to form a triangle. Repeat until all dough is used.

Put a rack in a steamer, and add 3 quarts water. Bring to a boil. Drop a coin into the water. When you can no longer hear the coin rattling, the water has evaporated. Add more water. Cover rack with a layer of corn leaves.

Place tamales on leaves in steamer, standing upright. Cover with a layer of leaves. Cover steamer tightly, and bring water to a boil. Steam tamales for about 1 hour or until the leaf can be easily peeled from the dough.

To serve, place 2 or 3 tamales, steaming hot, on individual plates. Unwrap, and cover with sauce. Spoon crème fraîche on top.

Makes about 30 tamales.

Ash Tamales, Michoacán Style are served on a copper plate from Santa Clara del Cobre.

BUNELOS
Fritters

Buñelos *are a traditional Mexican dessert, often served around Christmas. María Dolores Torres Yzabal, a Mexico City caterer, shared this recipe for a delicious dessert.*

FOR THE FRITTERS
1	tablespoon dry yeast
½	cup warm milk
1	pound flour
1	teaspoon salt
8	egg yolks, beaten until thick
4	egg whites, beaten until soft peaks form
2	tablespoons sugar
2	tablespoons butter, softened
1	teaspoon anise
2⅓	cups lard
½	to 1 cup boiling water, containing 10 tomatillo husks
2	quarts vegetable oil

FOR THE SYRUP
6	cones unrefined brown sugar, or 6 cups dark brown sugar
4	sticks cinnamon, each 4 inches long
6	guavas, thinly sliced

Prepare the fritters: Dissolve yeast in milk. Put flour, salt, egg yolks, egg whites, and yeast mixture in a bowl. In an aluminum bowl, mix sugar, butter, anise, and ⅓ cup lard. Add flour mixture, and knead dough with hands, adding a little boiling water. Continue kneading dough on a floured pastry board until elastic and not sticky. Form a ball, and grease with a little lard. Cover, and set dough aside until doubled in volume.

Heat oil and 2 cups lard in a large frying pan. Divide dough into 20 balls. Turn a clay pot upside down. Cover bottom with a dish towel. Sprinkle towel with flour. Roll out 1 dough ball on a floured surface to a circle 3 to 4 inches in diameter. Place on the floured dish towel, and carefully stretch circle until it measures 8½ to 9 inches in diameter. The dough will be very thin and almost transparent.

Fry in hot oil, turning once. When crisp, remove fritter from oil, and drain on paper towels. Repeat procedure for remaining 19 dough balls.

Prepare the syrup: In a medium saucepan, heat sugar, water to cover, cinnamon, and guava. Cook over high heat for 45 minutes to 1 hour or until a thick syrup is formed.

To serve, break buñelos into quarters, and place 4 quarters in each individual shallow bowl. Cover with hot syrup.

Makes 20 buñelos.

CHURROS
Long Fritters

Churros *are a typical Mexican sweet snack that originated in colonial times, when they were savored with a cup of piping hot chocolate or of coffee and milk.*

1	quart water
1½	to 2 teaspoons salt
3	cups flour
1	teaspoon baking powder
4	egg yolks
3	cups vegetable oil or corn oil
2	limes, halved
	Sugar to taste

Mix water and salt in a saucepan. Bring to a rolling boil. Remove from heat. Combine flour and baking powder, and add to water all at once. Stir to form smooth dough. Return to heat, and cook, stirring, until smooth. Remove from heat, and stir in egg yolks, one at a time. Continue to beat until the dough becomes smooth and elastic. Cool.

In a frying pan, heat oil and limes. Test with a bit of dough. When oil spatters, it is hot enough. Put dough in a churro mold or a pastry bag fitted with a star-shaped tip. Press out 4- to 4½-inch strips. Fry in oil until brown on all sides, turning to cook evenly. Drain on paper towels. Then roll in sugar.

To serve, place hot churros on a tray.

Makes about 25 churros.

GELATINA DE ZAPOTE NEGRO
Black-Zapote Gelatin

Zapote is a tropical fruit that grows abundantly in the state of Michoacán. The fruit is green on the outside and brownish-black on the inside. The soft pulp is used to make a compote, gelatin, and sherbet.

FOR THE SYRUP

1	quart hot water
2	sticks cinnamon, each 3 to 4 inches long
½	teaspoon ground cloves
1¾	cups sugar

FOR THE GELATIN

3½	cups black zapote, peeled, pitted, and strained through a sieve
2	cups fresh orange juice or tangerine juice
⅔	cup water
5	tablespoons unflavored gelatin
6	tablespoons dry or sweet sherry

FOR THE GARNISH

1¼	cups heavy cream, chilled in freezer for 45 minutes
1¼	cups crème fraîche or sour cream, chilled in freezer for 45 minutes
¾	cup sugar
2¼	pounds strawberries, washed and cut like an accordion

Prepare the syrup: Bring water to a boil. Add cinnamon, cloves, and sugar. Cook at slow boil for 35 minutes or until mixture forms a thick syrup. Cool.

Prepare the gelatin: Put zapote pulp in a glass bowl. Stir in orange juice and cool (not cold) syrup. In a saucepan, mix water and gelatin well. Heat dissolved gelatin over low heat, and strain. Add to zapote mixture. Stir in sherry, mixing well. Lightly grease a 9-inch ring mold with vegetable oil. Pour zapote mixture into mold, and refrigerate for 4 hours.

Prepare the garnish: Mix together chilled heavy cream and crème fraîche, and beat with an electric mixer or by hand until peaks form. Lower speed, and gradually add sugar. Continue beating until peaks form. Refrigerate for 30 minutes.

To serve, unmold gelatin by placing mold in hot water for a few seconds and inverting onto a platter. (If it melts slightly, refrigerate.) Spoon cream in center of gelatin. Garnish with strawberries.
Makes 8 to 12 servings.

JAMONCILLO DE LECHE
Milk Candy Fudge

Querétaro is famous for its wide variety of sweets, sold in doorways and marketplaces throughout the city. Among the homemade candies are peanut brittle, coconut patties, crystallized fruits, and fudges.

4	quarts milk
	Pinch of baking soda
10	cups sugar
1	cup pine nuts or pecans, chopped
½	cup ground pecans

Bring milk to a boil with baking soda in a copper or Teflon saucepan. Remove from heat, and cool. Pour half the milk into a bowl, and set aside.

Add sugar to the milk remaining in the saucepan. Bring to a boil, and gradually stir in reserved milk. Continue cooking over medium heat, stirring occasionally, until mixture forms a soft ball (about 240 degrees on a candy thermometer). Remove from heat, and beat by hand or with an electric mixer until thick. If the mixture becomes too thick, add a little water. Stir in pine nuts.

Line a 4- by 6-inch loaf pan with waxed paper. Spread the candy evenly in pan, and cool for 3 hours. Sprinkle with pecans, and remove from pan. Cut into squares.
Makes 70 to 80 candies.

CHONGOS ZAMORANOS
Curds in Syrup

Zamora is well known for its sweets and candies. Chongo, literally "chignon" in Mexico, refers to the curds that separate from the whey, which, with sugar, forms a syrup.

 4 egg yolks
 3 quarts raw milk (homogenized milk cannot be substituted)
 2 rennet tablets
 4 sticks cinnamon, each 6 inches long, in pieces
4½ cups sugar

Beat egg yolks with a little raw milk until smooth and light-colored. Add remaining raw milk, and mix. Pour mixture into a clay pot (must be earthenware).

In a large pot, dissolve rennet tablets in a little milk. Add raw-milk mixture. Set pot in a warm place (near stove pilot or oven), and allow milk to curdle overnight. Once milk is curdled, make an X-shaped cut into junket. Stick cinnamon pieces inside the incision. Sprinkle sugar over top, and let stand until sugar is absorbed by junket.

Place pot on very low heat for 3½ hours or until junket takes on a golden-brown color. Remove curds as they form, and cool. At the end of procedure, only syrup should remain in pot. Cook syrup for about 20 minutes or until thick. Refrigerate for 4 hours.

To serve, spoon chongos into small clay bowls, drench with syrup, and decorate with cinnamon pieces.

Makes 8 servings.

ARROZ CON LECHE
Rice Pudding

FOR THE PUDDING
 5   quarts water
1¾ cups unconverted long-grain white rice
 2   quarts scalded milk
 3   cups evaporated milk
 3   cups sugar, or to taste
 2   sticks cinnamon, each about 3 inches long
 ½ cup raisins, or to taste

FOR THE GARNISH
Ground cinnamon to taste

Bring 2 quarts water to a boil in a medium saucepan. Remove from heat, and add rice. Let stand for 20 minutes. Rinse rice well, and drain. Bring 3 quarts water to a boil in another saucepan, and add rice. Boil uncovered for 30 minutes or until the rice is tender. (Some rice will take considerably less time.) Be careful not to overcook. Drain off excess water.

Mix scalded and evaporated milk, sugar, and cinnamon in a medium saucepan. Cook for 45 minutes or until mixture begins to thicken and changes color. Add rice and raisins. Cook for 40 minutes or until pudding thickens. Remove from heat, and stir occasionally until pudding cools thoroughly.

To serve, spoon rice pudding onto a platter, and sprinkle with cinnamon.

The pudding can be cooked until it is very thick, if desired. It also can be shaped into patties and dipped in beaten egg and rolled in bread crumbs before frying in oil and butter until light brown. The patties are rolled in cinnamon and sugar before serving.

Makes 12 servings.

opposite: Rice Pudding, a traditional Mexican dessert, may be accented with orange leaves, cinnamon sticks, and raisins.
overleaf, clockwise from left: Fritters, Michoacán bread, pastries, earthenware mug filled with piloncillo (unrefined brown sugar) syrup to be poured over Fritters, chocolate rounds for Morelian Hot Chocolate, sugar-coated Long Fritters, Curds in Syrup in green dish, and guava paste.

PAN DE MUERTO
Bread for the Dead

This bread is typically served for All Saints' Day and All Souls' Day, November 1 and 2. In Patzcuaro, it is displayed on altars erected for the holiday as an offering to deceased relatives. The altars are elaborately decorated with sugar skulls, paper cuttings, candles, fruit, flowers, and the favorite foods of the deceased.

FOR THE DOUGH

½	cup warm water
¾	to 1 ounce dry yeast
2¼	cups flour
¾	cup sugar
½	teaspoon salt
4	eggs
8	egg yolks
1	cup butter
½	cup lard
1	tablespoon orange peel, grated
2	tablespoons orange-blossom extract
3	tablespoons anise extract
7½	tablespoons milk

FOR THE GLAZE

1	tablespoon flour
½	cup water
2	egg yolks
1	egg
	Sugar to taste

FOR THE GARNISH

Crystallized fruits, chopped (optional)

Prepare the dough: Put warm water in a glass bowl. Add yeast, stirring to dissolve. Set aside in a warm spot near the stove. Add 6 to 8 tablespoons flour to yeast and water to form a stiff dough. Set aside again in a warm spot until doubled in volume.

In a separate bowl, sift remaining flour and sugar. Add salt, 3 eggs, 7 egg yolks, butter, lard, orange peel, orange-blossom and anise extracts, and 6½ tablespoons milk. Mix well, and knead briefly.

Add yeast mixture, and knead until dough is smooth and elastic. Place in a greased glass bowl, and spread a little butter on the surface. Cover dough with a dish towel, and set aside in a warm spot for 12 hours or until doubled in volume.

Knead briefly again. From the dough, pinch 2 2-inch balls, 8 2-inch strips, and 8 1-inch balls. Divide remaining dough in half. Roll into 2 circles 6 inches in diameter. Place circles on a greased baking sheet.

Beat together 1 egg, 1 egg yolk, and 1 tablespoon milk. Brush circles with egg mixture. Place 2-inch ball in center of each circle, and decorate circumference with 1-inch balls and strips. Allow bread to rise for 1 hour in a warm place.

Preheat oven to 375 degrees. Bake bread for 30 to 40 minutes.

Prepare the glaze: Put flour, water, egg yolks, and egg in a small saucepan. Cook over medium heat, stirring constantly, for 5 minutes or until mixture thickens to consistency of heavy cream. Brush freshly baked bread with glaze. Sprinkle bread with sugar, and return to oven. Bake for 5 minutes. Remove from oven, and sprinkle with more sugar. Allow to cool.

To serve, place bread on platters. Decorate with crystallized fruits. Serve with hot chocolate.

Makes 2 round loaves.

The former hacienda of Santiago in the state of San Luis Potosí.

CHOCOLATE MORELIANO
Morelian Hot Chocolate

The drinking of hot chocolate originated in pre-Columbian times, when it was sweetened with locally produced honey and served in hollowed-out gourds decorated with filigreed gold. One of the traditional recipes for hot chocolate comes from Morelia, where it is flavored with vanilla beans.

FOR THE CHOCOLATE PASTE

2¼   pounds cocoa beans
1   ounce stick cinnamon, crushed
2   cups croissant, crumbled
2¼   pounds sugar

FOR THE HOT CHOCOLATE

4   quarts milk
1   stick cinnamon
1   vanilla bean
    Sugar to taste

Prepare the chocolate paste: Roast the cocoa beans on a hot comal until dark. Cool, and peel carefully, as you would shell nuts.

In a special mortar for grinding chocolate, heated with coals, grind beans until they form a smooth paste. The consistency of the paste varies, depending on freshness of beans. Spread paste on a tray.

In the same mortar, grind cinnamon, croissant, and sugar. Over medium heat, add cocoa paste to these ingredients, and regrind until a thick paste is formed. Make 2-ounce balls with your hands while mixture is still warm. Flatten to form little pancake rounds of chocolate. Cool rounds at room temperature until hardened. Store in a glass jar.

Prepare the hot chocolate: Heat milk in a clay pot. Add cinnamon and vanilla. Heat until milk boils. Add 5 chocolate rounds and sugar to taste. Heat until chocolate and sugar dissolve and milk boils again. Beat with a molinillo or rotary mixer until hot chocolate is thick and foamy.

Serve hot in clay mugs. Hot chocolate is good with churros or pastry.

Commercial Mexican chocolate rounds, which contain sugar, almonds, and cinnamon, can be substituted for the homemade chocolate rounds.
Makes 8 servings.

TUNAS Y PINA A LA MEXQUITIC
Prickly Pears and Pineapple, Mexquitic Style

This mezcal-flavored dish is very refreshing, especially in August, when the sun is hot and the air is pure and fresh.

FOR THE FRUIT

16   prickly pears
2   pineapples, about 3½ pounds each
¾   cup fresh pineapple juice

Cactus pads and red cardona prickly pears in a maguey leaf.

¾ cup sugar
½ cup mezcal or tequila

FOR THE GARNISH

2 bougainvillaea branches (optional)

Peel prickly pears, and quarter them. Halve pineapples. With a knife, carefully remove the fruit from the pineapple shell. Cut fruit in small triangles. Reserve shells. Put the fruits in a glass bowl, and add pineapple juice, sugar, and mezcal. Macerate at room temperature for 25 minutes, or refrigerate for 1 hour.

To serve, place pineapple shells on a tray, and fill them with prepared fruits. Sprinkle with a little additional sugar and mezcal. Refrigerate until serving. Decorate with bougainvillaea branches just before serving for dessert or at breakfast.

Makes 8 servings.

AGUA DE MELON
Melon Beverage

3 very ripe yellow or green melons, such as honeydew or Persian
6 quarts water
 Sugar or honey to taste
 Ice cubes

Peel melons, and remove seeds. Cut melon flesh into chunks. Mix with water, and let stand for 10 minutes. Strain, and sweeten water with sugar or honey. Add ice cubes, and stir.

To serve, pour melon beverage into a large pitcher, and serve in tall glasses.

Makes 1½ to 2 gallons.

Many Mexican beverages are made from fruit extracts.

CHAPTER FIVE

THE GULF

From the snow-capped peak of Orizaba, the inactive volcano whose summit is the highest point in Mexico, the westward view embraces the great central Mexican plains, the steeples of Puebla, and the icy crowns of the volcanoes Popocatepetl and Ixtacihuatl. Mexico City crowds the valley beyond.

Orizaba's eastward vista is still more dramatic. One of the longest mountain slopes in the world, the volcano's eastern side drops spectacularly from lofty glaciers to a lush, tropical landscape of palm trees and banana groves in barely 50 horizontal miles.

The balmy, easy-going world of the states that border the Gulf of Mexico is culturally, as well as geographically, an arm of the Caribbean, flanked by the Yucatán Peninsula to the east and by the state of Tamaulipas to the north. The essence of the Gulf of Mexico region—the heartland of eastern Mexican culture and cuisine—is found in the states of Tabasco, whose very name clings to the palate, and Veracruz, whose image is dominated by exquisite seafood, exotic carnival, and pulsating Latin beats.

A trip down the Gulf side of Orizaba is a passage through an array of climates and mouth-watering crops. Whereas the Gulf of Mexico provides the ingredients for the region's main dishes, the rugged Veracruz up-lands yield the greatest variety of dessert ingredients in Mexico. A third of the way down Orizaba, farmers tend orchards of pears and apples. Still farther down, the fragrant realm of Mexico's coffee plantations begins. The descent continues to the volcano's misty foothills, the habitat of Mexico's famous indigenous crops: cacao and vanilla. Vanilla extract is a Veracruz specialty, used in breads, liqueurs, and desserts, such as *natilla*, the prized vanilla stirred custard. Closer to the shore, coastal hills are covered with stands of coconut palms, groves of plantains (*plátanos machos*, as Mexicans call them), and fields of rich tobacco grown for Veracruz cigars. The rolling hills, divided by shallow estuaries that nurture fish and shrimp, end abruptly at the Gulf's edge in shifting, eroding dunes.

The passage down the mountain concludes most naturally a few city blocks shy of the seashore. Downtown Veracruz, the colonial port that is the unofficial capital of the Gulf region, is suffused with the sharp aroma of fresh highland coffee, the sweet fragrance of mangoes and other tropical fruits, and—most characteristically—the briny odors of a bewildering but enticing variety of mollusks, fish, and crustaceans.

Jarochos, as natives of Veracruz are called, are known throughout Mexico for three passions: celebration, conversation, and cuisine. For the essential *Jarocho* experience, claim a table at a sidewalk café facing the leafy central plaza and order a platter overflowing with *mariscos* (seafood), *salpicón de jaiba* (shredded crab), or *camarón para pelar* (shrimp for peeling). Then, simply the world stroll by. Musicians dressed in salt-white cotton serenade promenading lovers with brisk, elegant harp rhythms. Old men observing domino contests break into discreet step dances. Snatches of political gossip drift from the back tables. Ideally, the midday meal is huge and slowly savored. Three hours is about right, finishing around dusk. A typical repast starts with *sopa de camarón* (shrimp soup) and includes Veracruz-style red snapper and *picadas*—tortillas smothered with a spicy red sauce and garnished with chopped onion and beans or cheese. The rounds of accompanying beer eventually give way to steaming *café con leche* or *café de olla*, *natilla*, and a fat hand-rolled cigar haggled from a street vendor.

Veracruz has long been the preferred port of entrance for the many invaders of Mexico. Hernando Cortez first set anchor here in 1519, establishing the base from which he conquered Mexico. Since then, Veracruz has been successively victimized by more Spanish imperial troops, Dutch pirates, French sailors, and American marines. All these intruders left landmarks and descendants, which may explain why Veracruz seems the least typically Mexican of the country's major colonial cities. In many ways, Veracruz shares the Creole culture of the colonial Caribbean port towns—Havana, San Juan, Cartagena, and even New Orleans—as evidenced by such dishes as *calabaza criolla* (pumpkin in vinaigrette). Masterpieces such as Veracruz-style *huachinango* (red snapper) owe much to Mediterranean Spain and its green olives and capers. Yet other Veracruz specialties—oyster tamales swaddled in banana leaves and cucumber and *jícama* slices dusted with eye-opening *chile piquín*, for example—are uniquely and unmistakably Mexican.

While Veracruz offers a wide variety of foods from elsewhere in the area, purists insist on visits to the source. Tabasco, a state that embraces vast deltas and estuaries, offers much more than its famous hot sauce. The variety of Tabasco seafood is unmatched, with local waters teeming with several distinctive species of crabs and crayfish. The biggest crayfish here approach the size of Maine lobsters. Tampico, home to Mexico's most creative shrimp cooks, is a culinary center that rivals Veracruz in exuberance and invention and that preserves some of Mexico's most distinctive seafood traditions. Tampico *mariscos* are sometimes broiled in special chile pastes, adorned with delicate pumpkin-seed sauces, or stuffed into rich, fresh tamales. Shrimp sometimes are the stuffing for savory fried turnovers, such as *empanadas al achiote rellenas de camarón*.

Pilgrims seeking the Gulf's gastronomic heartland, however, will almost always be directed to smaller towns scattered across the great, marshy flat lands that define the coast—Mexico's bayou country. Here, flavors include not just the incendiary chiles of Indian Mexico and the garlic and onion bequeathed by Spain, but also the more subtle seasonings reminiscent of Creole and Cajun cookery.

Perhaps the most famous of these smaller towns is Tlacotalpan, a seventeenth-century shipbuilding port. Spanish colonists were drawn here by the deep, sheltered waters teeming with a unique mixture of marine and river fish. An island of graceful plazas and porticos in the flood plains to the south of Veracruz, Tlacotalpan was recently joined to the outside world by a highway bridge—an advance lamented by many of the town's admirers. Yet slapdash restaurants along the town's riverside quay still serve the local specialty—fresh turtle in green sauce. Also popular are fish sausage and giant, translucent shrimp. Families drive for hours just to dine here and amble afterward in the river breeze past the pastel façades and open, beckoning doors of the town's colonial-era homes. In Tlacotalpan, the best of the Gulf of Mexico shore is deliciously encapsulated.

SOPA DE CAMARON RINCONADA
Shrimp Soup, Rinconada Style

In Rinconada, a small village between the cities of Veracruz and Xalapa, food stands and restaurants serve this delicious shrimp soup as a hearty breakfast.

FOR THE SOUP

⅔	cup olive oil
4	medium white onions, sliced on the diagonal
6	large tomatoes, finely chopped
	Salt to taste
4	chiles jalapeños, sliced
2	quarts fish stock (see recipe on page 214)
3	sprigs epazote or cilantro, or 1 teaspoon dried
	oregano
120	shrimp, preferably fresh-water, unshelled

FOR THE GARNISH

Limes, sliced in wedges

Heat oil in a large saucepan or stock pot. Add onion, and sauté.

Add tomato, and simmer until mixture begins to thicken. Season with salt. Add chiles and fish stock.

When mixture begins to boil, add epazote and shrimp. Continue cooking over medium heat for 15 minutes.

To serve, divide shrimp among 8 soup bowls, and fill each bowl with soup. Garnish with limes. Serve with cold beer.

Makes 8 servings.

above: *Shrimp Soup, Rinconada Style.*
opposite: *Freshly boiled shrimp for peeling.*

CAMARON PARA PELAR
Shrimp for Peeling

Shrimp are served at ocean-front restaurants along the Veracruz coast or on the riverside in Boca del Río. And street vendors pile fresh shrimp into brown-paper cones.

FOR THE SHRIMP

6	quarts water
1	head garlic, halved
1	onion, halved
1	teaspoon annatto seeds
	Salt to taste
80	medium shrimp, unshelled

FOR THE GARNISH

15   limes, halved

Bring water to a boil in a large saucepan. Add garlic, onion, annatto seeds, and salt. Bring water to a rolling boil. Add shrimp, and cook for 8 minutes. Cool shrimp in water for 5 minutes.

To serve, arrange shrimp on a platter, and garnish with limes.

Makes 8 servings.

EMPANADAS AL ACHIOTE RELLENAS DE CAMARON
Shrimp-Stuffed Empanadas with Annatto Seeds

FOR THE DOUGH

1	pound, 6 ounces fresh masa or equivalent made with masa harina (see Basics)
6	tablespoons vegetable oil
1	tablespoon annatto seeds
1	tablespoon prepared annatto seeds (see recipe on page 267)
½	cup flour
	Salt to taste
3	cups vegetable oil

FOR THE STUFFING

½	cup olive oil
1	white onion, grated
4	cloves garlic, puréed or put through a press
2	tomatoes, roasted (see Basics) and puréed
2	cups shrimp, cooked and chopped
2	chiles jalapeños, finely chopped
1	teaspoon prepared annatto seeds
1	teaspoon freshly ground allspice
1	teaspoon oregano, dried and crushed
	Salt to taste

Prepare the dough: Put masa in a large bowl. Set aside.

Heat vegetable oil in a skillet, and add annatto seeds. Cook until seeds are soft and almost dissolved. Remove seeds from oil, and add prepared annatto seeds, mixing until a smooth paste is formed.

Add seeds to the masa with flour, a little water, and salt. Knead masa until smooth. Set aside.

Prepare the stuffing: Heat oil in a saucepan. Add onion and garlic. Sautée until translucent.

Add tomato purée, shrimp, and chiles. Season with prepared annatto seeds, allspice, oregano, and salt. Cook until the moisture has evaporated from the mixture. Cool slightly.

Using a tortilla press, make tortillas 2½ to 3 inches in diameter from the masa (see Basics). Spoon stuffing onto tortillas, and fold tortillas in half, sealing edges, to form the empanadas. Cover with plastic wrap. The empanadas can be refrigerated until serving time.

To serve, fry the empanadas in hot oil until golden. Drain on paper towels, and serve immediately. Serve with guacamole or cold tomato sauce.
Makes about 20 empanadas.

BOCOLES
Fresh Masa "Cakes" from Veracruz

Bocoles *are common to the Huasteca region of Veracruz.*

1½	pounds fresh masa or equivalent made with masa harina (see Basics)
½	cup water, approximately
¾	cup lard, at room temperature
	Salt to taste

Put masa in a bowl. Add some water and knead, being careful not to add too much water. Add lard and salt. Knead until dough is smooth and soft. Set dough aside for 1 hour.

Heat a comal or griddle for 30 minutes. With the masa, make 24 balls, each the size of an egg. Flatten with your fingers into a thick, round bocol.

Put bocoles on the comal, a few at a time. Cook over medium heat for 3 minutes or until golden; turn and cook until golden. The bocoles should be crusty with soft interiors.

Serve with eggs, roasted meats, and Mexican coffee. The bocoles may be filled with fresh cheese and chopped green chiles, chopped epazote, chorizo sausage, or beans.
Makes 24 bocoles.

Empanadas are stuffed with shrimp, tomato, chiles jalapeños, *and spices, then fried and served with guacamole.*

SALPICON DE JAIBA
Shredded Crab

Shredded crab is usually served before lunch as an appetizer, and in Mexico, appetizers are an institution. No gathering—public or private, with family or friends or for business—is considered complete without an hors d'oeuvre. This recipe is from Pardino's restaurant in the port of Veracruz.

¾ cup olive oil
6 tablespoons butter
6 cloves garlic, chopped
2 white onions, chopped
4 canned chiles jalapeños, chopped
½ cup chile juice, from can
⅓ cup canned pickled carrots, chopped
4 medium tomatoes, chopped
½ cup parsley, chopped
½ cup cilantro, chopped
   Salt and pepper to taste
2½ generous pounds crab meat, cleaned

Heat oil and butter in a frying pan. Add garlic and onion, and sauté.

Add chiles, chile juice, carrots, tomatoes, parsley, and cilantro. Season with salt and pepper, and cook over low heat until mixture thickens, about 25 minutes.

Add crab meat, and sauté until mixture thickens. Correct seasonings.

To serve, place crab on a platter. Serve with freshly made tortillas to roll into tacos.

The shredded crab may also be served in crab shells, sprinkled with bread crumbs, melted butter, and parsley, and baked in a hot oven for 25 minutes.
Makes 8 servings.

A fresh seafood bar in the port of Veracruz.

Crab meat is prepared in a variety of ways—breaded and fried, shredded and sautéed, or simply boiled.

MANITAS DE CANGREJO
Crab Legs

Oyster bars lining the municipal market in the port of Veracruz serve this delicacy piping hot from earthenware pots.

FOR THE CRAB LEGS
  5   quarts sea water or drinking water
      Salt to taste
 64   large crab legs

FOR THE GARNISH
 16   limes, halved

Bring water to a boil in a stock pot. Salt to taste if using drinking water. Add crab legs, and boil for about 25 minutes.

To serve, crack open crab legs using a nutcracker, and place on individual plates. Garnish with limes. The crab legs can be served hot or chilled over shaved ice.

Crab legs may also be cracked open, dipped in egg batter, and coated with bread crumbs. Refrigerate, and fry in vegetable oil. Drain, and serve with limes.
Makes 8 to 12 servings.

FILETE RELLENO DE SALPICON
Fish Fillet Stuffed with Crab Meat

FOR THE FISH

16   small cloves garlic, whole
12   black peppercorns
      Salt to taste
 8   thin red snapper, sea bass, grouper, or sole
      fillets, 5 ounces each

FOR THE STUFFING

½   recipe shredded crab (see recipe on page 174)
1¼   pounds small shrimp, shelled
1½   cups mayonnaise
 2   tablespoons fresh lime juice

FOR THE GARNISH

½   cup parsley, chopped
16   slices green bell pepper
 8   limes, halved

Preheat oven to 400 degrees. Grease a baking sheet.

Prepare the fish: Pureé garlic with peppercorns and salt. Spread on fish, and marinate for 1 hour.

Meanwhile, prepare the stuffing: Make half the crab recipe, adding shrimp. Cook until the mixture thickens. Spread crab over fish, and roll loosely. Place rolls on baking sheet. Mix mayonnaise with lime juice. Cover each fish roll with 3 tablespoons mayonnaise mixture.

Bake for 20 to 30 minutes or until fish is golden brown.

To serve, arrange fish rolls on a platter. Garnish with parsley, pepper, and limes. Serve with rice.
Makes 8 servings.

above: *Fillets of red snapper, sea bass, grouper, or sole are stuffed with a mixture of shredded crab and shrimp.*
left: *The fillet is rolled and baked until golden brown.*

PESCADO A LA VERACRUZANA
Fish, Veracruz Style

This dish is famous worldwide. The sauce combines Spanish olives and capers with the unmistakable flavor of Mexican chiles.

FOR THE TOMATO SAUCE

1½   cups olive oil
6   cloves garlic, whole, plus 8 cloves garlic, minced
4   cups white onion, finely chopped
4½   pounds tomatoes, finely chopped
1½   cups pimento-stuffed green olives, finely chopped
½   cup capers
12   fresh bay leaves or 6 dried bay leaves
1   tablespoon oregano, dried and crushed
3   sprigs thyme or 1 teaspoon dried thyme
3   sprigs marjoram or 1 teaspoon dried marjoram
  Salt to taste
1   teaspoon freshly ground pepper

FOR THE CHILTOMATE SAUCE

8   tomatoes, roasted (see Basics)
1½   white onions, halved
6   cloves garlic, whole
3   cups fish stock (see recipe on page 214)
¾   cup olive oil
4   bay leaves
3   sprigs thyme or ½ teaspoon dried thyme
3   sprigs marjoram or ½ teaspoon dried marjoram
  Salt to taste
1   8-ounce can chiles gueros or jalapeños
1   8-ounce can pickled chiles jalapeños with juice

FOR THE RED SNAPPER

1   6½-pound red snapper, very fresh
6   tablespoons lime juice
6   cloves garlic, puréed
4   bay leaves
1   teaspoon dried oregano

1½   cups olive oil
  Salt and pepper to taste

FOR THE GARNISH

4   fresh bay leaves
6   sprigs thyme
6   sprigs marjoram
⅓   cup chopped parsley

Prepare the tomato sauce: Heat oil in a saucepan or frying pan. Brown 6 garlic cloves, and discard. Add minced garlic and onion, and brown. Add tomato, olives, capers, bay sprig, oregano, thyme, marjoram, salt, and pepper. Simmer for 2½ hours, stirring occasionally. Sauce will be thick. Remove from heat. Set aside.

Prepare the chiltomate sauce: In a blender or food processor, blend tomatoes, onion, garlic, and fish stock. Strain mixture. Heat oil in a frying pan, and add blended tomato mixture. Season with bay leaves, thyme, marjoram, and salt. Add half the chiles güeros and pickled jalapeños and 1 cup pickling juices. Simmer for 1 hour.

Prepare the red snapper: Put fish in a baking dish. In a blender or food processor, blend lime juice, garlic, bay leaves, oregano, oil, salt, and pepper. Pour mixture over fish, and marinate for 1 hour in the refrigerator.

Preheat oven to 350 degrees.

Stir tomato and chiltomate sauces together, and cook for 25 minutes.

Remove fish from marinade. Place in another large baking dish. Baste with some sauce. Bake for 35 minutes, basting every 15 minutes, with more sauce. Then bake for 1¼ hours or until fish is done.

To serve, place fish on a platter, and cover with remaining sauce, warmed. Garnish with remaining chiles güeros, pickled jalapeños, bay leaves, thyme, marjoram, and parsley. Serve any remaining sauce on the side. Accompany with white rice.
Makes 8 servings.

overleaf: Fish, Veracruz Style is one of the most distinctive dishes from the Gulf region.

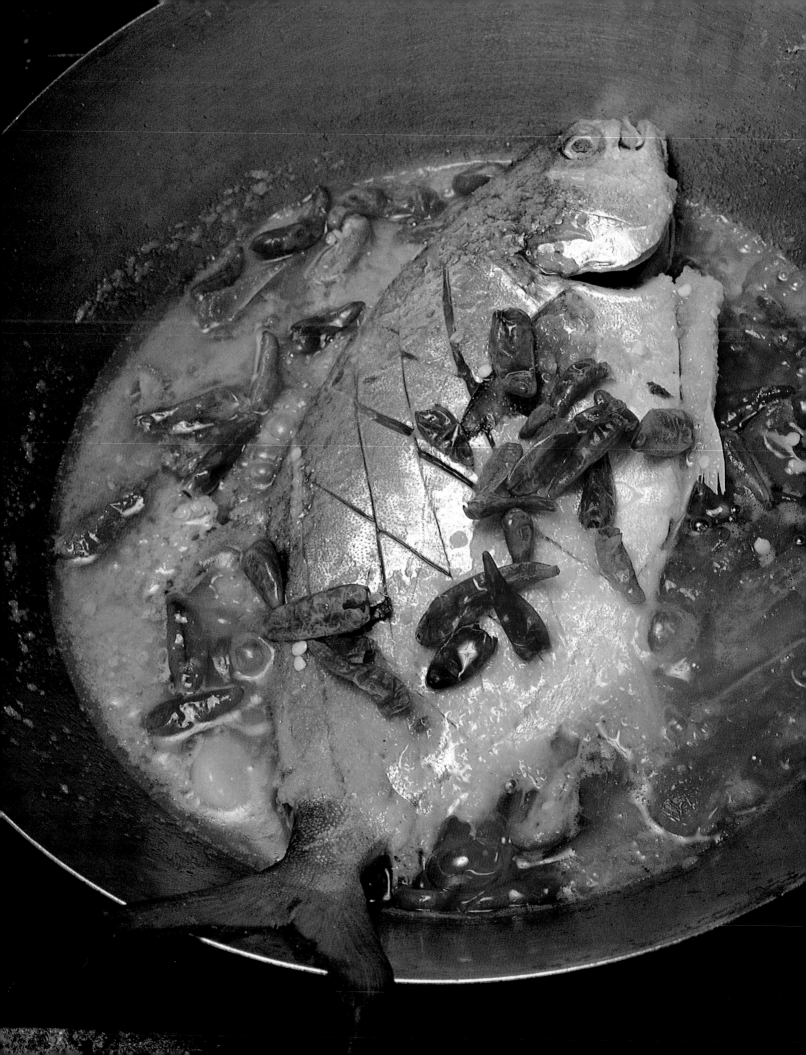

POMPANO AL AJILLO
Pompano in Garlic Sauce

The combination of ingredients from the Old World (olive oil and garlic) and from the New World (chiles) creates an inspired sauce for this fish dish.

I	pound butter
2	cups olive oil
24	cloves garlic, puréed, plus 24 cloves garlic minced
7	ounces chiles serranos
7	ounces dried chiles serranos or de árbol
	Salt and pepper to taste
8	pompanos, about 2 pounds each, cleaned

Place a paella dish over low heat. Heat butter and oil in the dish, and add garlic and fresh and dried chiles. Season with salt and pepper. Cook over low heat.

Place half the mixture in another frying pan. Add the fish, and cook over low heat for 20 to 25 minutes or until the fish is cooked.

To serve, cover the pompano with the garlic sauce. The sauce also can be served over shellfish or meat.
Makes 8 servings.

Pejelagarto is grilled until slightly charred. The fish is then shredded, garnished with chiles and limes, and served as an appetizer.

PEJELAGARTO
Fish Hors D'Oeuvre

Pejelagarto is a fish native to the state of Tabasco. It often is served as an appetizer.

FOR THE FISH

4	pejelagartos, red snappers, or bass, 4 pounds each, cleaned

FOR THE GARNISH

	Pickled chiles amashitos or chiles jalapeños
8	limes, halved

Prepare firewood or charcoal in a grill with a spit. Burn until coals turn white. Spear fish lengthwise on skewers, and cook over low fire, turning, for 2½ hours or until golden brown and slightly charred. They will look like smoked fish. Cut fish open, and shred.

To serve, garnish pejelagarto with chiles and limes. Serve with tortillas.
Makes 8 servings.

Pompano with Garlic Sauce uses fresh and dried chiles serranos.

Tapescan oysters are smoked on the seashore in the port of Ceiba.

OSTIONES AL TAPESCO
Smoked Oysters, Tapesco Style

Peppercorn leaves, used in smoking the oysters, give this seafood dish an exotic flavor.

FOR THE OYSTERS

40	banana leaves
10	sprigs peppercorn leaves
15	coconut-palm leaves, dried
160	oysters, unopened

FOR THE GARNISH

10	limes, halved
	Tabasco sauce

Prepare an open-air grill, with a raised platform. Cover grill with 20 banana leaves. Line with 5 peppercorn sprigs. Place oysters on top, and cover with remaining banana leaves and peppercorn sprigs. Put palm leaves under the grill, and douse with alcohol. Ignite, and burn the leaves, allowing oysters to smoke and absorb the aroma of leaves. Smoke for 30 minutes, and cool. Remove leaves, and pry open oysters with knives. Eat while hot, sprinkling with lime juice and Tabasco sauce.

The oysters can be prepared on a charcoal barbeque grill. Banana leaves can be substituted for peppercorn sprigs and palm leaves.

Makes 8 to 12 servings.

POLLO CUBIERTO DE MASA ESTILO LA HUASTECA VERACRUZANA
Chicken in Masa, Huasteca-Veracruz Style

FOR THE CHICKEN

2½	cups olive oil
20	cloves garlic, whole
10	large white onions, thinly sliced
30	fresh bay leaves or 15 dried bay leaves
20	sprigs thyme or 1½ tablespoons dried thyme
20	sprigs marjoram or 1½ tablespoons dried marjoram
1	teaspoon dried oregano
1	tablespoon whole allspice
2	tablespoons sugar
	Salt to taste
1	tablespoon pepper
8	chicken breasts, halved, bone-in
8	chicken legs
2½	quarts cider vinegar
1½	cups pimento-stuffed green olives
1	1-pound can chiles güeros or jalapeños, with juice
4½	pounds fresh masa or equivalent made with masa harina (see Basics)
2	cups warm water

FOR THE GARNISH

1	bunch mixed fresh herbs, such as thyme, bay leaves, and marjoram
1	cup pimento-stuffed green olives

The masa *dough creates a tight seal between the saucepan and the lid for the final stage of cooking the chicken.*

Heat oil in a wide saucepan or paella pan. Add garlic, and brown. Remove 10 garlic cloves, and purée. Return to saucepan. Add onion, bay leaves, thyme, marjoram, oregano, allspice, sugar, salt, and pepper. Simmer over low heat for 40 minutes or until onion is well cooked. Add chicken, and cook for 10 minutes, stirring occasionally. Add vinegar, olives, and half can chiles with juice. Bring to a boil.

Knead masa with 2 cups warm water or enough water to make a pliable dough. Roll out a layer on aluminum foil to cover top of the saucepan. Cut to size. Carefully cover saucepan, peel off foil, and seal edges of dough. Simmer for 45 minutes or until chicken is done.

To serve, place chicken on a platter, discard masa, and garnish with herbs, olives, and remaining chiles. The dish can be served hot or cold.

Makes 8 servings.

Misantla Chile—served from corn husks—is used as a spread for tortillas or bread; it is also served with meat, fish, and poultry.

CHILE DE MISANTLA
Misantla Chile

Misantla is a small village near the city of Xalapa in the state of Veracruz. This sauce or paste is made with ingredients that date to pre-Hispanic times. When blended, the pumpkin seeds, sesame seeds, and chiles form a delicious, piquant spread.

3   cups raw pumpkin seeds, hulled
1½ cups sesame seeds
3   chiles moritas or chipotles, soaked in water, seeded, and deveined (see Basics)
4   chiles anchos, lightly toasted, seeded, and deveined (see Basics)

Salt to taste
8   corn husks, soaked in water and dried (optional)

Toast pumpkin seeds on a griddle or comal. Blend well in a metate, blender, or food processor.

Toast sesame seeds on a comal or griddle. To pumpkin seeds, add sesame seeds, chiles moritas and anchos, and salt. Blend well to form a paste. Correct salt.

Divide chile paste in 8 portions, and wrap each in a corn husk like a tamale. (Or place paste in a glass bowl or jar, and cover tightly.) Refrigerate until ready to serve.

To serve, place corn husks on individual plates. Serve as a spread with freshly made tortillas or bread or with meat, fish, or poultry.
Makes 8 servings.

CHILES RELLENOS A LA HUASTECA
Stuffed Chiles, Huasteca Style

This version of the classic stuffed chiles is a delicacy typical of Veracruz. Instead of using the perennial chiles poblanos, the recipe calls for chiles jalapeños.

FOR THE CHILES
24 chiles jalapeños, roasted, peeled, seeded, deveined, and sweated in plastic bag for 8 minutes (see Basics)
2   quarts charcoal-ash water, or 2 quarts water mixed with ¾ cup vinegar and 1 teaspoon salt
24 thin slices mild Cheddar, Monterey Jack, feta, or fresh mozzarella cheese
    Flour

FOR THE SAUCE
25 tomatillos, husked
1   white onion, quartered, plus 1 white onion, coarsely chopped
9   cloves garlic, whole
3   chiles chipotles, preferably from Veracruz, or 2

Chiles jalapeños vary in intensity from pepper to pepper, making it difficult to determine the degree of spiciness of each Stuffed Chile, Huasteca Style.

whites until soft peaks form. Season with salt. In another bowl, lightly beat egg yolks with a bit of flour. Fold into whites.

Coat chiles with batter, and fry over medium heat, turning once. Remove chiles, and drain on paper towels. Keep hot in preheated oven.

To serve, divide hot sauce among 8 serving plates. Place chiles in center of plate, on top of sauce. Serve with hot tortillas. Chiles also may be stuffed with shredded beef flank steak fried with onion and chile or with mincemeat.

Makes 8 servings.

chiles pasillas, lightly fried
Hot water
⅔ cup vegetable oil
Salt to taste

FOR THE BATTER
1 quart vegetable oil
10 eggs, separated
Salt to taste
Flour

Prepare the chiles: Slit chiles open on one side, and soak for 1 hour in charcoal-ash water to remove some piquancy.

Remove chiles from water, and drain and dry them. Stuff with cheese, and roll in flour to coat.

Prepare the sauce: Put tomatillos in a saucepan with quartered onion, 6 garlic cloves, and chiles. Cover with hot water, and bring to a boil. Cook for 25 minutes over low heat. Cool and drain, reserving cooking water.

In a blender or food processor, blend these ingredients, adding chopped onion and 3 garlic cloves.

Heat oil in a saucepan, and fry sauce briefly. Reduce heat, and simmer for 30 minutes, seasoning to taste. If sauce thickens too much, add a small amount of cooking water. Keep warm.

Prepare the batter: Heat oil in a saucepan. Beat egg

CHILES ENCURTIDOS
Pickled Chiles

3 quarts water
2 cups strong vinegar
1 quart fruit vinegar (see recipe on page 128)
1 cup vegetable oil
15 bay leaves
2 small bunches marjoram
2 bunches thyme
2 tablespoons dried oregano
2 tablespoons pepper
Salt to taste
4 medium white onions, quartered
4 heads garlic, halved
2¼ pounds chiles jalapeños, manzanos, caribes, or amarillos, sliced
2¼ pounds carrots, peeled, sliced on the diagonal 1-inch thick, and cooked in water for 8 minutes

In a stock pot, combine water, strong and fruit vinegars, oil, bay leaves, marjoram, thyme, oregano, pepper, salt, onion, and garlic. Heat until mixture comes to a boil. Add chiles and carrots, and return to a full boil. Cover pot, and remove from heat. Let stand overnight. Store chiles in a sterilized, tightly covered glass jar. The chiles will keep indefinitely.

Makes 2 gallons.

The Cañamelar coffee plantation makes a dramatic setting for this house.

CALABAZA CRIOLLA

Creole Pumpkin

A wide variety of pumpkins are harvested in the region of Santa Maria Ixcatepec in Veracruz.

FOR THE VINAIGRETTE

2	cups green onion, sliced
3	cloves garlic, put through a press
1	tablespoon sugar
1½	to 2 tablespoons salt, or to taste
1	tablespoon freshly ground pepper
¾	cup vinegar
¾	cup safflower oil
1	cup olive oil

FOR THE PUMPKIN

4	quarts water
	Salt to taste
2¼	pounds green pumpkin, peeled and chopped
3	large chayote squash, peeled and chopped
6	carrots, chopped
2	cups fresh or canned hearts of palm, sliced
1	tablespoon lime juice

FOR THE GARNISH

⅓	cup green-onion tops or chives, chopped
1½	cup feta cheese, crumbled
6	canned chiles chipotles

Prepare the vinaigrette: Put onion in a bowl with garlic, sugar, salt, pepper, and vinegar. Mix well. Add safflower and olive oils slowly in a steady stream while mixing. Refrigerate for 3 hours.

Meanwhile, prepare the pumpkin: Put water and salt in a large pot. Bring to a rolling boil. Add pumpkin, and cook for 8 minutes. Remove pumpkin from water. Add chayotes to cooking water, and cook for 15 minutes or until tender, but not mushy. Remove from water. Add carrots to cooking water, and cook. Remove. Add hearts of palm to cooking water with lime juice. If using fresh hearts of palm, cook for 15 minutes; if using canned hearts of palm, heat through.

Pour vinaigrette over the drained hot vegetables, and let cool.

To serve, arrange vegetables on a platter, and garnish with onion tops or chives. Sprinkle with cheese and chiles. Serve with shredded chicken, sliced lettuce, and avocado.

Makes 8 servings.

FRIJOLES DE OLLA
Beans Cooked in a Pot

Beans traditionally are cooked in clay pots, a method that lends a special flavor.

4½	quarts water
1⅓	pounds dried black beans, washed and soaked overnight
2	white onions, halved
3	heads garlic, halved, or 10 cloves garlic, whole
	Salt to taste
30	epazote or cilantro leaves

Bring water to a boil in a large saucepan or clay pot. Add beans, onion, and garlic. Cook at a slow boil for 1½ hours or until beans are done. Add salt after 1 hour of cooking.

Blend 1 cup beans in a blender or food processor with a little cooking water. Add bean mixture to remaining beans. Stir in epazote.

Serve beans with chopped green onion, chile serrano, chopped cilantro, and tomato or with fresh cream and grated cheese.

Makes 8 servings.

FRIJOLES NEGROS ESTILO VERACRUZ
Refried Black Beans, Veracruz Style

In any Veracruz home, there are always beans available for this dish.

FOR THE BEANS

1	recipe frijoles de olla (see recipe on this page)
¾	cup lard or vegetable oil
1	large white onion, finely chopped
	Salt to taste

FOR THE GARNISH

2	to 3 quarts water
1	pound bacon
1½	cups feta cheese, crumbled
3	chiles jalapeños, chopped
	Totopos (crisply fried tortilla wedges)

Prepare the beans: Make frijoles de olla. Heat lard in a heavy frying pan. Add onion, and sauté until dark brown. Add beans little by little, and fry (refry). Correct salt to taste. Cool, and refrigerate for 1 day.

Before serving, prepare the garnish: Bring water to a boil in a saucepan. Add bacon, and cook for 10 minutes. Drain. Fry bacon in a frying pan. Reserve fat. Drain bacon on paper towels, and crumble. Set bacon aside.

Heat bacon fat in a frying pan. Add beans little by little, and mash, using the back of a spoon, until a thick purée is obtained. Tilt frying pan, and using a spatula, shape purée into an oblong roll.

To serve, place beans on a platter. Sprinkle roll with crumbled bacon, cheese, and chiles. Garnish with totopos. Serve with eggs, roasted meat, or chilaquiles.

Makes 8 servings.

HUEVOS REVUELTOS ESTILO DEL RANCHO SAN JOSE
Scrambled Eggs, Rancho San José Style

This Veracruz variation of traditional scrambled eggs is served for breakfast or a light dinner.

¾	cup vegetable oil
18	large fresh eggs
½	cup chile serrano or jalapeño, finely chopped
⅔	cup white onion, finely chopped
⅓	cup epazote or cilantro, finely chopped
	Salt to taste
3	cups frijoles de olla (see recipe on page 187)

Scrambled Eggs, Rancho San José Style is served over Frijoles de Olla (see recipe on p. 187) and is accompanied by Fresh Masa "Cakes" (see recipe on p. 173), enchiladas, and Sun-Dried Beef (see recipe on p. 190).

Heat a frying pan, and add oil. Beat eggs, and add chiles, onion, epazote, and salt. Pour the mixture into the hot oil.

Cook until eggs are softly scrambled, stirring with a fork so they cook evenly.

To serve, spoon beans onto a deep platter. Top with scrambled eggs. Serve with bocoles.
Makes 8 servings.

PAVO EN ESCABECHE
Pickled Turkey

Recipes that come from one state often are adapted in another. Such is the case with this Tabasco version of pickled turkey, which originated in Yucatán and Campeche.

FOR THE TURKEY

1	16- to 17-pound turkey
1	quart water
1	leek, sliced
2	turnips, sliced
4	carrots, sliced
2	white onions, quartered
6	to 8 ribs celery, coarsely chopped
	Salt to taste
1	tablespoon whole allspice
1	tablespoon black peppercorns

FOR THE ESCABECHE

1½	cups olive oil
6	white onions, sliced and wilted in hot water
6	cloves garlic, crushed
6	bay leaves, crumbled
1½	to 2 tablespoons dried oregano
1	tablespoon whole allspice
1	tablespoon pepper
	Salt to taste
2	tablespoons sugar

1½ to 2 cups vinegar
½   cup turkey stock

Prepare the turkey: Put turkey in a large stock pot with water, leek, turnips, carrots, onions, celery, salt, allspice, and peppercorns. Bring to a boil. Reduce heat, and simmer for 3 hours or until turkey is very tender. Let turkey cool in its broth.

Prepare the escabeche: Heat oil in a heavy saucepan. Add onions, garlic, bay leaves, oregano, allspice, pepper, salt, and sugar. Cook over medium to medium-high heat until onions are transparent, 4 to 5 minutes. Add vinegar and stock. Bring to a boil. Turn off heat, cover, and let stand for 20 minutes.

Place turkey on a deep platter, and pour hot escabeche over it. Let stand for 1 to 2 hours or overnight.

To serve, slice the turkey, and serve in sandwiches. Or shred turkey, and make tacos, taquitos (miniature tacos), or tostaditas (miniature tostadas).

Makes 12 servings.

GARNACHAS
Garnachas

Garnachas de Rinconada, *famous throughout Veracruz, can be savored at numerous roadside stands.*

FOR THE TORTILLAS
1¾ pounds fresh masa or equivalent made with masa harina (see Basics)
½   cup hot water, approximately
     Salt to taste
     Oil

FOR THE SAUCE
2   cloves garlic, puréed or put through a press
     Salt to taste
½   white onion, chopped
2   fried or canned chiles chipotles, or canned chiles

jalapeños
3   large tomatoes, roasted (see Basics)
½   cup water

FOR THE PORK
1   pound pork, cubed
2   quarts water
4   cloves garlic, whole
½   white onion, chopped
     Salt to taste

FOR THE GARNISH
2   white onions, chopped
2   potatoes, cooked and diced

Prepare the tortillas: Knead masa with hot water and a little salt. The consistency should be slightly moist and smooth, but not sticky. Set dough aside for 20 minutes.

Using a tortilla press, make 24 tortillas, each approximately 3 inches in diameter. Heat a comal or griddle, and cook tortillas on each side, turning once. Keep tortillas hot by wrapping in a napkin.

Prepare the sauce: Blend garlic and salt in a molcajete, blender, or food processor. Add onion, and continue blending with chiles and tomatoes. Add a little water so that the sauce is well blended, with a slightly thick consistency. Reseason.

Prepare the pork: Cook pork in water with garlic, onion, and salt for 1½ hours or until pork is tender. Allow to cool in stock. Shred meat finely.

To serve, heat a little oil in a frying pan. Quickly dip tortillas in the hot oil, and place them on a serving plate. Sprinkle with sauce and a bit of hot oil, shredded pork, chopped onion, and potatoes. Finally, sprinkle again with hot oil. Serve very hot.

The sauce can also be prepared with a pinch of ground cumin, cloves, allspice, or chile guajillo.

Makes 24 garnachas.

CARNE AL PASTOR CANAMELAR
Baked Pork, Cañamelar Style

The owner of the Cañamelar, an old hacienda near Xalapa, shared this recipe for juicy, baked pork.

FOR THE PORK

3⅓   pounds pork tenderloin, in 1 piece
     Salt and pepper to taste

FOR THE MARINADE

 8   chiles guajillos, roasted (see Basics)
1½   cups mild or fruit vinegar (see recipe on page 128)
 ⅔   cup vegetable oil
 2   cups canned pineapple juice
 6   cloves garlic, whole
     Salt to taste
 1   teaspoon freshly ground pepper

Prepare the pork: With a sharp knife, make shallow incisions in pork. Put pork in a glass bowl, and sprinkle with salt and pepper. Set aside.

Prepare the marinade: Blend chiles with vinegar, oil, pineapple juice, garlic, salt, and pepper in a blender or food processor. Pour mixture over pork, and marinate at room temperature for 1 hour.

Preheat oven to 350 degrees.

Place pork in a baking dish. Pour marinade over. Bake for 2 hours. Remove from oven, and cool pork in juices. Remove, and shred finely. Return pork to oven, and bake until crisp, about 20 to 30 minutes.

To serve, place pork on a platter. Serve with Mexican rice, guacamole, and tortillas. The pork may be served as an appetizer or as a stuffing for small tacos.

Makes 8 servings.

CECINA ESTILO XALAPA
Sun-Dried Beef, Xalapa Style

Sun-dried beef is prepared in different ways in different regions. In Xalapa, the beef sometimes is salted or seasoned with blended chiles, cumin, garlic, salt, and pepper. The beef is set aside for several days until it has matured completely in flavor. It is eaten at breakfast with fried eggs or as a main course at noon or in the evening.

FOR THE BEEF

16   strips boneless beef flank steak, butterflied to very thin strips of 7 to 8 ounces each
     Juice of 20 limes
     Salt to taste
     Vegetable oil

FOR THE GARNISH

 1   recipe guacamole (see recipe on page 33)
     Limes, halved
24   radishes, shaped like flowers

Flatten the flank strips by pounding them with a wooden mallet.

Layer the meat in a shallow dish, and sprinkle with lime juice and salt. Refrigerate for 2 days, or set in the sun for 2 days.

Preheat frying pan for 15 minutes. Sprinkle pan with oil, and brown the meat for 3 to 4 minutes on each side, being careful not to overcook.

To serve, place 2 strips of beef on each of 8 heated plates. Spoon guacamole on one side, and arrange limes on the other side. Garnish with radishes.

Serve with freshly made tortillas, refried beans, or bocoles.

Makes 8 servings.

CAFE DE OLLA
Mexican Coffee

Mexican coffee, sweetened with piloncillo (unrefined brown sugar), is one of the most popular hot beverages in Mexico. In Veracruz, where freshly ground local coffee is used, the drink has a distinctive flavor.

4	quarts water
4	sticks Mexican cinnamon, each 6 inches long
⅔	cup unrefined brown or dark brown sugar
2	cups medium-grind coffee, freshly ground

Put water in a 5-quart pot (preferably earthenware), and bring to a boil. Add cinnamon and sugar; let mixture boil for 20 minutes.

Add coffee. Stir, and bring to a boil. Remove from heat, and cover. Let steep for 5 minutes, and strain.

To serve, pour coffee into small clay mugs. This drink is often served with pastries or tamales.

Makes 8 servings.

JUGO DE PINA EN EL PLANTIO
Pineapple Juice Served in Pineapple Shells

Pineapple juice not only tastes good, but also is said to have medicinal properties that aid sluggish circulation.

8	ripe pineapples

Drop pineapples on the floor until soft and bruised. Cut around green crown with a sharp knife. Remove top, and core fruit carefully without penetrating the bottom of the shell. Over a bowl, squeeze pineapple shell with both hands, extracting as much juice as possible. Return juice to pineapple shells. Serve immediately, before juice can begin to ferment.

Makes 8 servings.

top: *The strong, rich flavor of Mexican Coffee goes especially well with breakfast pastries and braided bread.*
above: *Coffee beans are husked and ground at the Cañamelar coffee plantation.*

BUNUELOS A LA VERACRUZANA
Fritters, Veracruz Style

Fritters vary from region to region, but those from Veracruz are the most famous.

FOR THE FRITTERS

2	cups water
3	tablespoons butter
1	teaspoon salt
2	teaspoons sugar
1	tablespoon crumbled stick cinnamon
1	teaspoon anise seed
2¼	cups flour
6	medium eggs
2	cups corn oil or sunflower oil
2	cups lard

FOR THE SYRUP

3	cups dark brown sugar
1½	quarts water
4	sticks cinnamon, each 6 inches long
1	tablespoon anise seed

FOR THE GARNISH

Ground cinnamon

Prepare the fritters: Combine water, butter, salt, sugar, cinnamon, and anise in a saucepan. Bring to a boil. Boil for 8 minutes. Add flour all at once. Beat with a spoon until ingredients are well mixed. Simmer until mixture separates from sides of saucepan. Remove from heat, and cool for 3 hours. Add eggs one by one, beating by hand or with an electric mixer after each addition.

Measure 2 to 3 tablespoons dough. With greased hands, form a strip, and shape into a doughnut 4 inches in diameter, making sure the center hole is large.

Heat oil and lard in a deep frying pan. Test temperature with a piece of batter. Oil is ready when batter sizzles. Reduce heat, and fry fritters for about 3 to 4 minutes on each side, or until golden. Remove from oil, and drain on paper towels. Keep warm until serving time.

Prepare the syrup: Combine sugar, water, cinnamon, and anise in a saucepan. Boil until syrup thickens slightly, about 40 minutes.

Serve hot fritters in individual bowls in hot syrup. Or soak fritters in syrup for 1 or 2 minutes before serving. Garnish with cinnamon.

Makes about 24 buñuelos.

Fritters may be served in individual bowls with hot syrup and a garnish of cinnamon stick.

The ingredients for Fritters, Veracruz Style.

CHOCOLATE CHONTAL
Chontal Chocolate

The Aztecs considered hot chocolate to be a drink worthy of the gods. The emperor Montezuma drank hot chocolate from gold-filigreed gourds. The drink was believed to possess medicinal and aphrodisiac powers, increasing energy and vitality.

6	quarts milk
12	ounces vanilla-flavored chocolate or Mexican chocolate tablets (containing cinnamon)
10	ounces Mexican chocolate tablets (containing cinnamon)

Scald milk in a clay pot. Add chocolate, stirring to dissolve thoroughly. With a molinillo or rotary beater, beat the hot chocolate as it heats, until a thick layer of foam is produced.

To serve, pour hot chocolate into individual clay mugs. This drink is good with cake or conchas (Mexican sweet rolls).

Makes 16 generous servings.

FLAN DE CASTANAS
Chestnut Flan

The chestnut is native to the Tabasco region, where local Indians use it to flavor corn-tortilla dough. This recipe is a new version of a traditional Spanish dessert—flan—that uses local ingredients.

FOR THE CARAMEL

1½ cups sugar

FOR THE FLAN

2½ cups milk

2½	cups sugar
1	tablespoon vanilla extract
4	eggs, lightly beaten
4	egg whites, beaten until soft peaks form
4	egg yolks, lightly beaten
2	cups canned chestnut purée, or chestnuts, peeled, cooked, and puréed, or sweet potatoes, puréed

FOR THE GARNISH

½	cup heavy cream
1	cup sour cream or crème fraîche
½	cup sugar
16	cherries with stems, dipped in chocolate (optional)
1	cup raw almonds, skinned, sliced, and toasted

Preheat oven to 350 degrees.

Prepare the caramel: Put sugar in a heavy skillet, and heat, stirring, until sugar melts and turns dark brown. Pour into 8-inch round mold, quickly tipping mold so caramel spreads evenly. Set aside.

Prepare the flan: Put milk in a heavy saucepan with sugar and vanilla. Bring to a boil. Boil until mixture is reduced by half. Cool slightly.

Combine the eggs, egg whites, egg yolks, and chestnut purée. Add warm milk mixture. Mix. Pour into the mold over the caramel. Place mold in a water bath (bain-marie), and bake for 1½ hours or until a toothpick inserted in the center comes out clean.

Refrigerate for 4 hours before unmolding.

Prepare the garnish: Mix the heavy and sour creams, and chill in freezer for 1 hour. Beat cream mixture until frothy. Add sugar gradually, and continue beating until peaks form. Do not overbeat, or the creams may separate.

To serve, unmold flan onto a platter. Top with whipped creams. Decorate center with cherries, and sprinkle with almonds. Refrigerate until serving time.

Makes 8 servings.

Mexican chocolate tablets are used for making hot Chontal Chocolate.

NATILLA CON VAINILLA DE PAPANTLA
Vanilla Custard from Papantla

The vanilla plant requires abundant shade and grows in Mexico only in the northern mountain region of coastal Veracruz, in an area near Papantla and Gutiérrez Zamora. Used as a beverage flavoring since pre-Hispanic times, the vanilla bean was highly prized by the Totonacan Indians as a token of trade. After the conquest, when vanilla was first exported to Europe, nuns in convents in Veracruz began using it in foods, inventing delicious vanilla-flavored desserts. Today the bean is used to make a Veracruzian liqueur and, of course, as a flavoring extract for cooking.

FOR THE CUSTARD

1½ quarts milk
1   vanilla bean, whole
2   tablespoons vanilla extract, preferably Mexican
8   egg yolks
1½ cups sugar
¼   cup corn starch
2   tablespoons butter, melted

FOR THE GARNISH

Freshly ground cinnamon, preferably Mexican

Put milk, vanilla bean, and vanilla extract in a heavy saucepan. Bring to a boil.

In a large bowl, beat egg yolks and sugar until thick. Add corn starch, and stir. Add hot milk mixture, and mix well.

Pour into a saucepan, and cook over low heat, stirring constantly, until the mixture coats a metal spoon (almost at boiling point). Add butter. Remove from heat, and stir. Cool until skin forms, and skim off. Pour into large goblets. Refrigerate for 2 to 3 hours.

To serve, sprinkle with cinnamon. For variety, sprinkle with toasted almonds, or pour custard over cooked prunes.
Makes 8 servings.

LECHE DE MAMEY
Mamey Dessert

Mangoes may be substituted if mamey fruits are not available.

FOR THE MAMEY DESSERT

3   quarts milk
2   sticks cinnamon, each 4 inches long
4   cups sugar
8   egg yolks, beaten
2   cups raw almonds, skinned and ground
2   mamey fruits or 6 mangoes, puréed and strained

FOR THE GARNISH

½   cup raw almonds, skinned and finely chopped
3   tablespoons sugar
1½ tablespoons ground cinnamon

Bring milk and cinnamon to a boil in a heavy saucepan. Remove from heat, and cool to room temperature. Add sugar, and reheat, stirring constantly, until mixture thickens to the consistency of a light custard. Remove from heat, and slowly add to egg yolks, stirring constantly. Return to heat, and stir until bottom of pan shows when mixture is pushed aside with a spoon.

Add almonds, and remove from heat. Fold in mamey. Pour mixture into a serving bowl, and refrigerate for 2 hours.

Just before serving, sprinkle almonds, sugar, and cinnamon on top.
Makes 8 servings.

clockwise from top left: *Squashes,* pitahaya *fruits, green cocoa beans, and* mamey *fruits, called* zapote *in Tabasco.*

MEXICO CITY
AND THE STATE OF MEXICO

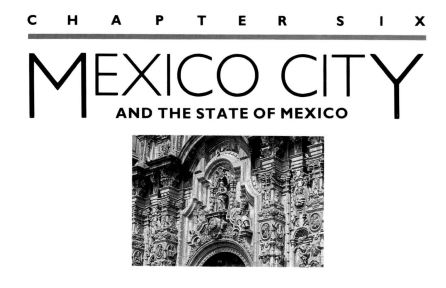

M exico City is indisputably the most heterogeneous city in Mexico. Successive waves of colonists and immigrants have had an enduring impact on Mexico City's culture and cuisine.

Today's overcrowded, ethnically diverse megalopolis has been a major urban center almost since its founding in the fourteenth century, when the Aztecs turned the town they called Tenochtitlán into the capital of what became the most extensive military empire in North American history. Even then, residents were exposed to the languages, art, and foods of peoples from far beyond their native valley. When the conquering Spaniards built their colonial headquarters on the rubble of Montezuma's palace, they expanded Mexico City's domination and ensured its emergence as one of the great cosmopolitan crossroads of the New World.

A significant result of Mexico City's variegated ethnic landscape is the wide choice of foods available in restaurants and markets. The diversity of international cuisine in the city has prompted local chefs to experiment with new approaches to Mexican fare, most recently with light, fresh *nueva cocina mexicana*. The results are eclectic, but unmistakably Mexican—a salad of artichoke and squash blossoms, for example, or a puff-pastry shell encasing fish rolls stuffed with *epazote*.

Yet the city's enduring culinary wealth is its traditional food, the fare of the millions of country people from every corner of Mexico who have come to the capital. Thousands of restaurants, humble and grand, specialize in every imaginable regional Mexican cuisine. And in affluent homes, maids from the hinterlands keep country cooking alive.

Nowhere is Mexicans' penchant for munching and snacking more blatant than in Mexico City. It is the place to see endless variations on the tortilla in terms of size, shape, and accompaniments. Stuffed, rolled, doubled, or folded. Oozing with cheese, succulent meats, vegetables, and chiles. Dabbed with green sauce, red sauce, or guacamole. There is hardly a neighborhood in Mexico City devoid of a snacker who ambles along a raucous, traffic-jammed street oblivious to all but the satisfaction of a tortilla snack.

Mexico City is blessed with huge, cornucopian markets. The La Merced and San Juan markets—both with roots in pre-Hispanic times—offer a dazzling array of vegetables, dozens of varieties of beans and corn, and fresh fish, mollusks, and crustaceans from both the Atlantic and the Pacific oceans. Neat mounds of brightly colored *masa* await the street vendors who transform the prepared corn dough into tamales, *gorditas*, tacos, *quesadillas*, *sopes*, and other snacks. Also piled high is light, crispy *chicharrón* (fried pork rind), which, when accompanied by the perfect sauce, delights the Mexican palate. Market booths overflow with stacks of fragrant yellow squash blossoms, the essential ingredient of a delicious Mexico City soup, and of stuffings for tacos or *empanadas*. Markets also sell such other central Mexican delicacies as *cuitlacoche*, a corn fungus disdained by United States farmers. *Cuitlacoche* has been cultivated as a delicacy since pre-Columbian times by Mexicans who consider the swollen, black kernels to be a rich and subtle improvement on the mushroom. *Cuitlacoche* is prized as a filling for crepes, a culinary legacy from the sorry rule of Maximilian and Carlota in the mid-nineteenth century.

The markets boast an endless supply of chiles, meticulously arranged for stunning contrasts in size, shape, and color. There are fresh varieties—such as *chiles güeros,* *serranos*, *jalapeños*, *chilacas*, and *poblanos*—and their dried counterparts. Alternatively, ground chiles or chile and spice blends are piled high in colorful mounds.

Tropical fruits are in abundance, their ripe, musky fragrance thick in the air. Mangoes are especially prized and are just as likely to be eaten on the spot from a Popsicle stick as they are to be used as an ingredient in an elegant dessert—*mangos con salsa de fresa y frambuesa* (mangoes in strawberry and raspberry sauce).

For what may be the world's most exotic food shopping, there is the Sonora market, with its stacks of herbs—some for seasoning (such as the irreplaceable *epazote* and cilantro), some medicinal, and some exclusively for sorcery. At the Plaza Garibaldi, crowded after midnight with dozens of free-lance mariachi bands, vendors in food booths offer broths billed as hangover remedies, such as *menudo* (tripe soup).

An indigenous Mexico City cuisine can still be found in small cantinas and in open-air markets. Much of this food recalls the long-gone days when the city was a waterfront town delighting in the aquatic delicacies of Lake Texcoco. Only vestigial fragments of the lake survive, but it was once a source of fish and of krill-like freshwater shrimp. Mexico City's *tortas de camarón* (dried-shrimp patties) are a remnant of the capital's Aztec heritage.

Part of the capital's pre-Hispanic market system is still intact in southern Mexico City, the renowned but misnamed "floating gardens" of Xochimilco. Neither floating nor gardens, the Xochimilco *chinampas* are intensively cultivated farm plots—tiny islands anchored by gnarled ancient trees—that have been built up by hand for six centuries along with a complex network of canals. The *chinampas* are like truck farms; more precisely, they are canoe farms, linked to marketplaces by narrow canals. Most of these waterways have long since disappeared beneath land fill, victims of urban sprawl. But as recently as a generation ago, many southern Mexico City neighborhoods regularly received their food by way of the canals. The poled, flat-bottomed boats arrived on market days laden with crates of fruits, vegetables, fresh corn, and beans. The canals and *chinampas* of Xochimilco still provide some of Mexico's choicest produce, luring vast crowds of Mexico City families to the wharfside markets and restaurants every Sunday.

The State of Mexico also offers a wide variety of delicious foods. The State's capital, Toluca, is famous for its pork *chorizo* (sausage), which is made in both red and green versions, as well as its dairy products. The marketplaces in the region are crowded with food stands displaying fresh produce and prepared foods, such as *tacos de plaza*, *barbacoa* (barbecued pork baked in underground pits), and *tlacoyos* (oval-shaped tortillas stuffed with beans or chickpea purée).

ENSALADA DE ALCACHOFA CON FLOR DE CALABAZA, CILANTRO Y ALBAHACA

Artichoke Salad with Squash Blossoms and Cilantro–Basil Dressing

The combination of cilantro and basil complements the flavor of fresh artichokes in this modern recipe. Squash blossoms are eaten uncooked—an unusual touch.

FOR THE ARTICHOKES

6	quarts water
	Salt to taste
8	large artichokes

FOR THE VINAIGRETTE

¾	cup mild cider vinegar
	Salt to taste
1	teaspoon freshly ground pepper
1	tablespoon sugar
1	cup fresh basil or ⅓ cup dried basil, chopped
1	cup cilantro, chopped
3	cloves garlic, chopped
1	cup olive oil
1	cup corn oil

FOR THE GARNISH

48	squash blossoms, washed, cleaned, and thick outer leaves removed

Squash blossoms can be used in salads, in a stuffing for crepes, or as the basic ingredient in a savory soup.

Prepare the artichokes: Bring water to a boil in a large saucepan. Add salt. When water is at a rolling boil, add artichokes. Boil for 40 minutes or until the leaves can be easily removed. Remove from water, and cool.

Prepare the vinaigrette: Blend vinegar, salt, pepper, sugar, basil, cilantro, garlic, and olive and corn oils in a blender or food processor for 4 minutes. Test for seasoning. Refrigerate for 1 hour.

To serve, place 6 large artichoke leaves on each of 8 plates. Center artichoke bottom on the plate. Arrange 6 squash blossoms on each plate (see photo). Pour vinaigrette over artichokes, or serve dressing in a bowl.

Makes 8 servings.

The markets in Mexico City offer a variety of fresh produce for salads. Squash blossoms and artichokes are combined with a cilantro and basil dressing.

CONSOME DE POLLO A LA MEXICANA
Chicken Broth, Mexican Style

Broths are a mainstay of Mexican cuisine. They can be transformed by varying just the ingredients used as a garnish. Caldo Tlalpeño is chicken broth filled with rice, chickpeas, carrots, zucchini, shredded chicken, avocado, and cilantro, and topped with a chile chipotle. Caldo Xochitl has a chicken-broth base, in which squash blossoms float. These are just two of countless variations.

FOR THE BROTH

6	quarts water
½	chicken, split lengthwise
4	chicken leg quarters
1	pound veal stew meat, in chunks
4	carrots, peeled and sliced
½	leek, sliced
6	cloves garlic, whole
1	large white onion, sliced
½	rib celery, sliced
12	black peppercorns
2	bay leaves
	Salt to taste

FOR THE GARNISH

6	knob-onion tops, or ½ cup chives, chopped
2	California avocados, peeled and chopped
2	tomatoes, finely chopped
10	sprigs cilantro, finely chopped
3	or 4 chiles serranos, finely chopped
10	ounces Oaxaca or mozzarella cheese, finely chopped

Bring water to a boil in a stock pot. Add chicken, veal, carrots, leek, garlic, onion, celery, peppercorns, bay leaves, and salt.

Simmer until soup foams. Skim, and simmer for 1½ hours.

Remove from heat. Set aside to cool, and skim off fat. Strain broth through a sieve.

To serve, pour hot broth into a soup tureen. Add garnishes immediately before serving.

Makes 8 servings.

ESQUITES
Fresh Corn Kernels

FOR THE ESQUITES

½	cup butter
1	tablespoon lard
1½	cups white onion, finely chopped
⅓	cup chile serrano, finely chopped
	Kernels from 12 ears corn
¾	cup epazote or cilantro, chopped
1	cup water
	Salt to taste

FOR THE GARNISH

2	tablespoons epazote or cilantro, finely chopped

Heat butter and lard in a saucepan over medium heat. Sauté onion and chile together until soft. Stir in corn kernels, epazote, water, and salt. Cover, and cook over low heat until corn is tender, about 20 minutes.

To serve, place esquites on a platter, and sprinkle with epazote or cilantro. This dish often is served with Mexican rice.

Makes 8 servings.

ARROZ DEL MONTON
Mexican Rice

Mexican rice is quite versatile and is served with many main courses or with tacos. It also accompanies such snacks as chalupitas, tostadas mineras, and comal quesadillas. Rice often serves as a bed for fried eggs.

FOR THE RICE

2½	quarts water, plus 3 cups hot water
2	cups long-grain white rice, washed
2	cups vegetable oil
1	white onion, halved, plus ½ medium white onion
10	cloves garlic, whole
3	large tomatoes (2½ pounds), roasted (see Basics)

Rice is a Mexican staple that accompanies countless dishes and is served here with beef, pork rind, fresh corn kernels, and avocado.

Salt to taste
2 chiles jalapeños or 4 chiles serranos
20 sprigs parsley

FOR THE GARNISH

4 chiles serranos
Several sprigs cilantro or epazote, chopped

Bring 2 quarts water to a boil in a medium saucepan. Remove from heat, let cool 10 minutes, and add rice. Soak rice for 20 to 25 minutes. Pour into a mesh strainer, and rinse under a stream of cold water until water runs clear. Drain the rice well.

Heat oil in a saucepan. Add halved onion and 6 garlic cloves, and brown lightly. Add drained rice, and stir to mix well with the oil. Cook over low heat until rice browns slightly, stirring occasionally (do not over-stir, or rice will become mushy).

Remove from heat, and drain off oil. Return rice to saucepan.

In a blender or food processor, purée tomatoes with ½ cup water, ½ onion, and 4 garlic cloves. Strain mixture, and mix with the rice. Return saucepan to heat, and cook until liquid has evaporated and sauce releases its fat. Then add 3 cups hot water and salt, stirring to mix.

Boil for 4 minutes. Place chiles and parsley on top of rice without stirring, and cover with a tight lid. Lower heat, and simmer for 40 minutes. Remove from heat, and let stand for 30 minutes without removing lid.

To serve, uncover rice and remove chiles and parsley. Place rice on a platter. Garnish with decoratively cut chiles, and sprinkle with cilantro.

Makes 8 servings.

SOPA DE TORTILLA A LA MEXICANA
Tortilla Soup, Mexican Style

Tortilla soup is basic to Mexican cuisine. The broth is standard, but the wide assortment of garnishes often makes the soup a surprise.

FOR THE BROTH

6   quarts chicken broth (see recipe on page 202), or canned beef broth

FOR THE SOUP

2   chiles pasillas, washed, seeded, deveined (see Basics), and fried in a little oil, plus 2 long chiles pasillas, fried in a little oil or lard
2   chiles anchos, washed, seeded, deveined (see Basics), and fried in a little oil
4   medium tomatoes, peeled
1   white onion, sliced
4   cloves garlic, chopped
⅔   cup olive oil or corn oil
2   sprigs epazote or cilantro
    Salt to taste

FOR THE GARNISH

2   cups vegetable oil
24 tortillas, sliced in thin strips and dried for 1 day
8   chiles pasillas, fried in a little oil or lard
2   California avocados, finely chopped
2   cups fresh cheese, such as panela or feta, finely crumbled
1   cup crème fraîche, or 1 cup sour cream mixed with ¼ cup half-and-half

Prepare the broth: Make broth according to the recipe. Cool, and skim fat. Reheat, and keep at boiling point.

Meanwhile, prepare the soup: In a blender or food processor, blend 2 chiles pasillas and anchos with tomatoes, onion, and garlic. Strain. Heat oil in a stock pot. Pour blended chile mixture into pot, and fry until

Tortilla Soup consists of a seasoned broth ladled over fried tortilla strips and topped with an assortment of garnishes, often including chiles, avocado slices, cheese, and crème fraîche.

it thickens and fat rises to the surface. Add epazote. Mix in the boiling broth and long chiles pasillas. Salt to taste, and simmer for 25 minutes.

Prepare the garnish: Heat oil in a frying pan, and fry tortilla strips until crisp. Drain on paper towels, and sprinkle with salt.

To serve, pour soup into a tureen. Divide tortilla strips among individual bowls. Ladle soup over tortilla strips. Serve chiles, avocado, cheese, and crème fraîche in separate bowls, allowing diners to season soup to taste.

Makes 8 servings.

ENSALADA DE ESPINACA ESTILO COYOACAN

Spinach Salad, Coyoacan Style

This salad combines several ingredients basic to the Mexican kitchen—cheese, sesame seeds, and spinach.

FOR THE VINAIGRETTE

2½ cups cider vinegar or wine vinegar
1 tablespoon freshly ground pepper
20 cloves garlic, chopped
6 bay leaves
1 teaspoon crushed allspice
4 sprigs thyme or 1 teaspoon dried thyme

FOR THE SALAD

32 medium spinach leaves, washed, dried, and chilled
½ cup olive oil
2 tablespoons butter
8 knob onions, thinly sliced
16 chiles serranos, sliced in strips
Salt and freshly ground pepper to taste

FOR THE GARNISH

8 plum tomatoes, 3 ounces each, sliced
1 pound, 2 ounces brie cheese, sliced in 16 slices
2 tablespoons sesame seeds, lightly toasted

Spinach Salad, Coyoacan Style includes slices of brie cheese.

Prepare the vinaigrette: Put all ingredients in a jar. Macerate at room temperature for 2 days.

Prepare the salad: Wash spinach leaves, and dry well. Refrigerate for 1 hour.

Heat oil and butter in a saucepan. Add onion, and sauté lightly. Add chiles and salt and pepper to taste.

Continue to sauté until ingredients are lightly browned.

To serve, place spinach in the center of a platter. On one side, garnish with alternate tomato slices, cooked onion slices, and cooked chile strips. Place cheese slices on other side. Shake vinaigrette to mix. Sprinkle with sesame seeds and vinaigrette. Serve immediately.

Makes 8 servings.

TRUCHAS EN CALDILLO
Trout in Broth

This recipe is from Taberna de León, one of the best-known restaurants in the resort town of Valle de Bravo. Chef Monica Patiño is well known for her sophisticated creations.

FOR THE TROUT
5⅓ tablespoons lard
2 tablespoons garlic, finely chopped
1½ cups white onion, finely chopped
6 trout, about ¾ pound each, sliced crosswise in 3 pieces
2 chiles guajillos, sliced in thin strips
3 chile guajillo veins (open chiles and remove veins with a sharp knife)
20 epazote or cilantro leaves
½ cup vinegar
   Salt to taste

FOR THE GARNISH
8 chile guajillo veins
24 epazote or cilantro leaves
4 limes, halved

Heat lard in a clay or ceramic pot. Brown garlic and onion until light brown. Add trout, and fry lightly. Add chiles, veins, epazote, and hot water to cover. Add vinegar and salt, and cook over medium heat for 40 minutes, being careful not to overcook fish.

To serve, ladle broth into soup bowls, placing 2 pieces of fish in each bowl. Garnish each serving with chile veins, epazote, and lime. Serve with blue tortillas or bread.
Makes 8 servings.

Trout is simmered in a spicy broth, seasoned with epazote, just until the fish is cooked.

AGUACATES RELLENOS AL ESTILO CALIXTLAHUACA
Stuffed Avocados, Calixtlahuaca Style

FOR THE AVOCADOS
¼ cup vinegar
1 tablespoon lime juice
   Salt and pepper to taste
½ cup olive oil or vegetable oil
3 medium California avocados, peeled, pitted, and halved

FOR THE STUFFING
¼ cup olive oil
5⅓ tablespoons butter
1 white onion, grated
5 cloves garlic, puréed
1¾ pounds cuitlacoche (corn fungus) or mushrooms, finely chopped
¼ cup epazote or cilantro, chopped
3 chiles serranos, finely chopped
   Salt and pepper to taste

FOR THE GARNISH
8 large lettuce leaves, washed, dried, and chilled
16 slices fresh cheese, such as panela, feta, or ricotta
16 slices tomato
8 epazote leaves

Prepare the avocados: Put vinegar, lime juice, salt, and pepper in a glass bowl. Add oil gradually, whisking until the ingredients are well mixed. Pour over avocados in a shallow baking dish. Refrigerate for 1 hour.

Meanwhile, prepare the stuffing: Heat oil and butter in a medium saucepan. Add onion, garlic, cuitlacoche, epazote, and chile. Season to taste with salt and pepper. Simmer, stirring occasionally, until mixture thickens, about 35 to 40 minutes. Cool.

To serve, place a lettuce leaf on each of 8 plates. Center avocados on lettuce. Garnish with cheese and tomatoes. Stuff avocado halves with cuitlacoche mixture, and place epazote leaves on top. Serve with tostadas and Mexican rice.
Makes 8 servings.

thick strips, or 3⅓ pounds small wild mushrooms
Salt to taste
1   teaspoon freshly ground pepper

Heat oil in a clay or ceramic pot. Add garlic cloves, and brown. Remove garlic from oil, and discard. Add chopped garlic, onion, and chiles. Sauté for 4 minutes. Stir in mushrooms, and continue cooking for 25 minutes. Season to taste with salt and pepper.

Serve the mushrooms in individual clay bowls or ramekins.

Makes 8 servings.

CREPAS
Crepes

Mexicans have adopted the French crepe, innovating with such native stuffings as squash blossoms, cuitlacoche, and jitomate sauce. Dessert crepes are filled with caramelized goat's milk and marmalade.

10   eggs
1   teaspoon salt
2   cups flour
3½   to 4 cups milk
½   cup butter, melted and cooled, plus ½ cup butter

In a blender or food processor, blend eggs, salt, flour, and milk, in batches, for 4 minutes. Pour batter into a bowl. Stir in melted butter. Let stand for 1 hour.

Heat a 12-inch frying pan over low heat for 5 minutes. Grease with a little butter, and heat for a few more seconds. Add 1 tablespoon batter over direct heat, tilting pan to spread well. Cook until edges of crepe begin to dry. Turn carefully with a spatula or with fingers. Cook for 2 minutes or until light brown. Remove from pan, and stack on a plate. Reheat frying pan before making another crepe.

Do not overcook crepes.

Makes about 40 crepes.

Mushrooms and Garlic, flavored with chiles, is served as an appetizer.

HONGOS AL AJILLO
Mushrooms in Garlic

Mexico boasts a wide variety of mushrooms. This bounty expands a recipe as basic as this. The flavor depends on the type of mushroom used.

1   quart olive oil
8   large cloves garlic, whole, plus 2 tablespoons garlic, chopped
1   cup white onion, finely chopped
10   chiles guajillos, sliced in strips
32   large mushrooms (3 pounds), sliced in 1-inch

Markets in the State of Mexico offer an array of mushrooms.

CREPAS DE FLOR DE CALABAZA CON QUESO GRUYERE FUNDIDO Y CREMA

Squash-Blossom Crepes with Melted Gruyère Cheese and Cream

Squash blossoms are a typical and important ingredient in Mexican cuisine. The vegetable is used as a stuffing for quesadillas *and crepes and as a base for soups.*

FOR THE CREPES

24   crepes (see recipe on page 209)

FOR THE STUFFING

⅓   cup olive oil
5⅓   tablespoons unsalted butter
1   medium white onion, finely chopped
4   cloves garlic, finely chopped
    Kernels from 3 ears corn, boiled in salted water
    for 8 minutes and drained
4   chiles poblanos, roasted, sweated, peeled, seed-
    ed, deveined, soaked in vinegar–water solution,
    and sliced in strips (see Basics)
3   tomatoes (1¾ pounds), peeled and chopped
2¼   pounds squash blossoms, washed, cleaned, thick
    outer leaves removed, and chopped
    Salt to taste
½   tablespoon freshly ground pepper

FOR THE TOPPING

1¼   cups sour cream or crème fraîche mixed with
    1¾ cups half-and-half
    Salt and pepper to taste
14   ounces Gruyère or Swiss cheese, grated
5   ounces Parmesan cheese, grated

Prepare the crepes: Make crepes according to the recipe. Set aside.

Preheat oven to 350 degrees.

Prepare the stuffing: Heat oil and butter in a saucepan. Sauté onion and garlic until soft. Add corn, chile strips, tomatoes, squash blossoms, salt, and pepper. Simmer for 40 minutes or until mixture thickens.

Spoon 1½ tablespoons of stuffing onto each crepe. Fold in half and half again to form triangles. Place crepes in a baking dish.

Beat sour cream with salt and pepper. Cover crepes with cream, and sprinkle with cheese. Bake for 40 minutes or until cheese is golden brown. If a crusty top is desired, place dish under the broiler until cheese browns.

Serve hot directly from the baking dish with a green salad.

Makes 24 crepes.

CREPAS DE CUITLACOCHE

Cuitlacoche Crepes

This recipe is an example of how native Mexican ingredients adapt to French crepes. If cuitlacoche (corn fungus) is not available, mushrooms can be substituted.

FOR THE CREPES

32   crepes (see recipe on page 209)

FOR THE STUFFING

½   cup olive oil
6   cloves garlic, puréed
2   white onions, grated
3   large tomatoes, finely chopped
1   or 2 chiles cuaresmeños or jalapeños, finely
    chopped
4   chiles poblanos, sliced in thin strips
2   pounds fresh cuitlacoche, finely chopped, or 4
    8- to 9-ounce cans cuitlacoche, or 2 pounds
    fresh mushrooms
    Salt to taste

1 teaspoon pepper
¾ cup epazote or cilantro, finely chopped
¾ cup cilantro, finely chopped

FOR THE BECHAMEL SAUCE

¾ cup butter
3 cloves garlic, puréed
½ white onion, grated
6 tablespoons flour
3 cups hot milk
2½ cups crème fraîche, or 1 cup sour cream mixed
with 1½ cups half-and-half
1½ cups dry white wine
2 bay leaves
1 teaspoon ground thyme
1 teaspoon ground nutmeg
Salt to taste

FOR THE TOPPING

9 ounces Gruyère cheese, grated
9 ounces manchego or creamy Monterey Jack
cheese, grated

Prepare the crepes: Make crepes according to the recipe. Set aside.

Prepare the stuffing: Heat oil in a frying pan. Add garlic and onion. Sauté well. Add tomatoes, chiles cuaresmeños and poblanos, and cuitlacoche. Cook over low heat for 40 minutes. Stir occasionally, adding salt and pepper to taste. Cook until thick, about 30 minutes. Add epazote and cilantro. Set aside.

Prepare the bechamel sauce: Melt butter in a saucepan. Add garlic and onion, and sauté. Stir in flour, and cook over low heat until mixture begins to bubble and turns light brown. Remove from heat, and gradually add hot milk to mixture, stirring with a whisk until it thickens. Add crème fraîche, wine, bay leaves, thyme, and nutmeg. Salt, and continue cooking over low heat for 45 minutes, stirring occasionally.

Preheat oven to 350 degrees.

Spoon 1½ tablespoons of stuffing onto each crepe. Fold in half and half again to form triangles. Place crepes in a large baking dish or on individual heat-resistant plates. Pour sauce over, and sprinkle with cheese. Bake for 45 minutes or until golden brown. Serve immediately.

The filling may be frozen and used for quesadillas as well as crepes. The crepes may be prepared and frozen. To serve, thaw and bake in a preheated 350-degree oven for 40 minutes.

Makes 32 crepes.

Cuitlacoche, *a fungus that grows on fresh ears of corn during the rainy season, is used in a flavorful stuffing for crepes.*

CREPAS RELLENAS DE HONGO AL CILANTRO
Crepes Filled with Mushrooms and Cilantro

Crepes filled with mushrooms are popular in Mexico. Each region of the country has its own variety of mushrooms, making this a dish whose character changes, depending on where it is prepared.

FOR THE CREPES

24 crepes (see recipe on page 209)

FOR THE STUFFING

½	cup olive oil
5⅓	tablespoons butter
4	cloves garlic, finely chopped
1	white onion, grated
4	chiles serranos or de árbol, fried in a little oil, drained, and finely chopped
2¼	pounds fresh mushrooms, finely chopped
3	tablespoons cilantro, finely chopped
	Salt and pepper to taste

FOR THE SAUCE

½	cup vegetable oil
½	white onion, grated
4	cloves garlic, finely chopped, plus 3 cloves garlic, chopped
1	pound fresh mushrooms, finely chopped
1	cup cilantro, finely chopped
1	cup parsley, finely chopped
	Salt and pepper to taste
1½	cups milk
1	cup crème fraîche or 1 cup sour cream
1½	cups half-and-half
11	ounces manchego, Chihuahua, or Monterey Jack cheese, grated

FOR THE TOPPING

6	ounces Monterey Jack cheese, grated

Prepare the crepes: Make crepes according to the recipe. Set aside.

Prepare the stuffing: Heat oil and butter in a saucepan. Sauté garlic and onion until transparent. Stir in chiles and mushrooms. Add cilantro, and salt and pepper to taste. Cook over low heat for 45 minutes or until mixture thickens. Remove from heat, and cool.

Prepare the sauce: Heat oil in a saucepan. Sauté onion and finely chopped garlic until light brown. Add mushrooms, and cook over medium heat for 25 minutes.

In a blender or food processor, blend chopped garlic, cilantro, parsley, salt, pepper, milk, crème fraîche, and half-and-half. Add this mixture to the sauce in saucepan, and cook over low heat for 40 minutes. Correct seasoning, and remove from heat. Stir in cheese.

Preheat oven to 350 degrees.

Spoon stuffing onto crepes, and roll up. Arrange a layer of crepes in a 9- by 12-inch baking dish. Pour some sauce over, and continue layering crepes and covering with sauce until all are used. Top with grated cheese, and bake for 40 to 45 minutes.

Serve crepes immediately, with a green salad.

Makes 24 crepes.

QUESADILLAS DE COMAL DE SANTIAGO TIANGUISTENGO
Comal Quesadillas, Santiago-Tianguistengo Style

These quesadillas are sold in the Santiago Tianguistengo market. The stuffings vary widely enough to satisfy the tastes of everyone. They range from fresh cheese and mushrooms cooked with epazote *to pork rind in red sauce and potato with sausage.*

FOR THE MASA

2½ pounds dried white or blue corn kernels, washed
10 quarts water
2 cups ground limestone
Salt to taste

FOR THE STUFFINGS

1 recipe squash-blossom stuffing (see recipe on page 210)
1 recipe cuitlacoche stuffing (see recipe on page 210)
1 recipe mushroom and cilantro stuffing (see recipe on page 212)
1 recipe mashed-potato stuffing (see recipe on this page)

FOR THE GARNISH

1 recipe red sauce (see recipe on page 74)
1 recipe green sauce (see recipe on page 104)

Put corn in a large stock pot. Add water, and stir in limestone and salt. Cook over low heat until the skin of the kernels puckers and can be easily removed. Remove from heat, and cool. Remove skin from kernels, and wash. Discard skins. Grind corn in a mill. Knead with enough water to form a pliant, elastic masa. You may substitute purchased fresh masa or masa made with masa harina.

Heat a brazier with coal or gas, and place a comal or griddle on top. Or heat a griddle on the stove. Make tortillas (see Basics), and cook on comal or griddle. Heat stuffings on the comal in clay bowls, or warm them in pans. Put 2 tablespoons of stuffing off-center on a tortilla, and fold in half to make a quesadilla. Continue to heat on comal until warmed through. Prepare the quesadillas with the various stuffings listed in ingredients.

Serve quesadillas hot with red and green sauces.
Makes about 60 quesadillas.

PAPA COCIDA (PARA QUESADILLAS DE COMAL)
Mashed-Potato Stuffing (for Comal Quesadillas)

2½ quarts water
8 medium red potatoes, unpeeled
Salt to taste
2 cups mozzarella cheese, shredded

Bring water to a boil, and add potatoes. Salt. Boil until potatoes are tender, about 30 minutes, depending on size of potatoes. Remove from water, peel, and mash well. Mix with cheese.
Makes stuffing for 18 quesadillas.

ACOCILES
Fresh-Water Shrimp

Acocil is the newborn fresh-water shrimp found in la-goons and river tributaries in the Valley of Mexico.

FOR THE SHRIMP

½ cup lard or butter
1½ white onions, minced
4 chiles serranos, minced
1 pound fresh acociles or tiny shrimp
    Juice of 4 limes
    Salt to taste

FOR THE GARNISH

3 ripe California avocados, mashed and seasoned with salt
1 recipe green sauce (see recipe on page 104)

Heat lard in a frying pan. Add onion and chile, and lightly brown. Add acociles, lime juice, and salt to taste. Cook over low heat until acociles begin to brown.

Serve acociles in a clay pot. Accompany with mashed avocado, freshly made blue or yellow corn tortillas, and green sauce.
Makes 8 servings.

CONCHAS DE PESCADO
Fish in Pastry Shells

This is an elegant dish that combines traditional Mexican cuisine with modern tastes.

FOR THE FISH STOCK

3 quarts water
2 cups dry white wine
4 chicken legs and thighs
2 fish heads, any variety
½ leek
1 turnip
4 carrots
1 white onion
½ head garlic
15 sprigs parsley
    Salt to taste
1 teaspoon freshly ground pepper

FOR THE SPREAD

⅓ cup olive oil
5⅓ tablespoons butter
1 medium white onion, grated
4 cloves garlic, finely chopped
8 cups watercress, cut in small sprigs, or 2¼ pounds fresh spinach, washed and chopped
    Salt and pepper to taste

FOR THE STUFFING

⅓ cup olive oil
5⅓ tablespoons butter
½ white onion, grated
4 cloves garlic, finely chopped
1 pound mushrooms, washed and finely chopped
2 chiles de árbol or serranos, fried in a little oil and finely chopped
    Salt and pepper to taste

FOR THE PASTRY SHELLS

2¼   pounds puff-pastry dough

FOR THE FISH

2¼   pounds fish fillets, preferably red snapper or
      bass, thinly sliced into about 48 strips
      Salt and pepper to taste
48   epazote or cilantro leaves
3   cups fish stock
½   cup butter, in small pieces

FOR THE SAUCE

3   cups fish stock, reduced to ¾ cup
2   cups half-and-half
2   cups crème fraîche
¾   cup Parmesan cheese
      Salt to taste
1½   tablespoons corn starch, dissolved in ½ cup fish
      stock
1   cup butter, in small pieces

FOR THE GARNISH (OPTIONAL)

½   cup butter
8   large carrots, peeled and julienned
      Salt and pepper to taste
8   epazote or cilantro leaves, whole, plus 24
      epazote or cilantro leaves, chopped

Prepare the fish stock: Bring water to a boil in a stock pot. Add wine, chicken, fish heads, leek, turnip, carrots, onion, garlic, and parsley. Season lightly with salt and pepper. Reduce heat, and simmer for 1½ hours. Remove stock from heat. Strain. Set aside.

Prepare the spread: Heat oil and butter in a saucepan. Add onion and garlic. Stir in watercress, and salt and pepper to taste. Cook for 20 minutes or until liquid is absorbed.

Prepare the stuffing: Heat oil and butter in a saucepan. Add onion, garlic, mushrooms, and chiles. Salt and pepper to taste. Cook over low heat for about 30 minutes, stirring occasionally, until mixture thickens.

Prepare the pastry shells: On a floured surface, roll dough ⅛ inch thick. Grease 8 serving shells (coquilles), and cover with dough, pressing dough against outside edges of shells. Freeze shells for 2 hours. Preheat oven to 350 degrees. Place shells on baking sheet. Bake shells for 25 minutes or until golden brown. Remove from oven. Carefully separate pastry from shell. Set aside.

Prepare the fish: Grease a baking dish. Sprinkle fish strips with salt and pepper. Place 1 epazote leaf on top of each. Spoon ½ teaspoon of mushroom stuffing on one end of strip, and roll up. Place fish rolls in baking dish, pour fish stock over, and dot with butter. Bake at 350 degrees for 6 to 8 minutes, depending on thickness of fillets. Reserve pan juices.

Prepare the sauce: Heat reduced stock. Add ½ cup pan juices, and stir in half-and-half and crème fraîche. Simmer for 40 minutes, and stir in cheese. Correct salt.

Add dissolved corn starch, and continue cooking for 8 minutes. Stir in butter. Remove from heat, and transfer sauce to a double boiler. Carefully add fish rolls to the sauce. Heat for 10 minutes.

Prepare the garnish: Heat butter in a saucepan. Add carrots, and cook over low heat for 25 minutes or until tender. Season to taste with salt and pepper.

To serve, place 1 pastry shell on each of 8 dishes. Spread with watercress mixture. Top with 6 fish rolls. Put 1 epazote leaf to the side, and spoon carrots onto it. Spoon sauce over. Garnish with chopped epazote, and serve additional sauce in a bowl on the side.
Makes 8 servings.

overleaf left: *Fish in Pastry Shells is a sophisticated dish from Mexico City.*
overleaf right: *Fish Tamales are wrapped in corn husks and steamed.*

PESCADO EN TAMAL
Fish Tamales

Fish tamales originated in pre-Hispanic times, when steaming was a common cooking method. This recipe is a modern version served in the San Angel Inn, a favorite restaurant of tourists and natives alike, located in San Angel, a suburb of Mexico City.

FOR THE STUFFING

¾ cup butter
2 tablespoons olive oil
3 cloves garlic, finely chopped
3 medium white onions, sliced on the diagonal
6 chiles poblanos or California (Anaheim) chiles, roasted, peeled, sliced in strips, and soaked in salted water (see Basics)
Salt and pepper to taste
½ teaspoon freshly ground allspice
½ cup crème fraîche

FOR THE SAUCE

½ cup olive oil
2 cloves garlic, whole
2 medium white onions, sliced on the diagonal
8 chiles poblanos, roasted, peeled, sliced in strips, and soaked in salted water (see Basics)
1½ cups fish stock (see recipe on page 214), reduced to ¾ cup
1 cup crème fraîche or sour cream
1½ cups half-and-half
1 tablespoon corn starch, dissolved in a little water
Salt to taste
1 teaspoon freshly ground pepper
½ cup butter

FOR THE FISH

8 whitefish, preferably from Patzcuaro, 7 to 8 ounces each, deboned, or 8 grouper or red snapper fillets, thinly sliced
Salt and pepper to taste

FOR THE HUSKS

48 fresh corn husks, whole, plus 8 fresh corn husks, sliced in thin strips

Prepare the stuffing: Heat butter and oil in a saucepan. Sauté garlic until light brown. Add onions, and sauté until transparent. Add chile strips, and cook over low heat for 20 minutes. Season with salt, pepper, and allspice. Add crème fraîche, and cook, stirring, until thick and creamy. Remove from heat.

Prepare the sauce: Heat oil in a saucepan. Brown garlic, and remove. Add onion, and brown; then add chile strips. Cook over low heat for 25 minutes, stirring occasionally. Stir in reduced fish stock. Add crème fraîche, half-and-half, dissolved corn starch, salt, and pepper. Cook over medium heat for 15 minutes, stirring, until sauce thickens. Remove from heat, and keep warm in a double boiler. Add butter, and stir.

Prepare the fish: Season fish with salt and pepper. Fill with 2 tablespoons of stuffing. (If using fillet slices, spread stuffing, and roll to enclose.)

Open 6 corn husks flat, overlapping ends. Place whole fish or rolled fillet in center. Cover fish with sauce, and fold husks over, wrapping well and tying closed with husk strips. Repeat until you have 8 packages. Place on a steamer rack lined with aluminum foil. Steam fish for 30 minutes or until tender. Do not overcook, and do not let boiling water come in contact with fish tamales.

To serve, place fish tamales on individual dishes. Unwrap, and cover with sauce. Serve remaining sauce in a bowl.

Makes 8 tamales.

TORTAS
Hard-Roll Sandwiches

Tortas, or hard-roll sandwiches, are sold on virtually every street corner throughout Mexico City. These Mexican-style hero sandwiches are filled with veal cutlets, shredded chicken, cheese and avocado, sausage, or ham, and, invariably, are topped with a chile jalapeño *or* chipotle.

FOR THE SANDWICH

8	teleras or French-bread rolls, about 4 inches long, slit lengthwise and with some bread removed
2	cups refried black beans (see recipe on page 187)
32	thin slices boiled ham
24	slices fresh cheese, such as panela or feta
16	slices tomato
2⅔	cups lettuce, shredded and well dried
½	cup California avocado, chopped
½	cup sour cream
16	canned pickled chiles jalapeños, sliced in strips (or see recipe on page 185)
	Salt to taste

FOR THE GARNISH

16	slices tomato
8	canned pickled chiles jalapeños, sliced in strips

Spread bread bases with refried beans. Top each with 4 ham slices, 3 cheese slices, and 2 tomato slices. Divide lettuce, avocado, and sour cream evenly among bread bases, garnishing each with 2 chile strips. Salt.

A variety of cold meats is available for Hard-Roll Sandwiches.

Place bread tops on sandwiches, and press. Slice sandwich in half with a sharp knife.

Serve on individual plates, garnishing each with 2 tomato slices and 1 chile strip.

Makes 8 sandwiches.

overleaf: Until fairly recently, many neighborhoods received regular deliveries of food via the network of Xochimilco canals.

CHICHARRON SUDADO EN SALSA VERDE
Pork Rind in Green Sauce

Pork rind is a traditional Mexican food, very common in city and countryside alike. Fried pork cracklings are served as a snack with lime, often to accompany a shot of tequila. Stewed pork rind is used to fill tacos. Chicharrón is seasoned with different chiles and sauces, depending on the region in which it is prepared.

FOR THE PORK RIND

2	quarts water
18	medium tomatillos, husked
1	medium white onion, halved, plus ½ medium white onion, plus 1½ white onions, finely chopped
10	cloves garlic, whole
8	chiles serranos or 3 chiles jalapeños
30	sprigs cilantro, plus ¾ cup cilantro, finely chopped
	Salt to taste
1¾	pounds pork rind, cut in 2½- to 3-inch cubes

FOR THE GARNISH

2	tablespoons knob onion, finely chopped
2	tablespoons cilantro, finely chopped

Bring water to a boil in a saucepan. Add tomatillos, halved onion, 6 garlic cloves, and chiles. Boil for 20 minutes. Remove from heat. Strain, reserving water. In a blender or food processor, purée cooked ingredients, 2 cups cooking water, ½ onion, 4 garlic cloves, cilantro sprigs, and salt. Blend for 3 minutes.

In a double boiler, place a layer of pork rind, green sauce, chopped onion, and chopped cilantro. Repeat layers. Cover pan, and simmer over low heat for 1½ to 2 hours or until pork rind is tender and well cooked.

Serve pork in a clay cazuela, garnishing with onion and cilantro. Accompany with Mexican rice, freshly made tortillas, and frijoles de olla.
Makes 8 servings.

TACOS DE PLAZA
Plaza Tacos

Plaza tacos are prepared and eaten in marketplaces. They usually are held so the end of the rolled tortilla is folded up to prevent the stuffing from dripping out.

FOR THE STUFFINGS

1½	cups pig's feet in vinegar (see recipe on page 90)
1½	cups avocado mashed with ½ pound pork rind
8	slices tomato
4	slices white onion
20	slices fresh cheese, such as feta, mozzarella, or ricotta
1½	cups cactus-pad salad (see recipe on page 245)
1½	cups pork, Santa Rosa de Jauregi style (see recipe on page 155)
1	cup fresh-water shrimp (see recipe on page 214)

FOR THE GARNISH

1	recipe green sauce (see recipe on page 104)
1	recipe red sauce (see recipe on page 189)
40	sprigs papalo or cilantro
30	sprigs cilantro
1½	cups sour cream

FOR THE TACOS

72	corn tortillas, freshly made

Assemble the stuffings: Place pig's feet on a platter. Arrange avocado and pork rind, tomato, and onion around them. Sprinkle with cheese. On separate platters, arrange cactus-pad salad, pork, and shrimp.

Assemble the garnishes: Pour red and green sauces into molcajetes or serving bowls. Place papalo, cilantro, and sour cream in separate bowls.

To make tacos, overlap 3 warm tortillas on each of 8 plates. Place 2 tablespoons of each stuffing in the center of each tortilla. Serve open-faced. Garnish tacos with green and red sauces, papalo, cilantro, and sour cream.
Makes 24 tacos.

Colorful boats cruise the Xochimilco canals.

Freshly gathered honey is often substituted for sugar in dessert recipes.

SORBETE DE HIGO
Fig Sherbet

FOR THE SYRUP

2½ cups sugar
 2 cups plus 1 tablespoon water

FOR THE SHERBET

3½ pounds fresh figs, peeled
    Ice cubes
    Coarse salt (kosher salt)

FOR THE GARNISH (OPTIONAL)

 ½ watermelon shell, sliced lengthwise
    Fig leaves
16 figs, halved

Prepare the syrup: Put sugar and water in a medium saucepan. Bring to a boil over high heat. Stir with a wooden spoon, making sure sugar is well dissolved. Stop stirring. Bring mixture to a rolling boil. Remove from heat, and immediately pour into a bowl. Cool.

Prepare the sherbet: The day before serving, purée figs in a blender or food processor, and pour into a glass bowl. Add cooled syrup, stir, and let stand for 10 minutes. Grind ice, and mix with salt. Place in a large bowl. Set figs in bowl on the ice to chill thoroughly. Beat mixture by hand or pour into an electric ice-cream maker. Process until sherbet sets. Freeze overnight.

To serve, place watermelon shell on a platter, and surround with fig leaves. Fill with scoops of sherbet, and garnish with figs.
Makes about 2 quarts.

A patio inside the renowned San Angel Inn Restaurant.

Throughout their country's history, Mexican cooks have adopted foods and adapted cuisines from foreign lands to suit their taste. Mangoes, formerly imported from the Far East, are now cultivated domestically.

MANGOS CON SALSA DE FRESA Y FRAMBUESA

Mangoes with Strawberry and Raspberry Sauce

Mangoes always can be found in Mexico City, although they are most abundant and inexpensive in May. They vary tremendously in size and flavor, depending on the variety.

FOR THE MANGOES

8 mangoes, peeled

FOR THE SAUCE

1 pound strawberries, washed and hulled
1 pound raspberries, washed and hulled
1 cup sugar, or to taste
½ cup Kahlúa or other coffee liqueur

FOR THE GARNISH

24 strawberries, sliced

Slice the mangoes, and refrigerate for 1 hour.
Prepare the sauce: Blend strawberries, raspberries,

sugar, and Kahlúa in a blender or food processor.
To serve, place the mango slices on each of 8 dessert plates. Drench with sauce, and garnish with strawberries.
Makes 8 servings.

MANGOS, ZARZAMORAS Y FRAMBUESAS

Mangoes, Blackberries, and Raspberries

Blackberries, raspberries, and boysenberries are cultivated in the Valle de Bravo region. They are combined to make a delicious, fresh, and refreshing dessert.

FOR THE FRUIT

8 mangoes, peeled, pitted, and halved
 Sugar to taste
1 pound blackberries or boysenberries, washed
1 pound raspberries, washed
½ cup Kahlúa or orange liqueur

FOR THE GARNISH

1½ cups heavy cream, chilled in freezer for 1 hour
1 cup sour cream, chilled in freezer for 1 hour
½ cup sugar
 Pecan brittle, ground (see recipe on page 59)

Prepare the fruit: Line a deep bowl with a layer of mango. Sprinkle with sugar, and cover with a layer of blackberries and raspberries.
Pour liqueur over. Repeat layers until all ingredients are used. Refrigerate for 2 hours.
Meanwhile, prepare the garnish: Beat heavy cream and sour cream together until stiff peaks form. Add sugar, and continue beating for a few seconds. Chill.
To serve, top fruit with whipped cream, and sprinkle pecan brittle on top. Serve immediately.
Makes 8 servings.

Mangoes with Strawberry and Raspberry Sauce makes an elegant dessert.

White-Chocolate Castle Cake is reserved for special occasions.

PASTEL DE CHOCOLATE BLANCO DEL CASTILLO
White-Chocolate Castle Cake

Maximilian, archduke of Austria, and Carlota, a Belgian princess, brought French cooking techniques and Austrian pastries to Mexico City in the mid-nineteenth century, when they briefly ruled as emperor and empress of Mexico.

FOR THE BATTER

10	egg yolks
1½	cups sugar
1¼	cups butter, melted and still warm
2	cups pecans, ground
2	cups raw almonds, skinned and ground
⅓	cup flour

¼ to ½	teaspoon almond extract
¾	teaspoon vanilla extract
10	egg whites

FOR THE SYRUP

1½	cups water
¾	cup sugar
¾	cup kirsch or rum

FOR THE FROSTING

8	egg yolks
1⅔	cups sugar
⅔	cup water
2¼	cups butter, at room temperature
9	ounces white chocolate, grated
¼	teaspoon almond extract
½	cup kirsch

FOR THE GARNISH

11	ounces white-chocolate curls

Preheat oven to 350 degrees. Grease and flour 2 9-inch round cake pans.

Prepare the batter: Beat egg yolks until foamy and lemon-colored. Gradually add sugar, and beat until mixture forms a ribbon when poured from a spoon. Add butter, a little at a time, until mixture forms a thick paste. Add pecans and almonds. Stir. Fold flour and almond and vanilla extracts into mixture, being careful not to overmix. Beat egg whites until they form stiff peaks, and fold into batter.

Fill cake pans equally with the batter. Bake for 45 minutes or until done. Remove from oven. Cool for 10 minutes, and remove from pans. Cool completely, and set on plate(s) with high rim.

Meanwhile, prepare the syrup: Heat water and sugar in a saucepan, and boil over medium heat for 20 minutes. Remove from heat, and stir in liqueur. Pour syrup over the cooled cakes, allowing the cakes to absorb the syrup totally.

Prepare the frosting: Beat egg yolks until foamy and lemon-colored. Set aside. Heat sugar and water in a saucepan, stirring until the sugar dissolves. Stop stirring, and heat until mixture reaches hard ball stage (260 degrees on a candy thermometer). Add sugar to eggs in a slow, steady stream, beating constantly with an electric mixer. Continue beating until mixture is cool. Gradually mix in butter and chocolate, alternating. Add almond extract and kirsch, and continue beating until thick and smooth.

Place 1 tablespoonful of frosting on a 12-inch serving plate in order to stabilize cake layers. Place one cake layer on plate, and frost. Top with second layer, and frost sides and top of cake. Swirl frosting with a spatula. Sprinkle with white-chocolate curls.

Makes 8 to 12 servings.

MOUSSE DE MANDARINA
Tangerine Mousse

FOR THE MOUSSE

5	egg yolks
1½	cups sugar
⅓	cup lime juice
3	cups tangerine juice
1	tablespoon tangerine peel, grated
1	tablespoon orange peel, grated
½	teaspoon lime peel, grated
3½	envelopes (⅞ ounce) unflavored gelatin
	Pinch of salt
1½	cups tangerine, chopped
1½	cups heavy cream, chilled in freezer for 1 hour
1½	cups crème fraîche or sour cream, chilled in freezer for 1 hour
3	egg whites
⅓	cup sugar

FOR THE GARNISH

⅓	cup powdered sugar
½	cup raw almonds, skinned, toasted, and chopped
6	kumquat branches, with leaves (optional)
	Orange leaves (optional)

With an electric mixer, beat the egg yolks until lemon-colored. Add sugar, and continue beating until mixture is thick. In a nonaluminum saucepan, heat the lime juice and 1½ cups tangerine juice to the boiling point. Add to egg-yolk mixture. Lower speed, and continue beating for 10 minutes, adding grated peels. The mixture must be thick.

Moisten gelatin and salt in 1½ cups tangerine juice for 20 minutes. Heat until the gelatin melts. Cool, and add to egg-yolk mixture. Refrigerate until the mixture begins to set. Fold in tangerine. Beat heavy cream and crème fraîche together until stiff. Fold into mousse mixture. Beat egg whites until stiff, then mix in sugar. Continue beating until the egg whites are shiny. Carefully fold into mousse.

Butter a 2-quart soufflé dish, and ring with a waxed-paper collar. Carefully pour mousse into dish. Refrigerate for 6 hours or overnight.

To serve, remove collar. Sprinkle with sugar and almonds. Decorate with kumquats and orange leaves.

Makes 8 to 12 servings.

Tangerines are used to make beverages, sherbets, and this delicious mousse.

SORBETE DE JAMAICA
Hibiscus-Blossom Sherbet

Hibiscus grows abundantly in the coastal state of Guerrero. The blossoms are commonly used to make fresh beverages and jellies, since their acidic flavor lends a special tang.

FOR THE SHERBET

1	pound dried hibiscus blossoms
1½	quarts water
1½	to 1¾ cups syrup, cooled (see recipe on page 224)
2	egg whites, beaten until stiff

FOR THE GARNISH

12	strawberries
8	mint leaves
8	small bunches green grapes

The day before serving, wash hibiscus blossoms, and soak in a bowl of water for 1 hour. Transfer blossoms and soaking water to nonaluminum saucepan. Bring to a boil, and boil for 10 minutes. Cool. Strain, reserving liquid. Reserve 24 blossoms for garnish. Measure 2½ cups liquid, and mix with syrup. Fold in egg whites.

To freeze, follow procedure for fig sherbet (see recipe on page 224).

To serve, mound sherbet balls one on top of another. Garnish with blossoms, strawberries, mint leaves, and grapes.

Makes 1 quart.

SORBETE DE MANGO
Mango Sherbet

Mango sherbet can be made from fresh or canned fruit. Fresh mangoes are plentiful from March to September.

In chinampas, or "floating gardens," brilliant flowers and choice vegetables are grown and then transported by boat to wharf-side markets.

Chinampas are located along the Xochimilco canals.

FOR THE SHERBET

3½	pounds mango pulp
2⅔	cups syrup, cooled (see recipe on page 224)

FOR THE GARNISH

24	strawberries
8	mint leaves

The day before serving, purée mango pulp in a blender or food processor. Strain through a mesh strainer. Combine with syrup.

To freeze, follow procedure for fig sherbet (see recipe on page 224).

To serve, mound sherbet balls one on top of another. Garnish with strawberries and mint leaves.

Makes 2 quarts.

SOMBRERO DE CHOCOLATE
Chocolate Hat

Chocolate is native to Mexico. Before the conquest, Indians used cocoa beans in hot drinks, enjoying chocolate for its natural bitter taste or sweetening it with locally produced honey.

FOR THE CHOCOLATE HAT

Parchment paper
1½ pounds bittersweet chocolate, in pieces
7 ounces sweet chocolate, in pieces
17 ounces milk chocolate, in pieces

FOR THE SAUCE

9 Manila mangoes, peeled, pitted, and sliced
1½ cups sugar
⅓ cup Kahlúa or other coffee liqueur
¼ cup tequila
1 teaspoon lime juice
3 cups fresh orange or tangerine juice

FOR THE GARNISH

1 quart lime sherbet
1 quart fig sherbet (see recipe on page 224)
1 quart blackberry sherbet
6 bougainvillaea branches or other flower branches (optional)

Prepare the chocolate hat: From parchment paper, cut a circle 15 inches in diameter (for base of the hat), a circle 8 inches in diameter (for top of the hat), and a rectangle 5 by 15 inches.

Bring water to a boil in a double boiler from which steam does not escape. Melt bittersweet, sweet, and 11 ounces milk chocolate together, stirring occasionally.

When chocolate reaches 85 degrees on a candy thermometer, remove from heat.

Pour half the chocolate onto a marble or metal surface. Keep remaining half warm in the double boiler. Cool chocolate on marble surface by stirring constantly with a spatula until it reaches 75 degrees. Add remaining chocolate, and mix well.

Using a spatula, spread chocolate ¼ inch thick over 15-inch parchment circle. Repeat procedure with 8-inch circle. Set aside for 3 hours to cool or until hard. Keep remaining chocolate melted in double boiler. *Do not* overheat. Spread warm chocolate over hardened chocolate circles, reserving some. Curl up sides of the large circle.

Form an 8¼-inch wide, 5-inch high cylinder with parchment rectangle, stapling to keep the form. Spread cylinder with melted chocolate. Cool slightly, and brush to give texture. Place upright on baking sheet, and cool. Peel off paper.

Peel paper from large circle, and place chocolate on a 16-inch round plate.

Melt remaining 6 ounces milk chocolate. Cover large circle with a thin layer of melted milk chocolate, and center the cylinder upright on top. Cover cylinder with a little melted chocolate. Peel paper from small circle, and place chocolate on top of cylinder.

Prepare the sauce: Purée all ingredients in a blender or food processor. Strain.

To serve, decorate brim of hat with scoops of sherbets and bougainvillaea branches. (You may substitute other fresh-fruit sherbets, such as pineapple, mamey, tangerine, zapote, lemon, guanabana, or grapefruit.) Serve mango sauce on the side to flavor sherbets.
Makes 24 servings.

Chocolate Hat is decorated with scoops of fresh-fruit sherbet, bougainvillaea blossoms, and strawberries.

CENTRAL MEXICO

No dish is more Mexican than *mole*, the rich concoction of spices, nuts, chiles, and chocolate that only the uninitiated would demean with the word *sauce*. Of the many *moles* prepared throughout Mexico, none is more widely served than *mole poblano*— Puebla-style *mole*. It has become a national standard. *Mole poblano's* unique mix of flavors epitomizes the central Mexican cuisine and culture, of which Puebla is the traditional center.

As with many Puebla specialties, the origin of *mole poblano* is traced by legend to a colonial-era convent. The nuns, daughters of Puebla aristocrats, were attended by Indian servants, and together they turned the Puebla convents into laboratories of gastronomic hybridization. The cavernous, tiled convent kitchens produced daring mixtures of indigenous and traditional Spanish ingredients, laying the basis for what are still some of the most complex dishes of Mexican cuisine. Similar experimentation flourished in Pachuca and Tlaxcala, which, like Puebla, were provincial capitals intensely proud of their Iberian culture, yet permeated by the influence of their Indian hinterlands.

Puebla tile makers, who craft the celebrated Talavera crockery, were originally renowned for their painted ceramic tiles.

One eighteenth-century Lenten Sunday, the legend goes, the bishop of Puebla invited the Spanish viceroy to dine at the convent of Santa Rosa, which was renowned throughout New Spain for its fine cuisine. The names of the bishop and the viceroy have long since been forgotten by most Mexicans, but not the name of Sor Andrea de la Asunción, the cook who was asked to impress the noble visitors with a meal unlike any they had ever tasted. Sor Andrea selected fresh spices from her walk-in cupboards: anise, clove, cinnamon, black pepper, and several varieties of dried Mexican chiles—*ancho, mulato, pasilla,* and *chipotle.* To these, she added fried garlic, *tomatillos,* tortillas, and sesame seeds; ground almonds and peanuts; and—the definitive touch—bitter Puebla chocolate, an ingredient that would have been an arresting novelty to the European palate. Carefully cooked and blended, the thick, gravy-like mixture was ladled over the convent's own corn-fed, chestnut-stuffed turkey. The bishop and his royal guest, chroniclers agree, were wildly enthusiastic. Word of this success spread quickly to other Puebla convents, each of which soon perfected its own distinctive variation of the rich new dish—and so *mole poblano* was born.

The tall mountains and lush valleys surrounding Puebla provide some of the most dramatic countryside in Mexico. A center of Mesoamerican culture for more than two millennia, the region boasts some of Mexico's finest pre-Columbian monuments, among them the magnificent Mayan murals of Cacaxtla and the massive Cholula pyramid, the largest such structure in the New World. On plots bordering these ruins, peasant farmers still cultivate the foods that were the bases of their ancestors' diet: corn, beans, tomatoes, chiles, and amaranth (a little-known but nutritious grain eaten widely today in candied *alegrías*, a kind of protein-rich alternative to the popcorn ball).

To the north of Puebla, in the states of Tlaxcala and Hidalgo, vast fields are planted with maguey, which has been cultivated for centuries as a source of food and clothing. The plant itself is not eaten, but the colonies of edible worms (*gusanos*) that it supports are. In one preparation, the worms are fried and served in tortilla shells. Maguey fibers make rough but durable thread, and its thorns provide serviceable needles. Maguey's primary attraction, however, is its sap, the raw material of the mild fermented liquor called *pulque*. The main cash crop of the region's great colonial estates, *pulque* is still drunk and is used as a cooking ingredient. It is the base for a marinade in a sophisticated roasted pork entrée typical of Hidalgo—*lomo de puerco en pulque*. Maguey has other culinary uses as well. The region's famous *mixiote* meats, including mutton, are wrapped in the plant's outer leaf during barbecuing to produce a very tender, succulent meat flavored with the aroma of maguey. Chicken and fish also are cooked *mixiote* style.

Nowhere in Mexico did the conquering Spaniards feel more at home than in the Puebla–Tlaxcala region. In fact, the city of Puebla was founded by the Spaniards, not by Mexican Indians. The Spaniards convinced local Indian leaders to join forces against their historic enemies, the Aztecs—or Mexicas—of the nearby valley that is now Mexico City. The fusion of Spanish and Mesoamerican culture in central Mexico produced an exuberant ecclesiastical architecture that was unequaled in the Americas. Riotous native color schemes transformed the Spaniards' Moorish-derived tile work into a distinctively Mexican style that still adorns the façades and domes of scores of colonial-era churches. Puebla tile makers also began to produce fine crockery, which came to be known as Talavera ware, after the celebrated Spanish dinnerware. The Mexican product—quite unlike the aristocratic Spanish original, with its subdued tones and elaborately illustrated scenes—is an uninhibited combination of Iberian, Islamic, and indigenous Mexican decorative influences. Throughout Mexico, Puebla's and Tlaxcala's Talavera pottery is considered to be the most elegant and appropriate dinnerware on which to serve a fine Mexican meal.

After Mexico won its independence from Spain, settlers from the Old World continued to put down roots in the region. The influence of these often non-Spanish immigrants can be tasted in the *pastes* of Pachuca, derived from the pasties and shepherd's pie favored by the Britons who once ran Hidalgo's silver mines.

Still, from the rugged mining districts of Hidalgo to the cactus fields of Tlaxcala and the orchards of the high sierra of Puebla, the central region's culture and cuisine remain aggressively, unquestionably Mexican. While *mole poblano* is the meal most representative of the area's gastronomic identity, another product of the Puebla convent kitchens best symbolizes the sense of indigenous inventiveness. *Chiles en nogada* is batter-fried chiles stuffed with assorted fruits, meats, and spices that challenge all stereotypes about Mexican cooking. *Chiles en nogada* is served cold and is sweet rather than spicy, and its presentation is a work of patriotic folk art: fresh pomegranate seeds and parsley sprinkled over a white, creamy walnut sauce. The presentation is a culinary version of the Mexican flag. An epicure seeking a definitive sampling of Mexican *haute cuisine* could do no better than a meal of *mole poblano* and *chiles en nogada*, preferably served on Talavera dinnerware. That these are all products of Puebla is telling evidence of the central region's seminal contributions to Mexican cooking—and to Mexican national culture.

Lush, verdant landscape provides grazing areas for central Mexico's livestock.

SOPA DE AGUACATE FRIA ESTILO ATLIXCO
Cold Avocado Soup, Atlixco Style

Atlixco is one of the most important avocado-producing areas of Mexico. What is known as the California avocado was developed from this Mexican fruit.

FOR THE BROTH

5	quarts water
4	chicken legs and thighs
6	chicken wings
I	white onion, sliced
I	head garlic, unpeeled and halved
3	carrots
6	ribs celery
2	bay leaves
6	mint leaves or ¼ teaspoon dried mint
6	black peppercorns
	Salt to taste

FOR THE SOUP

½	cup butter
I	white onion, puréed
2	cloves garlic, puréed
½	leek, puréed
I	carrot, puréed
6	ripe California avocados, peeled
I	cup crème fraîche or heavy cream
I	cup plain yogurt, beaten
	Salt to taste
2	tablespoons lime juice
½	cup olive oil

FOR THE GARNISH

¼	cup white onion, finely chopped
2	tablespoons cilantro, finely chopped

Prepare the broth: Bring water to a boil in a stock pot. Add chicken, onion, garlic, carrots, celery, bay leaves, mint, peppercorns, and salt. Simmer over low heat until mixture foams. Skim, and simmer for 1½ hours. Cool for 1 hour, and strain. Skim off fat, and refrigerate. If broth separates, reheat slightly.

Prepare the soup: Melt butter in a saucepan. Add onion, garlic, leek, and carrot with 3 cups broth. Cook until thick, about 25 minutes. Cool. Meanwhile, in a blender or food processor, blend avocados with 6 cups broth. (Blend in batches, if necessary.) Strain. Add crème fraîche and yogurt. Stir in vegetable mixture, and salt to taste. Add lime juice and olive oil. If the soup is too thick, add a little more broth. Chill in freezer for 1 hour.

To serve, pour cold avocado soup into soup bowls fitted in liners filled with crushed ice. Garnish with onion and cilantro.
Makes 8 servings.

HONGOS AL EPAZOTE ESTILO EL CHICO
Mushrooms with Epazote, El Chico Style

½	cup butter
½	cup olive oil
2	cups white onion, minced
½	cup chile serrano, minced
½	cup epazote, finely chopped
3⅓	pounds clavito or fresh, small mushrooms, cleaned and sliced
	Salt to taste

Heat butter and oil in a saucepan over medium heat. Sauté onion, chile, and epazote until onion is translucent. Add mushrooms, and continue to sauté.

Salt to taste, and cook for 25 minutes.

To serve, place the hot mushrooms on a platter, and accompany with freshly made corn tortillas.
Makes 8 servings.

ENSALADA ESTILO TEPEACA
Salad, Tepeaca Style

The town of Tepeaca is located in the Puebla Valley, near the resort town of Tehuacán. The marketplace, at the foot of Orizaba, an inactive volcano, is one of the most important centers of trade in the state. Merchants and farmers from near and far gather every Friday to sell their wares and produce. Women wrapped in traditional shawls carry knob onions, radishes, cabbages, cauliflowers, and chiles on their backs as they make their way to market stands.

FOR THE VINAIGRETTE

⅔	cup fruit vinegar (see recipe on page 128)
½	tablespoon ground thyme
⅓	tablespoon dried oregano
⅓	tablespoon avocado leaves, toasted and ground (optional)
4	cloves garlic, whole
2	tablespoons white onion, chopped
	Salt to taste
1	teaspoon freshly ground pepper
1½	cups olive oil or vegetable oil

FOR THE SALAD

3¼	pounds chivitos or dandelion greens
2	bunches papalo or cilantro, chopped
2	bunches watercress, chopped
1	bunch radishes, sliced
8	slices goat cheese, covered with ashes

Prepare the vinaigrette: Blend vinegar, thyme, oregano, avocado leaves, garlic, onion, salt, and pepper for 30 seconds in a blender or food processor. Lower speed, and gradually add oil. Correct seasoning, and refrigerate for 2 hours.

Prepare the salad: Place chivitos in the center of a platter. Surround with papalo and watercress. Garnish along sides with alternated radish and cheese slices. Refrigerate for 1 hour.

Serve salad with vinaigrette on the side.

Makes 8 servings.

MACHUCAS DE LA HUASTECA
Tortilla Chips, Huasteca Style

Machucas are typical of Mexican cuisine, since they were created using locally available ingredients, such as fresh cream, totomoste, tortillas, and chile.

2¾	cups lard or vegetable oil
50	small tortillas, about 2½ inches in diameter, sliced in squares
15	chiles serranos
1½	white onions, chopped
3	cloves garlic, whole
4½	cups water
2	cups heavy cream
1½	cups half-and-half
6	slices white onion
	Salt to taste
16	totomoste (hierba santa), Swiss chard, or spinach leaves

Preheat oven to 350 degrees.

Heat 2 cups lard in a frying pan to almost smoking. Fry tortilla squares until crisp. Remove, and drain on paper towels. Set aside.

In a blender or food processor, blend chiles, onion, garlic, ½ cup water, cream, and half-and-half. Set aside. Heat ¾ cup lard in another frying pan. Brown onion slices. Pour blended chile mixture into hot frying pan. Cook for 25 minutes at slow boil. Add tortilla chips, and salt to taste. Continue cooking until the chips absorb the sauce, about 10 to 15 minutes.

Meanwhile, bring 4 cups water and salt to a boil in a saucepan. Add totomoste leaves, and boil for 2 minutes. Remove, and drain well.

Butter 8 ramekins. Line each with totomoste leaves. Spoon the machucas into the ramekins. Fold edges of leaves over the stuffing to enclose. Bake for 25 minutes.

To serve, remove the machucas from molds. Place on individual plates with refried beans and a freshly broiled strip of beef sirloin. Serve immediately.

Makes 8 servings.

SOPA DE NOPALES
Cactus-Pad Soup

Nopales, or cactus pads, are commonly served in soup in Tlaxcala.

FOR THE BROTH

6	quarts water
1	5-pound stewing chicken
3	green or bulb onions, with tops
1	head garlic, unpeeled and halved
10	ribs celery
	Salt and pepper to taste

FOR THE NOPALES

3	quarts water
	Salt to taste
½	white onion, sliced, plus 1½ cups white onion, thinly sliced
¼	head garlic, unpeeled
	Skins from 10 tomatoes
4	corn husks, dried (optional)
16	large nopales (cactus pads), sliced in 2- by ½-inch strips
⅓	cup olive oil
8	dry chiles chipotles, fried in a little oil and drained

FOR THE GARNISH

2	cups fresh cheese, such as panela or feta, cubed, plus ⅔ cup fresh cheese, grated

Cactuses have been cultivated for centuries as a source of food and fibers. Nopales, the pads of the nopal cactus, are simmered in a spicy chicken broth and are served with fried pork rind for this soup.

Prepare the broth: Bring water to a boil in a stock pot. Add whole chicken, onions, garlic, and celery. Salt and pepper to taste.

Allow the broth to foam. Skim, and continue cooking over medium heat until the chicken is tender, about 1½ hours. Remove from heat, and cool chicken in broth. Remove chicken. Skim fat from and strain broth. Set aside. (The chicken can be used in taco fillings.)

Prepare the nopales: Bring water to a boil in a clay or ceramic pot. Add salt, sliced onion, garlic, tomato skins, corn husks, and nopales. Boil for 15 minutes or until the vegetables are tender. Strain through a sieve. Reserve vegetables, and set aside.

Heat oil in clay pot. Add thinly sliced onion, and cook until transparent. Add cooked vegetables and chiles. Stir. Add chicken broth, stir, and continue to simmer for 25 minutes.

To serve, pour soup into individual soup bowls. Garnish with cubed and grated cheeses, and serve immediately. Fried bacon or ham can be added as well.
Makes 8 servings.

NOPALES CURTIDOS
Pickled Cactus Pads

Like other cuisines, that of Mexico has changed over the years. Most recently, traditional dishes, such as pickled nopales, have been "lightened" to please proponents of fresh, nutritious foods.

FOR THE NOPALES

4¼	quarts water
1	head garlic, in pieces
6	green-onion tops
4	tomatillo peels or corn husks
¼	teaspoon baking soda
	Salt to taste
16	fresh nopales (cactus pads) or 6 cups canned nopales

FOR THE VINAIGRETTE

1	cup cider vinegar
	Salt to taste
	Sugar to taste
1	teaspoon freshly ground pepper
1	teaspoon black peppercorns
1	bunch fresh bay leaves (about 20 leaves) or 8 dried bay leaves
20	sprigs marjoram or 1 tablespoon dried marjoram
20	sprigs thyme or 1 tablespoon dried thyme
1	tablespoon dried oregano
32	knob onions, with tops, halved
1	head garlic, peeled and sliced
2½	cups safflower, corn, and olive oils, combined in equal quantities

Prepare the nopales: Bring water to a rolling boil in a large saucepan. Add garlic, onion tops, tomatillo peels, baking soda, salt, and nopales. Boil for 35 minutes or until nopales are tender. (Cooking time depends on freshness and size of nopales.) Strain through a mesh

The cathedral of Tlaxcala was built in the eighteenth century.

strainer, reserving 1 cup cooking water.

Prepare the vinaigrette: Put vinegar in a bowl. Add salt and sugar. Stir to dissolve well. Add pepper, peppercorns, bay leaves, marjoram, thyme, oregano, onions, and garlic. Stir in oils and reserved cooking water. Shake to mix, and pour vinaigrette over nopales. Marinate for 2 days in the refrigerator.

To serve, arrange 1 nopal on top of another. Garnish with onion, garlic, and fresh herbs, if desired. Pour vinaigrette over.
Makes 8 servings.

overleaf: The cardona cactus is identifiable by red prickly pears that sprout among its pads.

Cactus pads, garlic, tomatoes, and fresh herbs are the basic ingredients for a flavorful salad.

NOPALES EN ENSALADA
Cactus-Pad Salad

FOR THE SALAD

2½ quarts water
20 nopales (cactus pads), sliced in strips about ¼ to ½ inch wide
4 cloves garlic, whole
½ white onion
4 fresh corn husks (optional)
10 tomatillo husks
    Salt to taste
⅔ cup cider vinegar
1 cup olive oil
3 slices white onion, sliced on the diagonal

Cactus pads can be marinated for a tangy appetizer of Pickled Cactus Pads.

FOR THE GARNISH

2 California avocados, sliced
2 tomatoes, sliced
1½ cups cilantro, chopped
6 chiles de árbol, or any small dried red chile, fried in a little oil and deveined (see Basics)
2 cups fresh or feta cheese, crumbled extra fine

Bring water to a boil in a saucepan. Add nopal strips, garlic, onion, corn husks, tomatillo husks, and salt. Boil for 30 to 40 minutes or until nopal is tender. Strain through a metal sieve. While nopal is still hot, put it in a glass bowl. Mix salt, vinegar, oil, and onion slices. Pour over nopal, and marinate for 1 hour.

To serve, place nopal strips on a dish. On top, layer with avocado and tomato slices, cilantro, chiles, and cheese, finishing with cheese. Serve with freshly made corn tortillas.

Makes 8 servings.

ARROZ VERDE CON LANGOSTINOS
Green Rice with Crayfish

This dish, typical of Puebla and Veracruz, derives its flavor from the chiles poblanos *and bell peppers.*

FOR THE RICE

2½	cups long-grain white rice
2	cups vegetable oil
12	cloves garlic, whole
1	white onion, halved, plus 1½ white onions, chopped
4	chiles poblanos, cleaned, seeded, deveined (see Basics), and chopped
3	green or red bell peppers, chopped
3½	cups hot water
	Salt to taste
8	red snapper, grouper, or sea bass fillets, about 3½ inches wide and ½ inch thick
2	pounds clams, soaked and cleaned
8	large crayfish, cleaned

FOR THE GARNISH

4	green or red bell peppers, roasted (see Basics), peeled, and sliced

Soak rice in hot water to cover for 15 minutes. Drain and rinse in a mesh sieve until water runs clear. Drain well.

Heat oil in a deep skillet. Add 6 garlic cloves and halved onion. Fry until golden.

Add rice, and fry until brown, stirring frequently. Strain rice, and return to skillet.

In a blender or food processor, purée 6 garlic cloves, chopped onion, chiles, and peppers. Add to rice in skillet, and cook until fat begins to rise to the surface. Add water and salt to taste.

Add fish, clams, and crayfish. Correct seasoning. Cover skillet, and cook over low heat for 45 minutes. Remove from heat, and let stand, still covered, for 25 minutes.

To serve, place rice on a large platter, with crayfish on top. Garnish with pepper.

Makes 8 to 12 servings.

MIXIOTES ESTILO CACAXTLA
Pork in Maguey Leaves, Cacaxtla Style

FOR THE SAUCE

7	to 8 ounces thin chiles guajillos, roasted, seeded, deveined, and soaked in water for 20 minutes (see Basics)
½	cup lard
8	plum tomatoes, 3 ounces each, roasted (see Basics)
12	cloves garlic, whole
1½	white onions, coarsely chopped
¾	tablespoon cumin seeds
1	stick cinnamon, 4 inches long, toasted
	Salt to taste
1	teaspoon freshly ground pepper

FOR THE PORK

8	pork hocks
8	maguey leaves, 12 inches long, or 8 pieces parchment paper, 12 inches square

Prepare the sauce: In a blender or food processor, purée chiles, adding some soaking water if too thick. Add lard, tomatoes, garlic, onion, cumin, cinnamon, salt, and pepper.

Prepare the pork: Put 1 hock in the middle of a leaf. Generously cover with red sauce. Fold the corners of the leaf over hock to enclose it in a pouch. Trim protruding edges, and tie with string to secure. Repeat procedure for remaining 7 hocks.

Put a rack in a clay pot or steamer containing water. Cover rack with aluminum foil. Perforate foil with a fork all over. Place stuffed leaves on foil in an upright position. Cover with layer of leaves or foil and a dish towel. Put lid on steamer. Bring water to a boil, and steam for 2 hours or until pork is tender. If necessary, add more water during steaming. Do not let water boil onto mixiotes during cooking.

To serve, place 1 mixiote on each of 8 plates, and unwrap to expose pork hock. Serve with beans and yellow or blue corn tortillas.

Makes 8 mixiotes.

CHALUPITAS DE SAN FRANCISCO
Chalupitas, San Francisco Style

Chalupitas have become a tradition in the Pueblan town of San Francisco, where they are eaten for breakfast, lunch, and dinner, or as a light snack.

FOR THE PORK

5	quarts water
2¼	pounds boneless pork loin, in chunks
1	white onion
1	head garlic, halved
	Salt to taste

FOR THE CHIPOTLE SAUCE

3	cloves garlic, whole
½	white onion
	Salt to taste
2	dry chiles chipotles, fried and soaked in water for 10 minutes (see Basics)
2	dry chiles moritas, fried and soaked in water for 10 minutes (see Basics), or substitute 2 additional chiles chipotles
4	tomatoes, roasted (see Basics)
1	cup water

FOR THE GREEN SAUCE

1½	quarts water
15	tomatillos, husked
6	cloves garlic, whole
½	white onion, sliced, plus ½ white onion
7	chiles serranos
1½	cups cilantro
	Salt to taste

FOR THE DOUGH

1¾	pounds fresh masa or equivalent made with masa harina (see Basics)
1	teaspoon salt
4	cups lard

FOR THE GARNISH

1½	cups white onion, finely chopped

Prepare the pork: Bring water to a boil in a saucepan. Add pork, onion, garlic, and salt. Return to boil, and reduce heat to low. Cover, and cook for 2 hours or until the meat is tender. Cool pork in broth. Remove pork from broth, and shred it.

Prepare the chipotle sauce: Purée the garlic and onion in a molcajete, blender, or food processor. Salt. Add chiles chipotles and moritas, tomatoes, and a little water. Purée. Sauce should be thick, but add a little more water if it becomes very thick. Correct salt.

Prepare the green sauce: Bring water to a boil in a saucepan. Add tomatillos, 4 garlic cloves, sliced onion, and 6 chiles. Cook at slow boil for 25 minutes, and drain, reserving cooking water. Purée tomatillo mixture in a molcajete, blender, or food processor with 2 garlic cloves, ½ onion, 1 chile, and cilantro. Add a little cooking water so the mixture forms a thick sauce. Salt.

Prepare the dough: Put masa dough in a glass bowl. Add salt, and knead with a little warm water until pliable, but not sticky. Put dough aside for 20 minutes. Meanwhile, heat a comal or griddle.

Form balls 1½ inches in diameter, and make tortillas using a tortilla press (see Basics). Cook tortillas on the comal, turning once. The tortillas can be made a day ahead and refrigerated in a plastic bag.

To serve in the traditional manner, prepare a brazier with charcoal. Heat a square comal on brazier. Heat lard in a frying pan, and pour a little on the comal. Fry the tortillas in the lard. Top each with 1 tablespoon of either chipotle or green sauce, and add layers of finely chopped onion, shredded pork, and more onion. Dribble lard over chalupita, and continue to heat on the comal briefly, until it becomes slightly crisp. Serve immediately, alternating the red-sauce (chipotle) and green-sauce chalupitas on a platter.

The chalupitas can be prepared on a stove-top griddle as well as on a brazier.
Makes about 20 chalupitas.

LOMO DE PUERCO EN PULQUE
Pork Loin in Pulque

Jacqueline Saenz, a Mexico City scholar, professor, and art collector, shared this recipe for pork loin and also allowed photography with some of her priceless pre-Hispanic artifacts, dating to A.D. 900 to 1500.

FOR THE MARINADE

- 1   large white onion, puréed
- 6   medium cloves garlic, puréed or put through a press
- 2   cups pulque or beer
-     Salt to taste
- 1   tablespoon freshly ground pepper

FOR THE PORK

- 3¼   pounds pork loin, in 1 piece
- 1   strip pork rib chops, the same length as the pork loin
- ½   cup vegetable oil or lard
- 3   cups chicken broth (see recipe on page 202)

FOR THE SAUCE

- 6   chiles anchos, roasted, seeded, deveined, and soaked in hot water for 1 hour (see Basics)
- 4   chiles mulatos, roasted, seeded, deveined, and soaked in hot water for 1 hour (see Basics)
- 4   chiles guajillos, roasted, seeded, deveined, and soaked in hot water for 1 hour (see Basics)
- 4   chiles pasillas, roasted, seeded, deveined, and soaked in hot water for 1 hour (see Basics)
- 1   chile chipotle, roasted, seeded, deveined, and soaked in hot water for 1 hour (see Basics)
- 6   cloves, roasted (see Basics)
- 1   stick cinnamon, roasted (see Basics)
- 1   teaspoon pepper
- 1½   white onions, puréed, plus 2 white onions, sliced
- 6   cloves garlic, puréed or put through a press, plus 1 head garlic

Pork Loin in Pulque is served with a goblet of pulque. In the background are pieces from the collection of pre-Hispanic art belonging to the Saenz family.

- ¾   cup olive oil or lard
- 6   bay leaves
- 2   sprigs thyme
- 2   sprigs marjoram
- 1   teaspoon oregano, dried and crushed
- 1   cup unrefined brown sugar, chopped or grated, or dark brown sugar
- 1   teaspoon freshly ground allspice
-     Salt and pepper to taste

FOR THE GARNISH

- 16   radishes, shaped like flowers
- 16   knob onions, shaped like flowers
- 2   tablespoons sesame seeds

Prepare the marinade: Mix onion, garlic, pulque, salt, and pepper in a glass bowl. Place pork loin and rib in marinade, and let stand for 24 hours in the refrigerator.

Prepare the sauce: In a blender or food processor, blend chiles, cloves, cinnamon, pepper, puréed onion, and puréed garlic.

Heat oil in a saucepan. Add sliced onion and garlic head. Brown. Add blended chile mixture, stirring in bay leaves, thyme, marjoram, oregano, sugar, allspice, salt, and pepper. Cook over low heat until sauce thickens. Blend sauce in a blender or food processor. Pour over pork loin. Marinate at room temperature for 1 hour. Remove meat from sauce, and wipe dry.

Heat oil in a wide pan, and add loin and rib. Brown well on all sides. Add blended sauce and chicken broth. Cover pan, and cook until pork is tender, about 2 hours. If the sauce becomes too thick, add more chicken broth. Let pork cool for 20 minutes. Thinly slice ribs and loin.

To serve, place pork on a platter, and cover with sauce. Garnish with radishes, onions, and sesame seeds.

Serve remaining sauce hot, preferably from a molcajete. Accompany with fresh corn tortillas and fried plantains.

Makes 8 to 12 servings.

PIPIAN VERDE
Pork in Green Pipián Sauce

Pipián, or fricassee in a sauce of ground nuts, seeds, and spices, is a pre-Hispanic dish that survived the colonial period. Talented cooks at the convent of Santa Rosa em-bellished the original pipián-sauce recipe by combining the sauce with pork.

FOR THE PORK

5	quarts water
4½	pounds boneless pork loin, in chunks
1	head garlic, unpeeled and halved
4	knob onions
	Salt to taste

FOR THE SAUCE

1½	cups lard or vegetable oil
1	pound raw, unsalted pumpkin seeds
9	ounces raw peanuts, skinned
¾	cup sesame seeds
1½	white onions, sliced, plus ½ white onion, quartered
8	cloves garlic, whole
2	cups water
12	tomatillos, husked
8	chiles serranos
4	lettuce leaves
4	radish leaves
1	bunch cilantro or 2 totomaste (hierba santa) leaves, coarsely chopped, discarding stems
½	cup vegetable oil
2	slices white onion

FOR THE GARNISH

16	sprigs cilantro

Pork in Green Pipián Sauce.

Prepare the pork: Bring water to a boil in a saucepan. Add pork, garlic, onions, and salt to taste. Return to boil, and reduce heat to low. Cook for 2½ hours or until the meat is tender. Cool pork in broth.

Meanwhile, prepare the sauce: Heat a saucepan. Heat a little lard in the saucepan. Fry the pumpkin seeds, remove, and drain on paper towels. Add more lard, and fry the peanuts and sesame seeds. Remove, and drain on paper towels. Add more lard, brown the sliced onion and 4 garlic cloves, and remove.

In a separate saucepan, bring water to a boil. Add quartered onion, 4 garlic cloves, tomatillos, and chiles. Boil slowly for 25 minutes. Remove from heat, and drain. In a blender or food processor, blend tomatillo mixture, pumpkin seeds, peanuts, sesame seeds, and browned onion and garlic with lettuce leaves, radish leaves, and cilantro. Strain through a sieve, and set aside.

Heat oil in a saucepan, and brown the onion slices. Add pipián sauce, and cook until the fat rises to the surface.

Add pork broth to thin sauce to desired consistency. Add pork and salt. Simmer for 40 minutes.

To serve, ladle the pork in pipián sauce onto plates, and garnish with cilantro sprigs.

Makes 8 servings.

Cactus fiber is used to wrap seasoned meats for steam baking.

MIXIOTES DE POLLO ESTILO PAPATLA

Chicken in Maguey Leaves, Papatla Style

4	chicken breasts, halved and slightly pounded
8	maguey leaves, 7 inches long, or 8 pieces parchment paper, 6 to 7 inches square
	Salt and pepper to taste
48	tomatillos, husked and diced
4	to 6 chiles serranos, chopped
4	cups white onion, minced
2	cups cilantro, chopped
8	sprigs epazote
1	cup vegetable oil or lard

Preheat oven to 350 degrees.

Pour 3 cups water into a turkey roaster. Position rack in roaster, and cover rack with aluminum foil. Perforate foil with a fork. Put 1 chicken breast on a maguey leaf, and season with salt and pepper. Cover with a little tomatillo, chile, onion, cilantro, and epazote. Pour a little oil on top. Fold the corners of the leaf over chicken to enclose it in a pouch. Trim protruding edges, and tie with string to secure. Repeat procedure for remaining 7 chicken breasts.

Arrange mixiotes on roaster rack. Cover with lid or foil, and steam-bake for 45 minutes or until chicken is done.

To serve, place 1 mixiote on each of 8 plates, and unwrap to expose chicken. Serve with warm tortillas. ***Makes 8 mixiotes.***

MOLE POBLANO
Mole, Puebla Style

Mole *is the king of Mexican cuisine. The word* mole *comes from the Nahuatl root* mulli, *which means "sauce." This very special sauce originated in a colonial Puebla convent. Sor Andrea de la Asunción, a sister in the convent, invented it after raiding the cupboards for chiles and available spices and herbs. It was first served to the viceroy, Count Paredes y Marques de la Laguna, by host Bishop Don Manuel Fernández de Santa Cruz. In gratitude, the viceroy tiled the convent's kitchen with striking, handmade ceramic tiles, famous in Puebla. Today, this dish is served on special occasions, such as baptisms, weddings, and birthday parties. Its preparation is overseen by Saint Pascual Bailón, the patron saint of cooking!*

FOR THE SPICES

2	to 3 cups lard
2½	white onions, halved, plus 1 white onion, roasted (see Basics) and coarsely chopped
8	cloves garlic, whole, plus 1 head garlic, roasted (see Basics) and peeled
3	tomatoes, roasted (see Basics)
10	tomatillos, roasted (see Basics)
¾	cup sesame seeds
¾	cup raw almonds
¾	cup raw peanuts
¾	cup raisins
1	cup prunes, pitted
1½	ripe plantains, peeled and sliced ¼-inch thick
1	teaspoon coriander seed
1	teaspoon anise
2	sticks cinnamon, each 2 to 2½ inches long
1	stale croissant, in pieces
2	charred tortillas, in pieces
1½	quarts hot chicken broth (see recipe on page 202)
2	slices white onion
	Salt to taste

FOR THE CHILES

30	chiles mulatos, seeded, deveined, roasted or lightly fried, and soaked (see Basics)
16	chiles anchos, seeded, deveined, roasted or lightly fried, and soaked (see Basics)
6	long chiles pasillas, seeded, deveined, roasted or lightly fried, and soaked (see Basics)
1	chile chipotle, seeded, deveined, roasted or lightly fried, and soaked (see Basics)
1½	white onions, halved
6	cloves garlic, whole
	Salt to taste
8	ounces Mexican chocolate tablets (containing cinnamon), in pieces
¼	cup sugar
2	to 2½ quarts hot chicken broth

FOR THE CHICKEN

5	quarts water
6	chicken thighs
12	chicken breasts, halved, or 2 turkeys, 10 pounds each, in pieces
2	large white onions, halved
1	head garlic, halved
3	carrots, peeled
½	rib celery
6	bay leaves
	Salt to taste

FOR THE GARNISH

2	cups sesame seeds, toasted

Prepare the spices: Heat a little lard in a large, deep saucepan. Fry halved onion until transparent and lightly browned. Add garlic cloves, and brown. Remove garlic. Reserve. Add more lard, and fry chopped onion, garlic head, tomatoes, and tomatillos. Remove, and reserve. Add more lard, and fry sesame seeds, almonds, peanuts, raisins, prunes, plantains, coriander seed, anise, and cinnamon. Remove. Drain all fried ingredients on paper towels. Put fried ingredients, croissant, tortillas, and broth in a blender or food processor, and blend thoroughly. (It will be necessary to blend in batches.)

Heat remaining lard, and brown onion slices. Add blended ingredients and salt. Simmer over low heat for 1 hour, stirring occasionally.

Meanwhile, prepare the chiles: Blend chiles mulatos, anchos, pasillas, and chipotle in a blender or food processor with onion, garlic, and a little reserved soaking water. Salt. Strain chile mixture, and gradually stir into the simmering spice mixture, waiting about 10 minutes between each addition. Continue to heat mole, stirring occasionally. Add chocolate and sugar. Add salt if necessary.

Simmer mole for 2 to 3 hours. Cover saucepan with lid or aluminum foil to avoid splattering. (The mole also can be prepared outdoors on a brazier to avoid splattering or over firewood, which gives the sauce a rustic flavor.) Add broth until the mole is slightly thick. The mole is ready when it is very thick, with a thick top layer of fat. Taste, and add more salt if necessary.

Prepare the chicken: Heat water in a large stock pot. Add chicken, onions, garlic, carrots, celery, bay leaves, and salt. Cook over low heat for 30 minutes. Cool chicken in broth. Then add chicken pieces to the mole sauce, and cook for 30 minutes.

Serve mole, garnished with toasted sesame seeds, from a clay pot, or serve on individual plates, sprinkling sesame seeds over the mole-covered chicken. This dish often is served with red rice, frijoles de olla, and freshly made tortillas.

This mole recipe will yield more sauce than necessary for one meal. Use extra sauce to accent fried or poached eggs or in stuffings for enmoladas, mole-chicken pie, or chicken crepes with cheese and cream. It is an excellent complement to rice. The mole sauce freezes well.

Makes 24 servings.

LA BARBACOA EN BLANCO ESTILO TLAXCALA

Mutton, Tlaxcala Style

10 maguey or banana leaves, washed, tips removed, and roasted (see Basics), or 8 pieces aluminum foil, 8 inches square

1 11- to 12-pound sheep, in pieces

2 cups lard
Salt and pepper to taste

Preheat oven to 400 degrees. Fill a deep tray with cold water. Place on bottom oven rack.

Put 2 leaves on a large tray, and crisscross with 2 additional leaves. Place mutton on top of leaves. Spread lard over mutton. Sprinkle with salt and pepper, and cover with another layer of leaves, crisscrossing them until the meat is thoroughly covered. Tie closed with wire, and wrap in aluminum foil, sealing well.

Reduce oven to 350 degrees. Bake mutton for 6 hours or until the meat is tender and begins to shred.

To serve, place leaves on a platter, and arrange the mutton on top. Serve with red and green sauces, frijoles de olla, and corn tortillas.

Makes 8 servings.

above: *Grilled meat, Tlaxcala Style.*
overleaf: *Mole, Puebla Style is traditionally cooked on firewood stoves and served with a garnish of sesame seeds. The savory sauce can be eaten with red rice and is served with turkey, chicken, or enchiladas.*

SALSA DE CHILE DE ARBOL CON TOMATILLO
Chile de Arbol Sauce with Tomatillo

The tomatillos *from the state of Tlaxcala are used to make several hot sauces that accent many dishes.*

30	tiny tomatillos, husked and roasted (see Basics)
4	cloves garlic, roasted (see Basics), plus 2 cloves garlic, whole
	Salt to taste
4	to 6 chiles de árbol, fried
¼	cup white onion, chopped

In a molcajete, grind tomatillos and roasted garlic with raw garlic. Salt to taste, and add chiles. Grind. Add a little water to form a slightly thick sauce, and salt to taste. Stir. Add onion. Stir again.

Serve chile de árbol sauce from a molcajete. It usually accompanies avocado, cheese, or chicken tacos; tidbits of browned pork; and broiled or barbecued meat, poultry, or fish.

Makes 8 servings.

This fountain in the main square of Tlaxcala was given to Mexico by King Philip III of Spain.

CHILES EN NOGADA
Stuffed Chiles in Walnut Sauce

This famous dish, native to Puebla, commemorates Independence Day, August 21, 1821. It honors General Agustín de Itúrbide's defeat of the French, and its colors are those of the Mexican flag—green, white, and red.

FOR THE STUFFING

½	cup butter
1	cup olive oil
12	cloves garlic, whole, plus 10 cloves garlic, minced
2	large white onions, grated
1	pound ground pork
1	pound ground veal
1	pound ground beef
1	pound ground ham
1	cup raisins or currants
2½	cups prunes, pitted and finely chopped
1½	cups candied citron, finely chopped
1	cup dried apricots, finely chopped
6	large pears, finely chopped
6	peaches, finely chopped
4	apples, finely chopped
2	cups pineapple, finely chopped
1	plantain, finely chopped
6	large tomatoes (about 3½ pounds), finely chopped
1	tablespoon ground cinnamon
½	teaspoon ground cloves
½	teaspoon ground nutmeg
10	bay leaves
6	sprigs thyme
6	sprigs marjoram
1½	tablespoons freshly ground pepper
1	cup dry sherry
1	cup dry white wine
	Salt to taste

FOR THE CHILES

32	medium chiles poblanos, roasted, seeded, deveined, and soaked in salted water and vinegar for 6 hours (see Basics)
2	cups flour

FOR THE BATTER

20	eggs, separated
2	tablespoons salt
6	tablespoons flour
3	quarts vegetable oil

FOR THE SAUCE (WHEN FRESH WALNUTS ARE USED)

200	walnuts, shelled
80	raw almonds, shelled
14	ounces cream cheese
7	ounces goat cheese
3	ounces fresh cheese, such as feta
1	slice bread, crust removed and soaked in a little milk
2	cups heavy cream, or 1 cup heavy cream mixed with 1 cup half-and-half
1	cup milk
1	tablespoon white onion, grated
2	tablespoons sugar
1	teaspoon ground cinnamon
½	cup dry sherry
	Salt to taste

FOR THE SAUCE (WHEN PACKAGED WALNUTS ARE USED)

4	cups walnuts, soaked in cold water overnight
3	cups raw almonds, shelled
14	ounces cream cheese
7	ounces goat cheese
2	cups heavy cream
1	cup half-and-half
2	cups milk
2	tablespoons white onion, grated
¾	tablespoon ground cinnamon
½	cup dry sherry
	Salt to taste

FOR THE GARNISH

	Seeds from 6 pomegranates
1	bunch parsley, chopped

Prepare the stuffing: Heat butter and oil in a saucepan. Brown 12 garlic cloves, and discard. Brown minced garlic with onion. Add ground meats, and sauté until no longer red. Stir in raisins, prunes, citron, apricots, pears, peaches, apples, pineapple, plantain, and tomatoes. Cook until mixture begins to thicken, about 30 minutes.

Add cinnamon, cloves, nutmeg, bay leaves, thyme, marjoram, pepper, sherry, and white wine. Salt to taste. Simmer, stirring constantly, until the mixture thickens, about 1½ hours. Cool.

Fill prepared chiles with cooled stuffing. Put flour on a piece of waxed paper. Roll chiles in flour, and place on a tray. Refrigerate.

Prepare the batter: Make batter in 3 batches, as needed, or it will not remain fluffy. Beat one-third of egg whites with a little salt until stiff. Lightly beat one-third of egg yolks. Add yolks and 2 tablespoons flour to whites, folding in carefully.

Meanwhile, heat oil in a deep frying pan. Dip flour-coated chiles in batter, one at a time, and fry over medium heat. Do not crowd. Remove, and drain on paper towels.

Prepare the sauce: Boil walnuts in water to cover for 5 minutes. Remove from water. Peel skins. (Or soak walnuts in cold water overnight. Peel.) Boil almonds in water to cover for 25 minutes, and soak in cold water. Peel skins. Grind walnuts and almonds in a blender or food processor, adding cream cheese, goat cheese, feta cheese, bread, cream, milk, onion, sugar, cinnamon, sherry, and salt. The mixture will be very thick. Refrigerate.

If you are using packaged nuts, wash walnuts and almonds, and follow the procedure for fresh nuts.

To serve, place cold fried chiles on a platter. Ladle walnut sauce on top. Sprinkle with pomegranate seeds, and garnish with parsley.

There may be leftover stuffing, depending on the size of the chiles. It can be used to stuff empanadas, quesadillas, tacos, or poultry. It can be frozen.

Makes 16 servings.

overleaf: *Stuffed Chiles in Walnut Sauce, which is garnished with pomegranate seeds, is one of the best-known dishes from Puebla.*

ROMPOPE
Eggnog, Puebla Style

Rompope, *or Mexican eggnog, was created in the kitchens of the convent of Santa Clara in Puebla. A particularly flavorful version of this drink still can be savored in the Pasitas cantina located in this city.*

2   quarts milk
½   teaspoon baking soda

2   sticks cinnamon, each 6 inches long
3   cups plus 2 tablespoons sugar
12   egg yolks
1   cup grain alcohol (96 proof)

Bring milk, baking soda, and cinnamon to a boil in a heavy saucepan. Remove from heat, and cool. Bring to a second boil, and cool again. Add sugar, and stir to dissolve. Beat egg yolks, and add to milk mixture. Return mixture to heat, and simmer, stirring constantly

Rompope, Puebla's version of eggnog, is served as a liqueur.

Sautéed Ant Eggs, Pachuquilla Style is an exotic stuffing for omelets or tacos.

with a wooden spoon. Continue heating until eggnog is thick and reveals bottom of saucepan when pushed aside with the spoon. Remove from heat, and cool.

Stir in alcohol, and pour into 2 sterilized quart bottles.

To serve, pour rompope into liqueur glasses. Accompany with fresh blackberries or raspberries.

Makes about 2 quarts.

LOS ESCAMOLES ESTILO PACHUQUILLA
Ant Eggs, Pachuquilla Style

The cuisine of the state of Hidalgo is famous for exotic specialty dishes, such as ant eggs. The escamoles are eaten in several ways, including fried or as an omelet filling.

⅔	cup butter
⅓	cup olive oil
2	cups white onion, minced
½	cup chile serrano, minced
½	cup epazote or cilantro, finely chopped
6	cups ant eggs or red caviar
	Salt and pepper to taste

Heat butter and oil in a frying pan. Sauté onion and chile with the epazote. Add ant eggs, and cook over low heat for 10 minutes. Salt and pepper to taste.

To serve, spoon ant eggs into a clay pot. Serve with guacamole and green sauce in separate clay bowls and freshly made corn tortillas on the side for making tacos.

Makes 8 servings.

GUSANOS DE MAGUEY, ESTILO PACHUCA
Maguey Worms, Pachuca Style

Maguey worms, a Mexican specialty, are popular in the state of Hidalgo, where maguey grows abundantly. The worms were sold in cocoons on the street until a few years ago. Today, this dish is considered to be a delicacy.

FOR THE WORMS

5	cups vegetable oil
4	cups maguey worms, cleaned
8	tortillas

FOR THE GARNISH

8	balls fresh masa, 1 inch in diameter
8	limes, sliced
2	fresh cactus flowers (optional)

Heat 1 cup oil in a thick skillet, and fry worms until crisp. Remove, and drain on paper towels.

Heat 4 cups oil in a deep saucepan or deep fryer. Press tortillas in a mesh strainer, and fry one by one until they become crisp and take the shape of the strainer. Drain well on paper towels.

To serve, place a little ball of masa on each of 8 plates, and put tortilla "baskets" on top, pressing to fix in place. Fill tortillas with worms. Garnish with lime slices and flowers. Serve with guacamole and green sauce. This appetizer is good with tequila or pulque.

The worms also can be used as a taco stuffing.

Makes 8 servings.

The hacienda of Ixtafiayuca.

MOUSSE DE ALMENDRA Y CIRUELA PASA

Almond and Prune Mousse

This elegant recipe exemplifies European influence in Mexican cuisine. It is one of numerous, rich desserts coming from the Hidalgo region.

FOR THE MOUSSE

1	pound, 3 ounces prunes, pitted
1¾	cups red wine
2	strips orange peel, about 2 by 3 inches, or 1 stick cinnamon, 6 inches long
6	tablespoons plum jam
4½	envelopes unflavored gelatin
1	cup water
2½	cups raw almonds, soaked, skinned, and ground
6	egg yolks, lightly beaten
2	cups plus 1 tablespoon sugar
2½	cups milk
1	vanilla bean
½	teaspoon almond extract
1	cup heavy cream, chilled in freezer for 1 hour
1	cup sour cream, chilled in freezer for 1 hour

FOR THE GARNISH

Yellow and white chrysanthemums (optional)

Heat prunes with wine, orange peel, and jam in a saucepan. Cook until mixture thickens to consistency of a thick jam, about 25 minutes. Remove peel. In another pan, moisten 1½ envelopes gelatin in ½ cup water for 20 minutes. Heat until dissolved. Stir in prune mixture, mixing well.

Wet and grease a 9-inch gelatin mold with oil. Pour prune mixture into mold, and refrigerate for 40

The church of the convent of San Gabriel is the background for an array of Puebla sweets.

LECHE QUEMADA
Caramelized Milk

Puebla is one of the leading milk-producing regions in Mexico. Some of the finest pudding recipes originated there.

FOR THE PUDDING

2½	quarts cow's or goat's milk
¼	teaspoon baking soda
2	sticks cinnamon, each about 2 inches long
2¾	cups sugar
10	egg yolks, beaten
2	tablespoons corn starch, dissolved in ½ cup water
1½	cups walnuts, chopped

FOR THE CARAMEL

6	to 8 tablespoons sugar
5⅓	tablespoons butter, melted

FOR THE GARNISH

⅔	cup walnuts, chopped or ground

Heat milk in a saucepan. Add baking soda and cinnamon. Bring to a boil over high heat, and remove from heat. Cool. Repeat procedure 3 times. Add sugar, and stir to dissolve. Return to low heat, stirring until pudding thickens. Remove from heat, and cool. Beat egg yolks with dissolved corn starch. Stir into pudding. Return to heat, stirring constantly. Cook and stir until pudding is very thick and separates when stirred to reveal the bottom of pan. The milk will turn dark brown. Add walnuts, and cook for 5 to 10 minutes, stirring constantly.

Spoon pudding onto a deep heat-resistant platter. Sprinkle generously with sugar, and top with butter. Heat the broiler, and brown top of pudding. Sprinkle generously with chopped walnuts, and cool for 4 to 5 hours before serving.

Makes 8 servings.

minutes.

Meanwhile, purée almonds, egg yolk, sugar, and milk in a blender or food processor. Pour into saucepan. Add vanilla bean and almond extract. Cook over low heat, stirring constantly, until mixture comes to a boil. Remove from heat, and cool slightly.

Moisten 3 envelopes gelatin in ½ cup water for 20 minutes. Heat until dissolved. Stir in almond mixture. Chill for 30 minutes or until gelatin begins to set.

Combine heavy cream and sour cream, and whip until peaks form. Carefully fold into almond mixture. Pour into mold over prune mixture. Chill for 4 hours or overnight.

To unmold, dip mold into warm water briefly. Turn mousse onto a platter. Decorate with chrysanthemums.

Makes 8 servings.

CHAPTER EIGHT

THE SOUTH

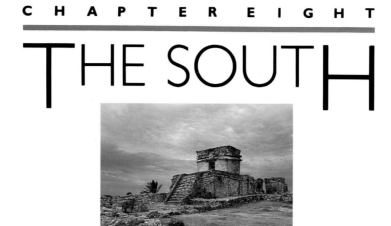

When Mexicans from other parts of the country visit the Yucatán, they often remark that they feel like foreigners. With its unique landscape, language, and culture, the Yucatán Peninsula—including the states of Yucatán, Campeche, and Quintana Roo—possesses a sense of identity that is almost national. Not only is it like nowhere else in Mexico, but also, as Yucatecos enjoy reminding outsiders, it is like nowhere else in the world.

Neither is its food. Unlike the rest of Mexican cooking, Yucatecan cuisine was heavily influenced by the foods and cookery of Cuba and other Caribbean islands, Europe, and Asia well into recent times. Remote from central Mexico, the Yucatán had a unique bond with foreign countries, which the Caribbean Sea and Gulf of Mexico made accessible. Its most popular chile—the *habanero*—is rumored to have come from Java. In Mexico, it is grown only in the Yucatán. Some of the best restaurants in Mérida—capital of the state of Yucatán—are Lebanese. But the food of Yucatán reflects unmistakably the legacy of the indigenous Mayas, whose sophisticated civilization was already in decline at the time of the conquest.

From the beginning, Yucatecan agriculture and food have been intertwined with ritual. The Mayas attributed divinity to seeds, tended plants with prayerful reverence, and regarded agriculture as a cosmic miracle. When corn was domesticated in Mesoamerica, it was born a god.

The terrain does not favor agriculture. The Yucatán is a vast, flat sheet of limestone relieved just slightly by low karst hills. Strangely, the peninsula is porous; its only major rivers, fed by thunderstorms, run far underground. Above, the abrasive bedrock is oddly pockmarked with hundreds of perfectly cylindrical sinkholes. Known as *cenotes*, these deep natural wells are usually found within a short walk of the legendary Mayan temples, which rise above the Yucatán plain. For many locals, *cenotes* are still the sole source of fresh water.

The Mayas have planted corn by the same method for almost 3,000 years. A farmer cuts the trees on his *milpa* (plot) and burns the vegetation. With a stick, he pokes holes in the ground, dropping in the corn and, around it, some beans. No one is sure when the method for making *masa* was developed, but the Indians' fascination with it—and, more important, with the tortilla—almost equaled their religious zeal.

Among the many uses to which *masa* is put is as an ingredient in *tamalitos* in the Yucatecan style. The *tamalito*, or small tamale, is filled with ground pumpkin seeds and is rolled in *chaya* leaves, which are similar to spinach and chard. The tamale is steamed and basted with one of the Yucatán's classic sauces—*chiltomate*. The basic ingredients are tomatoes, roasted garlic, the herb *epazote*, roasted onion, and *chile habanero*.

A knowledgeable cook can identify the food markets of the Yucatán simply by their fragrances, prominent among them oregano, cilantro, *recados* (spice blends), and *epazote*. *Epazote* originated in Spain, but it was—and is—best loved in the Yucatán. Although it is used in other regions, such as Oaxaca, nowhere is it so important as in the Yucatán. *Epazote* is essential to the famous *papadzules* of the Yucatán, fresh corn tortillas rolled with a stuffing of hard-cooked eggs. The tortillas are covered with a pumpkin-seed sauce that is flavored with *epazote*.

Absolutely basic to the Yucatecan kitchen are the *recados*, seasoning mixtures based on such spices and seasonings as allspice, black pepper, chiles, oregano, cumin, and roasted garlic. The most widely used Yucatecan *recado* is *achiote*. Its basis is the red annatto seed, and it is used to season and color the pit-roasted meats of the Yucatán, such as *cochinita*, or pork cooked by the *pibil* method.

Second only to *achiote* is *recado de chilmole*, made of dried and charred *chiles xcatiks*—another chile peculiar to the Yucatán. Black and pungent, *chilmole* also contains roasted garlic, oregano, and allspice. It is often used to flavor meatballs.

The Yucatán's interior is blanketed by North America's densest surviving tropical woodlands. Ranging from the high-canopied rain forests of the south to the agave-studded bush of the more arid northern coast, the Yucatán selva remains a refuge for the varied and exotic wildlife that is central to the peninsula's personality, mythology, and food. Yucatecan food features more game and wild herbs than does any other Mexican regional fare.

For centuries, Yucatecos have savored vension. Wild grouse and turkey are favored by hunters and eaters alike. Some of the Yucatán's oldest recipes are based on wild turkey. As in the rest of Mexico, animals were not domesticated in the Yucatán, although beekeeping is an ancient occupation. Many Yucatecan desserts and a famous liqueur are flavored with the local honey.

Along the coast, manatees and small crocodiles pa-troling mangrove swamps and coral inlets feed on one of the world's most varied supplies of fish. Fishermen still reap the bountiful catches praised four centuries ago by Bishop Diego de Landa in his *Relación de las cosas de Yucatán*. The Spanish friar, who also lauded the local habit of "seasoning and dressing the fish so as to make them both savory and wholesome," especially approved of the native bream, pike, skate, and squid, all of which might be found today in a good *ceviche* from Quintana Roo.

From the Gulf of Mexico comes seafood for the cocktails of Campeche, which feature oysters, crab, shrimp, or a combination of all three in a devilish tomato sauce punctuated with chiles and lime juice. The Gulf provides an amazing array of shrimp, from petite varieties that fit ten on one human fingernail to the giant variety for which Ciudad del Carmen is famous.

The most important fish in Campeche kitchens is the *cazón*, a small dogfish shark. *Pan de cazón* is a byword in this region. It is a sophisticated layering of puffed tortillas filled with refried black beans and *cazón*, first cooked with onion and *epazote*, and then garnished with *chiltomate* sauce and *chile habanero*.

The Yucatán's stunning beaches and Mayan ruins make it one of Mexico's most visited areas. The ancient Mayan heritage is evident in the magnificent, partially restored ruins of the cities of Chichén Itzá, Uxmal, Tulum, and Coba—each of which is an architecturally distinct reminder of the classic civilization that vanished a millennium ago. The modern Mayas, with their broad foreheads and deep-brown, almond-shaped eyes set in almost flawless complexions, are temple art come to life. The women are striking; many still dress in the colorful, embroidered white *huipils* of their ancestors. Nowhere is the Yucatán's living Mayan influence more apparent, however, than in a restaurant menu. Even in Mérida, the most European of Yucatecan cities, the best dining rooms offer tacos of pickled venison, *chile xcatik* sauces, and *huevos motuleños*—the Yucatán's own version of *huevos rancheros*. The culture that once created the greatest of New World civilizations still survives in a hospitable, gentle people and their distinctive, sophisticated cuisine.

RECADO DE ADOBO
Adobo Seasoning

Several seasonings are commonly used in the Yucatecan kitchen. These regional seasonings are used to perk up a wide variety of dishes. Basic ingredients—dry spices—are purchased in the marketplace in Mérida.

1 tablespoon pepper
12 dried Yucatecan oregano leaves or 1 tablespoon oregano, dried and crushed
1 small head garlic, roasted (see Basics)
6 small cloves
1 heaping teaspoon ground cumin
1 teaspoon cilantro seeds
   Pinch of saffron
1 tablespoon ground cinnamon stick
1 teaspoon salt
   Juice of 1 medium Seville (bitter) orange or 1/4 cup grapefruit juice

In a mortar, a food processor, or an electric spice grinder, grind pepper, oregano, garlic, cloves, cumin, cilantro seeds, saffron, cinnamon, and salt. Add juice to bind spices. Allow paste to dry a little before storing in a glass jar in the refrigerator.
Makes about 1/2 cup.

RECADO DE CHILMOLE O RELLENO NEGRO
Chilmole or Black Seasoning

This seasoning is used in stuffings for turkey, shrimp, and Cornish hens, as well as in meatballs.

2 1/4 pounds chiles anchos or costeños, washed, seeded, and deveined (see Basics)
   Grain alcohol
6 whole large allspice
1/2 teaspoon cumin seeds
1 1/2 tablespoons black peppercorns
1 1/2 tablespoons annatto seeds, soaked overnight in

   Seville (bitter) orange juice or grapefruit juice
1 head garlic, roasted (see Basics) and peeled
20 Yucatecan oregano leaves or 1 tablespoon oregano, dried and crushed
2 tablespoons salt

Dry the chiles. Sprinkle chiles with grain alcohol, and char them on a hot griddle.
   Purée chiles in a blender. In a blender or spice grinder, grind allspice, cumin, peppercorns, annatto seeds, garlic, oregano, and salt. Mix well with chiles. Store in a glass jar in the refrigerator.
Makes about 2 cups.

RECADO PARA BISTEC
Seasoning for Steak

Although the Spanish meaning of the name of this seasoning is "a seasoning for steak," its uses are much broader. It is added to pickling solutions and marinades for poultry, seafood, and fish and is also used to flavor broths.

1/4 cup black peppercorns
2 tablespoons whole allspice
1 stick cinnamon, about 2 1/2 inches long, broken
1 teaspoon cumin seeds
20 Yucatecan oregano leaves or 1 1/2 tablespoons oregano, dried and crushed
2 heads garlic, roasted (see Basics), peeled, and put through a press
   Salt to taste

In a mortar, a food processor, or an electric spice grinder, grind peppercorns, allspice, cinnamon, cumin, oregano, garlic, and salt. Allow paste to dry a little before storing in a glass jar in the refrigerator.
   To use, dissolve seasoning in a little Seville (bitter) orange juice or vinegar or in a mixture of equal amounts of orange and grapefruit juices.
Makes about 1 1/2 cups.

Various recados, or spices, are blended to flavor Yucatecan cuisine.

The most popular seasoning used to flavor and color roasted meats is made from the reddish seed of the annatto tree.

RECADO DE SALPIMENTADO
Salt and Pepper Seasoning

This seasoning is used to flavor broths and turkey.

1	teaspoon black peppercorns
4	cloves
8	cloves garlic, whole, plus 8 cloves garlic, roasted (see Basics) and peeled
20	Yucatecan oregano leaves or 1½ tablespoons oregano, crushed and dried
2	sticks cinnamon, each about 2 inches long
1	teaspoon coriander seeds
1½	tablespoons salt
1	large white onion, puréed
	Leaves from 8 sprigs parsley, puréed

In an electric spice grinder or a mortar, grind peppercorns, cloves, raw and roasted garlic, oregano, cinnamon, coriander, and salt. Stir in onion and parsley. Store in a glass jar in the refrigerator.
Makes ¼ to ½ cup.

RECADO DE ACHIOTE
Annatto-Seed Seasoning

This is the principal Yucatecan seasoning used to flavor meat roasted in a pit (pibil).

3	tablespoons annatto seeds
5	cloves garlic, whole
1	tablespoon black peppercorns
1	tablespoon oregano, dried and crushed
1	white onion

Simmer annatto seeds in a little water for 10 minutes. Let stand overnight to soften seeds. Drain. Combine seeds with garlic, peppercorns, oregano, and onion, and grind to a fine consistency in an electric spice grinder or a mortar. Store in a glass jar in the refrigerator.

To use, dissolve seasoning in a little Seville (bitter) orange juice or vinegar or in a mixture of equal amounts of orange and grapefruit juices.
Makes about ½ cup.

RECADO DE ADOBO COLORADO
Seasoning for Red Marinade

This seasoning is used to spice pork cooked in the Yucatecan style and, indeed, to flavor any kind of baked meat.

- 12 cloves garlic, whole, plus 12 cloves garlic, roasted (see Basics) and peeled
- 20 Yucatecan oregano leaves or 1½ tablespoons oregano, dried and crushed
- 1½ tablespoons cumin seeds
- 1 teaspoon coriander seeds
- 2 cloves
- 2 heaping tablespoons annatto seeds, soaked in ½ cup mild vinegar for 1 hour
- 1 tablespoon black peppercorns
- 4 whole allspice
- 1½ teaspoons salt
- ½ cup Seville (bitter) orange juice, or ¼ cup orange juice mixed with ¼ cup grapefruit juice

In an electric spice grinder or a mortar, grind raw and roasted garlic, oregano, cumin, coriander, cloves, annatto seeds, peppercorns, allspice, and salt. Place in a bowl. Add juice, mix, and form into a round, about the size of a pancake. Let dry. Store in a glass jar in the refrigerator.
Makes about ¾ cup.

SALPICON DE CHILES HABANEROS
Yucatecan Table Sauce of Chiles Habaneros

This typical sauce graces almost all tables in southeastern Mexico.

FOR THE SAUCE
- 3 chiles habaneros or güeros, roasted (see Basics)
- 2 medium chiles xcatiks or 4 chiles serranos, roasted (see Basics)
- 4 green onions, finely chopped
  Juice of 2 Seville (bitter) oranges or 1 grapefruit
  Juice of 1 orange

Juice of 1 lime
- 20 sprigs cilantro, chopped
  Salt to taste

FOR THE GARNISH
- 2 small limes, thinly sliced
- 20 sprigs cilantro, chopped

Slice chiles habaneros and xcatiks in thin strips, and place in a clay, ceramic, or glass bowl. Add onion. Add Seville orange juice, orange juice, lime juice, cilantro, and salt. Stir. Macerate for 2 hours.

Garnish with limes and cilantro. Serve with meat, Yucatecan specialties, and fish.
Makes 1 cup.

ENSALADA DE NARANJA, JICAMA Y CILANTRO
Orange, Jícama, and Cilantro Salad

FOR THE SALAD
- 16 seedless oranges
- 2 red onions, finely chopped
- 1 large jícama, finely chopped, or 2 cups water chestnuts
- 1½ cups cilantro, chopped
  Salt to taste
  Chile piquín or any very hot red dried chile, finely ground, to taste

FOR THE GARNISH
- 1 cup cilantro leaves
- 1 red onion, thinly sliced

Peel the oranges, and thinly slice in rounds. Place half the slices on a platter. Layer half the onion, half the jícama, and half the cilantro on the orange. Repeat layers of orange, onion, jícama, and cilantro. Season with salt and chile. Garnish with cilantro leaves and onion. Refrigerate for 2 hours.
Makes 8 servings.

An austere dining room in the hacienda of Yaxcopoil.

HUEVOS MOTULENOS
Eggs Motuleños Style

This is the Yucatán's delicious version of huevos rancheros.

FOR THE EGGS

8	tortillas, freshly made and warm
2	cups vegetable oil or corn oil
8	large eggs
2	cups refried black beans, warm (see recipe on page 187)
6	cups chiltomate sauce, warm (see recipe on page 280)
	Salt to taste

FOR THE GARNISH

2	cups frozen peas, or canned peas, cooked
1½	cups boiled ham, chopped
2	cups fresh cheese, crumbled
8	chiles habaneros or serranos, fried lightly in a little oil

Keep the tortillas warm. Heat oil in a frying pan, and fry eggs, a few at a time. Keep warm. Meanwhile, daub the tortillas with beans, and place on individual plates. Place an egg on each tortilla. Salt to taste. Ladle sauce over egg. Sprinkle peas around the egg, and top with ham and cheese. Garnish with a chile.

Makes 8 servings.

Valladolid, the second-largest city in the state of Yucatán, lends its name to the chicken dish it made famous.

POLLO VALLADOLID
Chicken, Valladolid Style

FOR THE CHICKEN

4½ quarts chicken broth (see recipe on page 202)
8 chicken legs and thighs
½ cup plus 1 teaspoon seasoning for steak (see recipe on page 266)
½ teaspoon coarsely ground pepper
8 whole allspice
Salt to taste
Vegetable oil

FOR THE GARNISH

8 chiles xcatiks or güeros, or any mild fresh yellow chile
2 large white onions, quartered and roasted (see Basics)

1 cup pickled onions (see recipe on page 280)

Put 1 quart broth in a large saucepan, and heat. Add chicken, 1 teaspoon steak seasoning, pepper, allspice, and salt. Cover, and cook over low heat for 25 minutes or until the chicken is cooked, stirring occasionally. Cool chicken, and skin.

Heat a griddle for 30 minutes. Rub each chicken part with 1 heaping tablespoon steak seasoning. Sprinkle with oil. Roast on a hot comal or griddle, turning to brown on all sides.

Reheat broth.

To serve, divide broth among 8 soup bowls. Place chicken in bowls, and garnish each with 1 chile, roasted onion, and pickled onion. Serve with freshly made warm tortillas.

Makes 8 servings.

CEVICHE DE CARACOL MARINO
Conch Ceviche

The state of Quintana Roo has its own version of lime-marinated fish cocktail. It is made with conch, which is plentiful in Caribbean waters. The sea snails are prepared in the fishing boats, immediately after being caught.

FOR THE CONCH

6	conch, cleaned, pounded, and chopped
	Juice of 16 limes
3	red onions, finely chopped
10	plum tomatoes, finely chopped
1½	cups cilantro, finely chopped
5	chiles xcatiks or serranos, chopped
¾	cup olive oil
	Salt to taste
1	tablespoon freshly ground pepper

FOR THE GARNISH

3	California avocados, peeled and chopped
1	cup red onion, finely chopped
½	cup cilantro, finely chopped
	Freshly ground pepper to taste
16	slices lime
	Soda crackers

Put conch in a glass bowl. Pour the lime juice over, and marinate for 2 to 3 hours. Drain. To conch, add onions, tomato, cilantro, chiles, oil, salt, and pepper. Mix well. Refrigerate for 2 hours.

To serve, spoon conch into 8 crystal goblets. Garnish each with avocado, onion, and cilantro. Sprinkle with pepper. Hang 2 lime slices on the rim of each goblet. Serve with soda crackers.

Makes 8 servings.

LANGOSTA AL EPAZOTE Y AL AJO
Lobster in Epazote and Garlic

Lobster is eaten frequently in the Caribbean, since it is abundant and relatively inexpensive. This dish is prepared with local seasonings, making an already delicious crustacean a real treat.

FOR THE LOBSTER

16	cloves garlic, roasted (see Basics) and peeled, plus 4 cloves garlic, minced
1	cup epazote or cilantro, finely chopped
4	chiles serranos, finely chopped
⅓	cup vegetable oil
1¼	cups butter
	Salt and pepper to taste
8	lobster tails, underside removed and shell left in place, or 4 fresh lobsters, halved lengthwise

FOR THE GARNISH

¾	cup vegetable oil
1	teaspoon salt
80	epazote or cilantro leaves, cleaned and dried
24	cherry tomatoes
4	limes, halved
½	cup clarified butter, melted

Prepare the lobster: Purée roasted garlic, minced garlic, epazote, and chiles in a blender or food processor. Add oil and butter, and blend. Season with salt and pepper to taste. Spread butter mixture over lobster, and refrigerate for 2 hours.

Heat a comal or griddle for 30 minutes. Cook lobster for 15 minutes. Turn, and cook for 8 to 10 minutes, depending on size of lobsters.

Prepare the garnish: Heat oil and salt in a frying pan, and fry epazote until crisp. Remove, and drain on paper towels.

To serve, place lobster on a bed of fried epazote leaves, and garnish with tomatoes and limes. Drench lobster with clarified butter. Serve hot.

Makes 8 servings.

SOPA DE CANGREJO Y PESCADO ESTILO MERIDA
Crab and Fish Soup, Mérida Style

This recipe is from Doña Monina Garcia Ponce, a specialist in Yucatecan cuisine.

FOR THE BROTH
6 quarts water
Salt to taste
4 crabs, each cut in 3 pieces
2 fish heads
½ head garlic, roasted (see Basics), plus ½ head garlic
8 Yucatecan oregano leaves or 1 teaspoon dried oregano
3⅓ pounds fresh tuna, grouper, red snapper, or bass fillets

FOR THE SAUCE
¾ cup olive oil
2 large white onions, sliced on the diagonal
3 large potatoes, sliced in thin strips
¾ cup parsley, chopped
8 plum tomatoes, chopped
8 green or red bell peppers, chopped
2 heads garlic, roasted (see Basics) and peeled
6 bay leaves
1 tablespoon ground cayenne pepper
Salt to taste

FOR THE GARNISH
4 or 5 slices white bread, crusts removed and cut in 1-inch cubes
2 cloves garlic, whole
½ cup olive oil
¼ cup parsley, chopped

Prepare the broth: Bring water and salt to a boil in a stock pot. Add crabs, fish heads, roasted and raw garlic, and oregano. Cook over medium heat for 45 minutes. Add fish, and cook for 20 minutes. Remove from heat, and cool. Strain broth, and reserve. Shred fish and crab, and set aside.

Prepare the sauce: Heat oil in a frying pan. Sauté onion, and add potatoes, parsley, tomato, peppers, garlic, bay leaves, cayenne pepper, and salt. Cook until fat rises to the surface, about 35 minutes. Add shredded crab and fish. Heat reserved broth, and add to sauce gradually, stirring. Correct seasoning.

Prepare the garnish: Fry bread cubes and garlic in oil until cubes are crisp. Drain croutons on paper towels.

To serve, pour soup into a tureen, and garnish with croutons and parsley.
Makes 8 servings.

TIKIN XIC PESCADO
Grilled Fish in the Mayan Tradition

From unrecorded time, the Maya have cooked fish, marinated with annatto seeds, over an open fire.

FOR THE MARINADE
6 tablespoons annatto seeds, soaked overnight in water and drained
1 tablespoon black peppercorns
½ tablespoon whole allspice
1 head garlic, roasted (see Basics) and peeled, plus 10 cloves garlic, whole
1 tablespoon oregano, dried and crushed
1 teaspoon cumin seeds
½ teaspoon cloves
1 stick cinnamon 1½ to 2 inches long, in pieces
Salt to taste
1 cup vegetable oil or lard
2 cups Seville (bitter) orange juice, or mixture of 1 cup orange juice, ½ cup grapefruit juice, and ½ cup mild vinegar

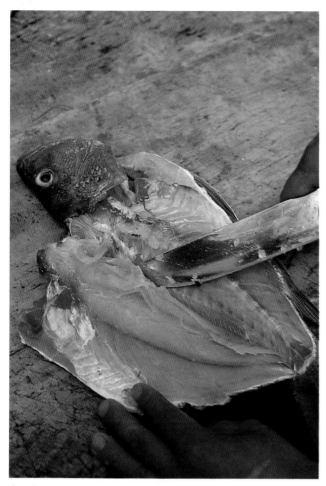

A red snapper is cleaned before being cooked over an open fire in the Mayan tradition.

A banana leaf is placed under a tikin xic fish to catch the marinade during the grilling.

FOR THE FISH

6 pounds grouper or snapper, halved lengthwise, deboned, and scaled
Bay leaves to cover

FOR THE GARNISH

1 recipe pickled red onions (see recipe on page 277)
8 plum tomatoes, sliced
16 limes, halved

Prepare the marinade: With a mortar and pestle or an electric spice grinder, grind annatto seeds. Add peppercorns, allspice, roasted and raw garlic, oregano, cumin, cloves, cinnamon, and salt. Grind to a paste. Dissolve paste in oil, and add orange juice.

Prepare the fish: Put fish in large glass or ceramic dish. Pour the marinade over, and cover fish with bay leaves. Marinate for 3 hours or overnight.

Prepare a grill with charcoal and mesquite (or preheat oven to 375 degrees). Put a banana leaf or foil on the grill. Place fish on top, reserving marinade in dish. Cook over low coals until fish flakes easily, basting frequently with marinade (or bake in a dish in oven for 45 minutes to 1 hour, basting frequently).

To serve, place fish on a platter, and garnish with onions, tomatoes, and limes. Serve with white rice.
Makes 8 to 12 servings.

CAZON EN CHILES XCATIKS
Xcatik Chiles Stuffed with Baby Shark

Baby shark is commonly eaten in southeastern Mexico. It has a smooth texture and subtle flavor, lending itself to various treatments. This method is adapted to locally available chiles.

FOR THE SHARK

1	quart water
10	sprigs epazote or cilantro
1	white onion, roasted (see Basics), plus 1 white onion
½	head garlic, roasted (see Basics), plus ½ head garlic
1	tablespoon black peppercorns
3⅓	pounds baby shark, sole, or flounder fillets

FOR THE STUFFING

1½	cups olive oil or vegetable oil
3	cloves garlic, whole
2	white onions, finely chopped
4	large plum tomatoes, chopped
¾	cup green olives, chopped
½	cup capers
3	cloves, ground
1	teaspoon ground allspice
½	teaspoon ground cumin
½	stick cinnamon, ground
	Salt to taste

FOR THE CHILES

½	cup olive oil
4	cloves garlic, crushed or put through a press
32	chiles xcatiks or güeros, or any mild fresh yellow chile, seeded and deveined (see Basics)

FOR THE MARINADE

½	cup vegetable oil
4	cloves garlic, whole

3	medium white onions, thinly sliced
2½	cups wine vinegar
1	tablespoon whole allspice
1	stick cinnamon, about 3 inches long
2	sprigs thyme or pinch of dried thyme
2	sprigs marjoram or pinch of dried marjoram
2	bay leaves
10	sprigs parsley
1	tablespoon dried oregano
	Salt to taste
1	tablespoon sugar, or to taste

FOR THE GARNISH

2	red onions, halved and sliced on the diagonal
¾	cup Seville (bitter) orange juice, or mixture of ½ cup grapefruit juice, ⅓ cup orange juice, and juice of 1 lime
1	teaspoon dried oregano
	Salt to taste
20	small radishes, shaped like flowers
8	small radishes, thinly sliced in rounds

Prepare the shark: Put water, epazote, roasted and raw onion, roasted and raw garlic, and peppercorns in a medium saucepan. Bring to a boil, and add shark, placing fillets on top of ingredients so they poach for 20 minutes. Cool shark in broth, and shred. Set aside.

Prepare the stuffing: Heat oil in a frying pan, and sauté garlic. Discard garlic, and add onion. Sauté until transparent. Add tomato, olives, capers, cloves, allspice, cumin, cinnamon, and salt. Cook over medium heat for 40 minutes or until sauce thickens and fat rises to the surface. Add shredded shark, and cook until sauce thickens. Correct seasoning.

Prepare the chiles: Heat oil in frying pan, and brown garlic. Discard garlic, and add chiles. Sauté for 2 minutes. Cover, and cook for 2 minutes, being careful not to overcook or the chiles will fall apart. Remove from heat, and cool, uncovered, in pan.

Prepare the marinade: Heat oil in a frying pan, and

brown garlic. Discard garlic, and add onion. Sauté until soft. Add vinegar, allspice, cinnamon, thyme, marjoram, bay leaves, parsley, oregano, salt, and sugar. Cook over low heat for 35 minutes. Cool.

Prepare the garnish: Marinate onions in mixture of juice, oregano, and salt for 1 hour.

Remove chiles from frying pan, and stuff with shark mixture. In a 9- by 13-inch baking dish, arrange a layer of chiles. Pour half of marinade over chiles. Add another layer of chiles, and pour remaining marinade over. Garnish with onion, radish flowers, and radish rounds. Refrigerate for 2 hours. Serve cold.

Makes 8 servings.

A Yucateca wearing a huipil, *or hand-embroidered blouse.*

ARROZ BLANCO
White Rice

Rice was introduced to Mexico by the Spaniards. The grain was quickly embraced and is a staple side dish.

FOR THE RICE

- 2   cups long-grain white rice
- 2   cups vegetable oil
- 6   cloves garlic, whole, plus 3 cloves garlic, puréed
- 1   medium white onion, halved, plus ½ white onion, puréed
- 3   cups water, at the boiling point
-     Salt to taste
- 20 sprigs parsley
- 4   chiles serranos or 2 chiles jalapeños

FOR THE GARNISH

- 1   small bunch parsley, stems trimmed
- 3   chiles serranos or 2 chiles jalapeños

Soak rice in hot water to cover for 15 minutes. Drain in a mesh sieve. Rinse in cold water until water runs clear. Drain well.

Heat oil in a deep frying pan or saucepan. Add 6 garlic cloves and halved onion. Fry briefly. Add rice, and fry, stirring with a wooden spatula until golden. Be sure the rice does not stick to the bottom of the pan. Drain off oil, and remove garlic and onion. Lower heat, and add puréed garlic and onion to rice in pan. Fry until dry. Add boiling water, and allow to boil with rice for 3 minutes. Season with salt, and place parsley and chiles on top of rice. Do not stir. Cover tightly, and simmer over low heat for 25 minutes. Remove from heat. Allow to set for 30 minutes without removing lid. The rice will puff.

Shake saucepan, and remove lid. Discard parsley.

To serve, place rice on platter, and decorate with parsley and cooked and fresh chiles.

Makes 8 servings.

PAN DE CAZON
Layered Tortilla, Shark, and Tomato Sauce, Campeche Style

This layered casserole from Campeche is in the Mayan tradition. The puff of the tortilla is split, and the tortillas are filled with beans and shark, layered, and covered with tomato sauce.

FOR THE SHARK

2   quarts water
8   sprigs epazote or cilantro, or 1 tablespoon oregano, dried and crushed
2   white onions, sliced
6   cloves garlic, whole
8   black peppercorns
    Salt to taste
3   pounds shark steaks or other firm fish fillets

FOR THE SAUCE

½   cup lard or vegetable oil
1½ white onions, finely chopped
1   chile habanero or 4 chiles serranos or jalapeños, chopped
5   large tomatoes or 14 plum tomatoes, cooked in boiling salted water for 2 to 3 minutes, then peeled and chopped
⅓   cup grapefruit juice
    Salt to taste
1   tablespoon sugar
1   teaspoon coarsely ground pepper
4   sprigs epazote, or ½ tablespoon oregano, dried and crushed

FOR THE STUFFING

4   cups refried black beans (see recipe on page 187)

6   tablespoons lard
    Epazote or cilantro sprigs to taste, or oregano, dried and crushed, to taste
½   chile habanero or 1 chile serrano
24 tortillas, 3 inches in diameter, freshly made

FOR THE GARNISH

8   chiles habaneros or serranos

Prepare the shark: Bring water to a boil in a stock pot. Add epazote, onions, garlic, peppercorns, and salt. Keep at slow boil for 20 minutes. Add shark, and cook for 15 minutes. Remove from heat, and cool in broth for 10 minutes. Remove fish from broth, skin the steaks, and shred the fish. Set aside shark, and reserve the broth.

Prepare the sauce: Heat lard in a saucepan. Add onion, and sauté for 5 minutes. Add chile, tomatoes, and grapefruit juice. Season with salt, sugar, and pepper. Add epazote. Stir. Cook over low heat until sauce thickens, about 20 minutes. Thin with fish broth if it becomes too thick. Keep sauce hot.

Preheat oven to 350 degrees. Grease 2 9- by 13-inch baking dishes.

Prepare the stuffing: In a frying pan, cook beans with lard, epazote, and chile until thick, about 20 minutes.

Heat the tortillas on a hot griddle until they puff (see Basics). Slit the puff, and fill tortilla with refried beans and shredded fish. Close puff loosely. Put the filled tortilla in baking dish. Cover with sauce. Continue process, filling tortillas and adding layers of the filled tortillas covered with sauce, until each dish contains 3 layers. End with sauce, reserving some for garnish. Bake for 10 minutes.

To serve, place casserole on a plate. Garnish with reserved sauce and chiles.
Makes 8 servings.

COCHINITA PIBIL
Pork, Pibil Style

If there is a quintessential Yucatecan dish, this is it. Pibil denotes "pit roasting," a method used for chicken, venison, and game as well as pork. A pit is dug and lined with stone. A fire is lighted, and the meat is slowly roasted in banana leaves.

FOR THE PORK

3	pounds boneless pork loin or leg, in 1 piece
1	cup annatto-seed seasoning (see recipe on page 267)
6	cloves garlic, roasted (see Basics) and puréed
1	tablespoon dried oregano
1	tablespoon freshly ground pepper
¾	cup lard or vegetable oil
2	cups Seville (bitter) orange juice, or 1 cup orange juice mixed with 1 cup grapefruit juice
	Salt to taste
1½	quarts water
2	packages banana leaves, roasted until pliable (see Basics), or 1 package corn husks, soaked overnight in water to cover and drained or fresh corn husks
4	red onions, sliced on the diagonal
16	bay leaves
1	bouquet garni of 1 tablespoon dried thyme and 1 tablespoon dried marjoram

FOR THE PICKLED RED ONION

6	medium red onions, thinly sliced on the diagonal
¾	cup olive oil
10	bay leaves
6	sprigs marjoram or 1 teaspoon dried marjoram
1½	tablespoons oregano, dried and crushed
1	teaspoon coarsely ground pepper
10	whole allspice
	Salt to taste
¾	cup vinegar

FOR THE TACOS

32	fresh, hot tortillas

Prepare the pork: Put pork in a bowl, and score.

In another bowl, mix annatto-seed seasoning with garlic, oregano, and pepper. Add lard and juice, and stir to dissolve the seasoning. Salt. Rub meat with the mixture, and marinate for 4 hours in the refrigerator or overnight.

Pour water into a stock pot or large saucepan that can be used as a steamer. Place rack inside, and line with a large sheet of aluminum foil. Line foil with some banana leaves. Cover banana leaves with half the onion, topped with a layer of bay leaves and the bouquet garni. Place pork on the leaves. Pour marinade over. Cover with remaining onion and another layer of bay leaves. Top with a layer of banana leaves. Wrap tightly with the aluminum foil.

Cover pan with tight-fitting lid. Bring water to a boil, and steam for 2½ to 3 hours, turning meat package occasionally so pork cooks evenly. Add more water if necessary.

(The pork may be baked in a 350-degree oven for 2½ hours as an alternative to steaming. It should be wrapped in banana leaves and covered with aluminum foil.)

Remove pan from heat, and let stand, covered, for 1 hour. Remove lid. Drain pan juices, and reserve. Shred pork. Set aside.

Meanwhile, prepare the pickled red onion: Soak onions in salted water to cover for 10 minutes. Drain. Heat oil in a skillet. Add onions, and sauté with bay leaves, marjoram, oregano, pepper, allspice, and salt. When onions are tender, remove from heat, and stir in vinegar.

To serve, heat pan juices with a little lard or oil. Add shredded pork, and heat through. Spoon meat and pickled onions onto tortilla. Roll into a taco. Stack tacos on a platter, and garnish with remaining pickled onions. Serve pork with beans and beer.
Makes 32 tacos.

overleaf left: *Pork, Pibil Style is wrapped in banana leaves and roasted for several hours.*
overleaf right: *The ingredients for Papadzules, unique to the Yucatán.*

PAPADZULES
Papadzules

Papadzules, or Yucatecan tortillas with pumpkin-seed and chiltomate sauces, is an indigenous dish dating to Mayan times.

FOR THE PICKLED ONIONS

1½ quarts water
3   large red onions, thickly sliced on the diagonal
3   large white onions, thickly sliced on the diagonal
2   cups cider vinegar
    Salt to taste
1   tablespoon ground allspice
1   tablespoon dried oregano
6   bay leaves

Papadzules, tortillas stuffed with hard-cooked eggs, are covered with pumpkin-seed and chiltomate sauces and garnished with pickled onions.

4   sprigs marjoram or ¼ teaspoon dried marjoram
4   sprigs thyme or ¼ teaspoon dried thyme
6   chiles xcatiks or güeros

FOR THE TORTILLAS

3   pounds fresh masa or equivalent made with masa harina (see Basics) or 24 fresh tortillas
¾   cup water
    Salt to taste

FOR THE CHILTOMATE SAUCE

8   medium, firm tomatoes or 16 plum tomatoes, roasted (see Basics) and peeled
2   white onions, roasted with skins (see Basics) and peeled, plus ½ white onion, coarsely chopped
8   cloves garlic, roasted (see Basics) and peeled, plus 2 cloves garlic, whole
½   cup olive oil or lard
4   chiles habaneros, xcatiks, or güeros
    Salt to taste
½   cup chicken broth or water

FOR THE PUMPKIN-SEED SAUCE

6   cups raw pumpkin seeds
1   quart water or chicken broth (see recipe on page 202)
6   sprigs epazote or cilantro
1   white onion, quartered
½   head garlic, unpeeled
2   chiles habaneros or 6 chiles serranos
    Salt to taste

FOR THE STUFFING

8   hard-cooked eggs, finely chopped

Prepare the pickled onions: Bring 2 cups water to a boil. Add red and white onions, and boil for 3 minutes. Drain well, and put onions in a glass bowl. Mix together remaining ingredients, and pour over onions. Macerate for 2 days at room temperature or in the refrigerator.

Prepare the tortillas: Put masa in a bowl. Add water

Flamingos in the Lagartos River.

and salt to form a pliable dough. Knead until masa forms a firm ball. With a tortilla press, make tortillas 3 inches in diameter (see Basics). Keep warm.

Prepare the pumpkin-seed sauce: Heat a heavy skillet. Add pumpkin seeds, and toast (they will jump in the pan), being careful not to burn. Place in a blender or food processor, and blend seeds until a paste forms. Set aside.

Put water in a pot with epazote, onion, garlic, chiles, and salt. Cook for about 15 minutes or until the water is strongly flavored. Cool a little, discarding vegetables. Mix a little of this water with the pumpkin-seed paste, adding enough to be able to work mixture with hands to form a slightly thick sauce. Do not overcook, or the sauce will curdle.

Prepare the chiltomate sauce: Coarsely chop roast-ed tomatoes, onions, and garlic. In a blender or food processor, purée roasted ingredients with chopped onion and 2 garlic cloves until smooth. Heat oil in a skillet, and add tomato mixture. Add chiles and salt to taste. Boil sauce until fat rises to the surface. Stir in a little chicken broth to thin.

Pour about one-third of the pumpkin-seed sauce into a deep dish. One by one, dip hot tortillas in sauce (adding more if necessary). Put a spoonful of egg on each tortilla. Roll like an enchilada.

To serve, place 3 papadzules on individual warmed plates. Cover with hot pumpkin-seed sauce, and garnish with hot chiltomate sauce. Garnish with pickled onions.

Makes 24 papadzules.

CHOCOLATE DE SURESTE
Southeastern Hot Chocolate

This dish is a favorite at the hacienda of Yaxcopoil, located on the road between Campeche and Mérida. Local Mayan Indians prepare and enjoy this hot beverage.

2¼   pounds cocoa beans, toasted, peeled, and ground

Follow procedure for chontal chocolate (see recipe on page 195), but grind the cocoa beans twice (to a fine paste), without sugar, on a metate. Form chocolate patties, and place on squares of brown wrapping paper. With fingertips, make indentations to decorate patties.

    Southeastern hot chocolate can be prepared with water and honey instead of milk and sugar. Beat the hot beverage with a molinillo until frothy.

Makes 8 servings.

HORCHATA
Rice Beverage from Yucatán

This refreshing drink is particularly welcome in the scorching climate of the Yucatán Peninsula.

 3   cups long-grain white rice
      Rain or spring water to cover, plus 6½ quarts rain or spring water
 2   cups raw almonds, unshelled
⅓   cup freshly ground cinnamon
2½   cups sugar, or to taste
      Ice cubes

A typical Yucatecan kitchen.

Wash rice. Cover with rain water, and soak for 12 hours. Drain in a mesh sieve. Wash almonds, cover with water, and soak for 4 to 6 hours. Shell almonds, and discard skins. Purée the rice in a blender. Set aside. Purée the almonds to a fine paste in a blender.

    Mix rice, almond paste, cinnamon, sugar, rain water, and 16 ice cubes in a large glass jar or clear pitcher. Serve rice beverage in tall glasses over more ice cubes.

Makes about 7 quarts.

Sweet, rich Southeastern Hot Chocolate is enjoyed by Yucatecos and visitors alike.

PASTEL MARGARITA CON MAZAPAN DE ALMENDRA
Marzipan Daisy Cake

This dessert, combining local fruits and nuts, was invented during the eighteenth century by nuns in convents.

FOR THE MARZIPAN

2½	cups raw almonds, unskinned
3	cups powdered sugar
3	small egg whites
I	to 2 tablespoons butter, softened

FOR THE CUSTARD

1½	quarts milk
3	sticks cinnamon, each 6 inches long
8	egg yolks
1⅓	cups sugar
⅓	cup corn starch
¼	cup flour
I	cup fresh or frozen unsweetened coconut, finely shredded
½	cup butter
1½	cups heavy cream, chilled in freezer for 30 minutes

FOR THE GARNISH

Yellow food coloring
Powdered sugar
Ground cinnamon

Prepare the marzipan: Boil almonds in water to cover for 10 minutes. Let stand for 10 minutes. Drain, and remove skins. Dry on a baking sheet for 1 hour. Grind almonds in a blender or food processor until fine. Add sugar, and blend until mixture forms a thick paste. Do not overblend, or almonds will turn to oil.

Put almond paste into a bowl, and add egg whites. Mix until ingredients are blended. Add butter, stirring well. Set aside.

Prepare the custard: Bring milk to a boil with cinnamon. Remove from heat. Repeat process 3 times. Remove from heat, and cool. Meanwhile, beat egg yolks with sugar until they turn pale yellow. Slowly add corn starch, flour, and coconut, mixing well. Gradually add cooled milk. Heat mixture and simmer, stirring constantly, until consistency of thick cream. Remove from heat, and stir in butter. Press greased waxed paper onto custard to prevent a film from forming. Refrigerate for 2 hours.

Beat heavy cream until thick. Fold into chilled custard.

Pinch off 3-tablespoon portions of marzipan, and shape daisy petals. Make 3 daisies, joining petals with a dab of egg white and pressing firmly with the tip of scissors. Place flowers on waxed paper. Pinch off 1 tablespoon of marzipan, and color with yellow food coloring. Shape 3 balls, and place 1 in the center of each flower.

Grease a 9- or 10-inch oval pan. Measure and cut a piece of waxed paper the size of the pan. Roll out a ⅛-inch layer of marzipan on the waxed paper. Turn over into the pan, and peel off waxed paper. Spread custard over marzipan. Roll out a second layer of marzipan on the waxed paper, and turn over onto the custard, removing waxed paper. Sprinkle with sugar and cinnamon. Garnish with the marzipan daisies, and refrigerate for 6 hours before serving.
Makes 8 servings.

Marzipan is used in many Yucatecan desserts. These delicate candies are made from almond and egg pastes.

ACKNOWLEDGMENTS

I owe a great deal of thanks to the people who collaborated with me on this book. It would not have been possible to even consider taking on this gigantic task without the total support of Antonio Enrique Savignac, Secretary of Tourism, and Guillermo Grimm, Undersecretary of Promotion and Development. Alejadro Mornes, Undersecretary of Operations, and the State Tourism Offices strongly supported this project by introducing me to the native tastes of a wide variety of places.

I would also like to thank Reneé Lopez, photographer's assistant; Lorenza Caraza, prop coordinator and photostylist; Augustin Monsreal, Maria Lozon, Lynda Finegold, and Camille Grossdidier for translating and editorial help in Mexico; and the secretaries at the Tourism Ministry.

Hundreds of other people participated in the creation of this book in one way or another. Because of space limitations, it is impossible for me to list all the names here. However, I would like to specifically mention the following people for the important role they played during the preparation of *The Taste of Mexico:*

THE NORTH

Baja California Sur

State Tourism Office
Jorge Talamás
Bismark Restaurant
Pichilingue Restaurant
Las Palmas Restaurant in Cabo San Lucas
Lucha de Garaizar in Loreto
Kemil Rizk, Fonatur Office
M. Atamoros, Fonatur Office
Ruben Jaime

Chihuahua

Federal Tourism Office
Patricia Ruiz and Yolanda Vazquez
El Aguila Creamery
Santa Cruz Family Ranch
La Estancia Cinégetico Ranch
El campo 6 1/2 of the menonitas
Calesa Restaurant

Monterrey

Federal and State Tourism Offices
Rafael Chaib
José G. Treviño Castillo
Margarita East de Fernández
Arturo Fernández
Margara Garza Sada de Fernández
Alberto Fernández
Martha Chapa
Catalina de Fernández
Jorge Fernández
Cecilaide Garza Sada
Ismael Garza T.
El Tio Restaurant

Sonora

Federal Tourism Office
Manuel Antillón
El Mezquital del Oro
Carmelita Gutierrez de Pesqueira
Doña María in Villa de Seris
Palomino Restaurant
Cesar Paulovich

THE NORTH PACIFIC COAST

Colima

Federal Tourism Office
Ricardo J. Malagón y de Parres
Mésico Lindo Restaurant
L'Recif Restaurant
Las Hadas Hotel
Doña Chayo Restaurant
Guillermo Trujillo Nova

Jalisco

Federal Tourism Office
Canirac
Los Otates Restaurant
Brass Restaurant
de Dios La Libertad Marketplace in San Juan
Tizoc Restaurant
Los Cazadores Restaurant
La Casa Canela in Tlaquepaque
Las Palomas Restaurant
Le Bistro Restaurant

Sinaloa

Javier Gaxiola
Carmen María Bustamante, State Tourism Office
Canirac
Daniel Viesca
Los Arcos Restaurant
El Paraje Restaurant
La Pradera Restaurant
Mama Licha
El Pargo Restaurant
Lupita Rojas
Margarita Rivero Acosta
Escuinapa Cooperative
Lay S. A. Products
Los Pelicanos Restaurant
Camino Real Hotel

THE SOUTH PACIFIC COAST

Chiapas

Federal and State Tourism Offices
José Luis Zebadua
Miguel Angel Reyes
Canirac in San Cristobal de las Cadas
Diego de Mazariego Hotel
Gertrudis Duby de Blom
Nabolon Hotel
Capril Hotel

Guerrero

Federal Tourism Office
Alejandro de la Cerda
Las Brisas Hotel
Susana Palazuelos
Tres Fuentes Restaurant
Betos Restaurant in Acapulco
Barra Vieja Beto Godoy

Oaxaca

Federal Tourism Office
Jacqueline and Josué Saenz Collection
Ana María Vasquez Colmenare's book, *La Cocian Oaxaqueña*
Presidente Hotel, formerly the Santa Catalina Convent
Mi Casita Restaurant
Margarita East de Fernández
Chabela Vasseur
Jaime Saldivar's retablo painting

THE BAJIO

Guanajuato

Federal Tourism Office
Hidalgo Marketplace
Las Bugambilias Restaurant in San Miguel de Allende
Sierra Nevada Hotel
Parador San Javier Hotel

Michoacán

Federal Tourism Office
Armando Arriaga
Carmen Arriaga de Zavaleta

Regional Museum in Patzcuaro
Handicraft Museum in Morelia
Villa Montaña Hotel
Posada Don Vasco Patzcuaro Hotel
Los Comensales Restaurant

Queretaro

Federal and State Tourism Offices
Francisco Herrera
Marco Antonio Velazquez Zepeda
Patricia Silva
Fernando Urquiza and Family
El Salto Agustín Urquiza Ranch
La Caperucita Cheeses
El Sauz Cheeses
Queretaro Cheeses
Vogue Magazine, June 1986, recipe for Pork from Santa
　　Rosa Jaure by Patricia Quintana

San Luis Potosi

Federal and State Tourism Offices
La Virreina Restaurant
La Lonja Restaurant
José Garfias
Isabel Montero de Garfias

THE GULF

Tabasco

State Tourism Office
Yolanda Osuna
Nilda Al Jordán
Doña Marí Restaurant on the road to Puerto Ceiba
Chon Cupón Restaurant
Chef Ferneti at the Hyatt Hotel
Puerto Ceiba Seafood Cooperative
Chocolate Factory Chontal

Veracruz

Federal Tourism Office
Canirac
Luis Lara
Pardiño's Restaurant
Café Cathedral Restaurant

Carlos Prieto
García Saenz Luna Family
Chapopote Hacienda
Quintana Fernández Family
Perez-Quintana Family Ranch in San José
Caraza-Barrencechea Family Ranch in Cañamelar
Margaria Fernández de Quintana
Laura Caraza
Lorenza Caraza

MEXICO CITY AND THE STATE OF MEXICO

Mexico City

Antonio Enrique Savignac, Secretary of Tourism
Guillermo Grimm, Undersecretary of Promotion and
　　Development
Undersecretariat of Operations:
　　Alejandro Morones
　　Fonatur
　　Kemil Rizk
　　Eduardo Saenz
　　Javier Rivas
　　Rodolfo Pria
Mexicana de Aviación
Aeroméxico
María Orsini Grocery Store
Guadalupe San Vicente
San Angel Inn Restaurant
Cabayo Bayo (Grupo Loredo) Restaurant
Lula Beltran
Lila Lomelí
Dolores Torres Ysabal
Susana Luna Parra de Urquiza
Ana Rosa Seoane de Urquiza
Eduardo Rangel Rams for transportation
Jakeline Saenz
Josue Saenz
Janet Solis

State of Mexico

Carmen Maza de del Mazo
Monica Patiño
Granadina Grocery Store

Taberna de León Restaurant
Santiago Tianguistengo Marketplace
State of Mexicoš Handicraft Store in Toluca

CENTRAL MEXICO

Hidalgo

Jacqueline and Josué Saenz Collection
Rosana Cortina de Quintana
Elvira Harsh de Quintana
Vogue Magazine, July 1984, recipe for Pickled Cactus Pads
    by Patricia Quintana

Puebla

State Tourism Office
Salomón Jauli
José Luis Bretón
Fonda de Santa Clara Restaurant
San Francisco Restaurant
Santa Rosa Convent Museum
El Lirio Candy Shop
Lolita Ramón

Tlaxcala

State Tourism Office
Felipe Mazarraza

Hernández Family Restaurant
Saldivar Restaurant
Hacienda Ixtafiayuca

THE SOUTH

Campeche

Malena Cuesta
Dolores Lanz de Echeverria

Quintana Roo

Playa Car Hotel
Oscar Viera
Poberto Pineda

Yucatan

Federal Tourism Office
Jorge Gamboa Patrón
Chacha de García Ponce
María del Mar García Ponce
Barbachano Family
Pilar García Ponce
Doña Monina García Ponce

SOURCES FOR INGREDIENTS

In certain parts of the United States where Hispanics of Mexican origin have settled—such as California, the Southwest, and the Chicago area—ingredients for Mexican cookery are plentiful and easy to find. In other regions, Mexican ingredients are often still difficult to locate, although their availability has increased with the heightened interest in Mexican cuisine.

Stores that carry fresh produce usually have chiles, cilantro, and *tomatillos*. Depending on the season, the kinds of chiles that are available may be limited. Markets in Chicago, Houston (and other Texas cities), and Los Angeles usually stock a large variety of fresh chiles. Almost all the stores listed here sell fresh or frozen tortillas and *masa harina*.

The following list of markets and shops that sell Mexican foods and ingredients is arranged by city and covers all regions of the United States.

AKRON

West Point Market

1711 West Market Street
Akron, Ohio 44313
(216) 864-2151
Dried and canned ingredients, some frozen foods, such as tortillas.

ATLANTA

Rinconcito Latin

Limburg Plaza
2581 Piedmont Road
Atlanta, Georgia 30324
(404) 231-2329
Dried and canned ingredients.

BOSTON

Common Market

1383 Commonwealth Avenue
Boston, Massachusetts 02134
(617) 254-9519
Some fresh produce; dried chiles and spices; canned *salsas* and pickled chiles; frozen tortillas.

Le Jardin

248 Huron Avenue
Cambridge, Massachusetts 02138
(617) 492-4534
Fresh produce in season, including most varieties of chiles, corn husks, cilantro, black and red beans, *tomatillos*, plantains, red bananas, and papaya.

CHICAGO

Armando's Finer Foods

2627-2639 South Kedzie Street
Chicago, Illinois 60623
(312) 927-6688
Fresh produce, including chiles and tropical fruits (mango, papaya); fresh spices, including tamarind and stick cinnamon; dried chiles and beans; *chorizo* and meats; Mexican-style cheeses from Illinois and Wisconsin; baked goods; Mexican candies and cookies.

LaCasa del Pueblo

1810 South Blue Island
Chicago, Illinois 60608
(312) 421-4640
Fresh produce; dried ingredients; complete line of canned *salsas* and pickled chiles; meats and homemade *chorizo* and tamales; *tacqueria* for take-out.

DENVER

Johnnie's Grocery and Market

2030 Larimer Street
Denver, Colorado 80205
(303) 297-0155
Fresh produce in season; dried chiles; canned and pickled chiles; Mexican macaroni; homemade *chorizo* (sells to supermarkets in area).

DETROIT

Honey Bee Market (La Colmena)

2443 Bagley Street
Detroit, Michigan 48216
(313) 237-0295
Some fresh produce; dried and canned ingredients; homemade and other *chorizo*.

HOUSTON

Fiesta Mart

Twelve stores in the Houston area
(713) 869-5060

Fresh produce, including *nopalitos* and *tomatillos*; fresh spices; thirty-five varieties of dried chiles; dried and canned ingredients; Mexican baked goods; fresh tortillas.

LOS ANGELES

Grand Central Market

317 South Broadway
Los Angeles, California 90013
(213) 624-2378
More than fifty independent vendors carry a great variety of fresh and dried Mexican ingredients, including most varieties of chiles year-round, meats and fish, and baked goods.

El Mercado de Los Angeles

3425 East 5th Street
East Los Angeles, California 90063
(213) 269-2953
Fresh tortillas; dried chiles and beans; *salsa*; *tomatillos*; complete line of spices including *cilantro* and *epazote*.

NEW YORK

Casa Moneo

210 West 14th Street
New York, NY 10021
(212) 929-1644
Fresh produce; complete line of dried and canned ingredients. Mail-order catalogue available on request.

OMAHA

Jacobo's Grocery

6330 South 30th Street
Omaha, Nebraska 68107
(402) 733-9009

3702 South 24th Street
Omaha, Nebraska 68107
(402) 733-4507

Fresh produce in season, including cilantro, *tomatillos*, *chayotes*, and *chiles poblanos*; dried chiles and spices; canned ingredients, including *tomatillos*, *salsas*, and stuffed *chiles jalapeños*; fresh tortillas and baked goods, including rolls such as *conchas*, *bolillos* and *semitas*.

ST. LOUIS

Tropicana Market
5001 Lindenwood Street
St. Louis, Missouri 63109
(314) 353-7328
Fresh produce; dried chiles and beans; canned *salsas* and other ingredients; fresh tortillas.

ST. PAUL

Joseph's Market
736 Oakdale Street
St. Paul, Minnesota 55107
(612) 228-9022
Fresh produce in season; dried chiles and spices; meats, including cuts for *fajitas* and *menudo* (tripe soup); fresh tortillas.

Morgan's Mexican Lebanese Foods
736 South Robert Street
St. Paul, Minnesota 55107
(612) 291-2955
Fresh produce, including chiles, *tomatillos*, root vegetables, yucca, *nopalitos*, and squash; spices; dried chiles; frozen meats; complete line of tortillas and chips.

SAN DIEGO

Taylor's Herb Gardens
1535 Lone Oak Road
Vista, California 92084
(619) 727-3485
Potted herbs (retail), about a dozen herbs used in Mexican cooking, including lemon verbena and *epazote*. Mail-order catalog available for $1.00.

SAN FRANCISCO

La Palma Mexicatessen
2884 24th Street
San Francisco, California 94110
(415) 647-1500
Fresh produce, including chiles, *nopales*, and *epazote*; dried ingredients, including chiles, beans, lentils, red and white corn, cilantro, and plantains; canned chiles, *salsas*, baby corn, garbanzos, and *menudo*; *burritos*, tacos, *chiles rellenos*, *tortas*, and *carnitas* for take-out; fresh tortillas and *masa*.

SEATTLE

Mexican Grocery
1914 Pike Place
Seattle, Washington 98104
(206) 682-2822
Dried and canned ingredients; Mexican-style cheeses from California; fresh tortillas.

TULSA

Petty's Fine Foods
8221–I East 61st Street
Tulsa, Oklahoma 74133
(918) 254-0993

1964 Utica Square
Tulsa, Oklahoma 74114
(918) 747-8616
Fresh produce in season; spices; dried chiles and corn husks; fresh tortillas.

WASHINGTON, D.C.

Mixtec
1792 Columbia Road, N.W.
Washington, D.C. 20009
(202) 332-1011
Fresh produce; dried and canned ingredients.

INDEX